90667

PN
2277
N5
B46
1984

Botto, Louis
    At this theatre

'M 18 '85	DATE DUE		
NOV 18 1986			

AT THIS THEATRE

AT THIS THEATRE

An Informal History of New York's Legitimate Theatres

LOUIS BOTTO

Dodd Mead & Company • New York

All photographs in this book are from the archives of the Theatre Collection, Museum of the City of New York. These include the following photographs by Martha Swope:

Pg. 8: *Your Arms Too Short To Box With God* and *Morning's At Seven; Pg. 15: Oh! Calcutta!;* Pg. 16: *Ain't Misbehavin';* Pg. 22: *Peter Pan;* Pg. 24: *Private Lives;* Pg. 31: *Cats;* Pg. 49: *Woman of the Year;* Pg. 57: *Ain't Misbehavin'; Children of a Lesser God;* Pg. 66: *A Chorus Line;* Pg. 73: *Butterflies Are Free;* Pg. 74: *For Colored Girls Who Have Considered Suicide When the Rainbow is Enuf;* Pg. 85: *Dancin';* Pg. 94: *Plaza Suite;* Pg. 95: *Piaf;* Pg. 101: *A View From the Bridge;* Pg. 114: *Lena Horne: The Lady and Her Music;* Pg. 123: *Side By Side By Sondheim;* Pg. 132: *Pippin;* Pg. 133: *Dreamgirls;* Pg. 143: *The Little Foxes;* Pg. 151: *1776;* Pg. 156: *Candide;* Pg. 157: *Evita;* Pg. 190: *Same Time, Next Year; The Dresser;* Pg. 199: *Joseph and the Amazing Technicolor Dreamcoat;* Pg. 213: *The Wiz;* Pg. 214: *The Act;* Pg. 233: *Annie;* Pg. 249: *Sugar Babies;* Pg. 251: *The Man Who Came To Dinner;* Pg. 252: *The Caine Mutiny Court-Martial;* Pg. 257: *The Pirates of Penzance.*

Author's Note: All PLAYBILL covers in this book are from the magazine's archives and the author's private collection. Unfortunately, the people at PLAYBILL had no sense that someday these covers would be used in a book and stamped them with dates and other marks. We show the covers exactly as they appear in our archives.

☙ CONTENTS ❧

⚓ PREFACE ⚓

PLAYBILL Magazine is commemorating its centennial in 1984. As part of such celebrations it is considered traditional to put out "the book." Being a quite traditional company and a bit of an institution in our own right, we have published "At This Theatre." There is no shortage of books about the theatre. However, our volume is special in several ways.

First and foremost, we are privileged to have Louis Botto, senior editor on our staff, bring his astonishing knowledge to this project. In addition, many of the most interesting illustrations are reproductions of items in his fabulous personal collection of theatre memoribilia.

The organization of this volume is unique. Our popular "At This Theatre" feature reflects the organization of the day to day life at PLAYBILL Magazine where, in reality, we do not serve shows, we serve theatres. Our thinking, printing, deliveries, and files are all organized by theatre. It results in an unusual and interesting slant on theatre history.

We have chosen to illuminate the history of only those theatres now served by PLAYBILL Magazine for any other choice would result in an encyclopedic project. Even so, it was possible to include only a fraction of the interesting and amusing material available.

We are grateful to be part of the tradition and to be able to look through this volume and be able to say, without exception, "PLAYBILL was there!"

ARTHUR T. BIRSH

Publisher

⚜ INTRODUCTION ⚜

At This Theatre is an expanded version of the popular feature of the same name that has appeared since the 1930s in PLAYBILL Magazine, which serves as the program of the legitimate theatre in New York City. When attending a Broadway show, theatregoers are fond of reading this page to discover the names of other productions and stars they have seen in the past at this same theatre. The feature offers instant nostalgia and that is the primary purpose of this book.

It was the idea of Joan Alleman, Editor-in-chief of PLAYBILL, to expand "At This Theatre" to book form as one of the observances of the magazine's centennial in 1984. PLAYBILL, which was founded by Frank Vance Strauss, an Ohio advertising man, has brought a century of playgoing pleasure to theatregoers by combining magazine features with a theatre program, offering a rich memento of the show they have seen.

This expanded *At This Theatre* contains the informal history of thirty-four theatres that were built as either legitimate houses or movie palaces and that are currently operating as legitimate theatres. Theatres that were originally night clubs or temples are not included, nor are theatres that have been demolished or that have reverted to showing films, such as the Apollo on 42nd Street. The magnificent Art Nouveau palace, the New Amsterdam, currently being restored to legitimacy by the Nederlander Organization, is also omitted since its official reopening has been delayed.

Even in this expanded form, *At This Theatre*, is not a complete history of all shows that these thirty-four theatres have housed. Hundreds of short-lived productions are omitted. Some shows have moved from theatre to theatre; these productions are listed at the theatre where they first played and also in other theatres if they had extended runs after they moved.

A number of legitimate theatres have had name changes in their long years of operation. The names that appear in the chapter headings are the current names of these theatres, but all name changes are included in each history.

It has not been possible to chronicle ownership changes of each house. The original builders and owners are noted, as well as the current owners, but many who came in-between are not mentioned.

The entire cast of a show is not listed, unless the production had a very small cast. Other credits—author, director, producer, set designer, composer, lyricist, librettist, costume and lighting designers, and choreographers—are listed when their contribution was notable.

Unfortunately, due to a fire, PLAYBILL Magazine's "theatre-by-theatre" listing of productions that have played in each house only goes back as far as 1924. To determine shows that played in theatres before that year, it has been necessary to refer to the following sources: *Notable Names in the Theatre; The New York Times Theater Reviews; The Best Plays* annuals edited by Burns Mantle; *A Pictorial History of the American Theatre* by Daniel Blum; *Twentieth Century Theatre* by Glenn Loney; *American Musical Theatre* by Gerald Bordman; *Encyclopaedia of the Musical Theatre* by Stanley Green; *Broadway* by Brooks Atkinson; *The City & the Theatre* by Mary C. Henderson; *Documents of American Theater* by William C. Young; and *Our Theatres To-day & Yesterday* by Ruth Crosby Dimmick.

Other sources include: the *Theatre World* annuals, edited successively by Daniel Blum and John Willis; the *Best Plays* annuals, edited successively by Burns Mantle, John Chapman, John Kronenberger, Henry Hewes and Otis L. Guernsey Jr.; *The World of Musical Comedy* and *Ring Bells! Sing Songs!*, both by Stanley Green; *The Tony Award* by Isabelle Stevenson; *The Magic Curtain* by Lawrence Langner; *Vintage Years of the Theatre Guild 1928-1939* by Roy S. Waldau; *A Pictorial History of the Theatre Guild* by Norman Nadel; *Revue* by Robert Baral; *Complete Book of the American Musical Theater* by David Ewen; *Matinee To-morrow* by Ward Morehouse; *Stage* and *Theatre Arts magazines*; the *Rodgers and Hammerstein Fact Book*, edited by Stanley Green, and *The Passionate Playgoer* by George Oppenheimer.

All PLAYBILL magazines are from the files of PLAYBILL and from my own collection; souvenir programs, sheet music, "heralds" (inserts placed in theatre programs to advertise a show playing in another theatre) are from my own collection.

All photographs are from the collection of The Museum of the City of New York. Unfortunately, not all actors are credited on vintage photographs and, in some cases, it has been impossible to verify their names. Some actors changed the spelling of their names or changed their names entirely and these changes are noted.

I have many people to thank for the completion and publication of this book. First of all, I am grateful to Arthur Birsh, publisher of PLAYBILL for allowing me the use of his files and for the publication of this work. I am also grateful to Joan Alleman for her help and for relieving me of some of my staff duties in order to write this book.

I am especially indebted to Linda Smith, who spent months researching material and collecting photographs at The Museum of the City of New York for this project. Deadlines would not have been met without her diligent work.

My thanks to Mary C. Henderson, Curator, Theatre Collection, The Museum of the City of New York and her extremely helpful staff: Robert Taylor, Camille Croce Dee, Prudence Farrow, and Wendy Warnken.

I am grateful for the editorial assistance of Bruce Macomber, Gilda Abramowitz, and Jane Hawke Warwick; for the skillful assistance of the book's designers, Gilda Hannah and Camilla Filancia; and for Stanley Stark's excellent theatre sketches.

Musical theatre historian Stanley Green has offered inestimable editorial aid with his vast knowledge of theatrical data. Finally, I wish to thank actor Alan Hewitt and other eagle-eyed theatregoers who have, through the years, written to or called me at PLAYBILL whenever they spotted an inaccuracy in PLAYBILL Magazine's feature "At This Theatre." They have helped to diminish the errors that usually occur in a theatrical history of this genre.

LOUIS BOTTO
Senior Editor, PLAYBILL

❧ LYCEUM THEATRE ❧

When the famed impresario Daniel Frohman opened the Lyceum Theatre on November 2, 1903, on West Forty-fifth Street, east of Broadway, he called it the New Lyceum to distinguish it from the old Lyceum that he formerly owned on Fourth Avenue. The opening of his new theatre brought much publicity, and the day before its premiere the New York *Tribune* ran a feature article on the splendors of the new house. One of the unusual features was a ten-story tower at the rear section of the theatre containing such departments as a carpenter shop, scene building and painting studios, wardrobe sections, and extra dressing rooms.

The paper praised the theatre's decorative scheme by architects Herts and Tallant; its gray limestone façade with Roman columns; the marble staircases in the lobby; the width of the auditorium, which brought seats closer to the stage; the absence of posts, giving all theatregoers an unobstructed view of the stage; and Mr. Frohman's elegant quarters above the theatre with a concealed window that permitted him to supervise rehearsals from above and to telephone directions to his stage manager below.

Ideal for dramas and comedies, the New Lyceum opened with *The Proud Prince*, starring the distinguished American actor E.H. Sothern, who had appeared in many fine plays at the downtown Lyceum. Later in 1903 another illustrious star, William Gillette, sparkled in James M. Barrie's *The Admirable Crichton*.

In 1905 a tremendous hit came to the Lyceum. Charles Klein's *The Lion and the Mouse* was an attack on big business and in particular on John D. Rockefeller. The drama was about a judge whose career was unjustly ruined by a tycoon named John Burkett Ryder (the Rockefeller character, played by Edmund Breese). The judge's daughter, who exposes the injustice (a character based on the true-life Ida Tarbell), was acted by Grace Elliston. Her boyfriend was played by Richard Bennett, father of the future stars Constance and Joan Bennett. The play caused a sensation and ran for 686 performances.

In 1907 Daniel Frohman presented his wife, Margaret Illington, and Kyrle Bellew in Henri Bernstein's play *The Thief*. During the run of this hit, Frohman and his wife discovered a way to control her performance in the explosive second act. Margaret would look up, and if she was overacting, Frohman would wave his handkerchief frantically from his secret window above the theatre.

During the early years of the Lyceum, the theatre presented a parade of beauteous stars in plays that were regarded more as star vehicles than as great dramas. Billie Burke, a British beauty, soon became a Lyceum fixture in a series of these vehicles, many produced by Daniel Frohman's celebrated brother, Charles Frohman. Among these plays were *Love Watches* (1908); *Mrs. Dot* (1910); *Suzanne* (1910); *The Runaway* (1911), with C. Aubrey Smith and Henry Miller, Jr.; and *The "Mind the Paint" Girl* (1912). The beautiful young Ethel Barrymore starred in *Our Mrs. McChesney* (1915), by Edna Ferber and George Hobart; the steamy Lenore Ulric heated the house with Pedro de

Cordoba in David Belasco's *Tiger Rose* (1917); and the coruscating Ina Claire made sparks in *The Gold Diggers* (1919), another hit Belasco production. It ran for 720 performances.

The Roaring Twenties continued to bring hits to the Lyceum. In September 1921 Belasco revived Eugene Walter's shocker *The Easiest Way*, starring the revered actress Frances Starr. In his autobiography, *Present Indicative*, Noel Coward relates how he attended this opening night while on his first visit to New York. He was introduced to the acerbic critic Alexander Woollcott, and Coward confessed to the critic that he found the performance of one of the actresses in the cast "vexing." Woollcott thought the remark hysterically funny and he and Coward became lifelong friends.

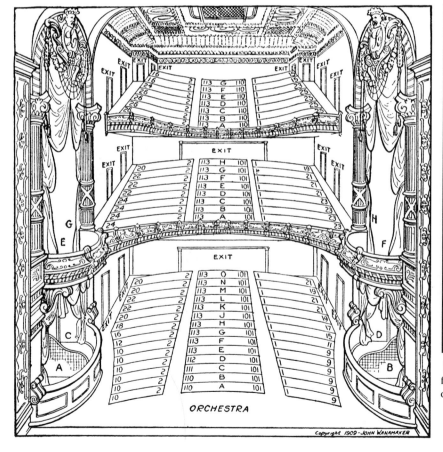

LEFT: Sketch of the Lyceum Theatre in 1909 from *The Wanamaker Diary*. ABOVE: Daniel Frohman, original owner-manager of the theatre.

ABOVE LEFT: E. H. Sothern in *The Proud Prince* (1903). RIGHT: Lenore Ulric in the sultry hit *Tiger Rose* (1917). BOTTOM LEFT: Billie Burke, a Lyceum favorite, in *Mrs. Dot* (1910). RIGHT: regal Ethel Barrymore in *Our Mrs. McChesney* (1915).

David Belasco continued to provide the Lyceum with hits. In November 1921 he presented actor Lionel Atwill and popular Lina Abarbanell in one of those Sacha Guitry romantic comedies, *The Grand Duke*, about royalty mingling with peasantry. It worked for 131 performances. In the summer of 1922 Belasco produced a naval comedy, *Shore Leave*, starring James Rennie as a romantic gob and Frances Starr as his girl in a New England port. This amusing comedy later was turned into the smash musical *Hit the Deck*, and still later into the enchanting Rogers/Astaire film musical *Follow the Fleet*.

Belasco's 1924 hit was *Ladies of the Evening*, a Pygmalion tale about a man (James Kirkwood) who makes a lady out of a prostitute (Beth Merrill) and then falls in love with her.

Charles Frohman returned to producing at the Lyceum in 1925 and presented *The Grand Duchess and the Waiter*, with Elsie Ferguson as the royal dame who falls for a waiter (Basil Rathbone) who turns out to be the son of the president of the Swiss Republic. Later in the year, Frohman produced another continental comedy, *Naughty Cinderella*, with the vivacious French star Irene Bordoni as an amorous secretary.

In 1926 revue genius Fanny (she spelled it Fannie at this point) Brice starred in a comedy called *Fanny* with Warren William, but despite the Belasco production and Brice's clowning, it only lasted sixty-three performances. In 1928 Walter Huston gave a comical performance as baseball pitcher Elmer Kane in Ring Lardner's *Elmer the Great*, produced by George M. Cohan, but the unpopularity of baseball as a stage topic resulted in only forty performances.

One of 1929's ten best plays (as chosen by critic Burns Mantle for his annual *Best Plays* volumes) opened at the Lyceum and became one of its most fondly remembered experiences. The prestigious producer Gilbert Miller and actor Leslie Howard coproduced a fantasy called *Berkeley Square* by John L. Balderston. It starred Mr. Howard as a contemporary American whose spirit is transported back to his ancestors' home in London in 1784, where he engages in a fateful romance with a lovely British woman (Margalo Gillmore). The enchanting play ran for 227 performances and was made into a successful film with Mr. Howard.

The depression had its effect on the Lyceum as Daniel Frohman's career declined, and he was threatened with eviction in the early 1930s. In 1939 the Lyceum was in danger of being demolished, but a group of theatre titans, who loved the old theatre, banded together and bought it. They were playwrights George S. Kaufman and Moss Hart, producer Max Gordon, and others. They bought the theatre in 1940 with the stipulation that Daniel Frohman be permitted to live in his quarters above the house for one dollar a year. It was a fitting gesture for the aged impresario, who died on December 16, 1940. The Kaufman/Hart group sold the Lyceum at a profit in 1945 and it is currently owned by the Shubert Organization.

Highlights of the 1930s at this theatre included the American debut of Charles Laughton with his wife, Elsa Lanchester, in a murder thriller, *Payment Deferred* (1931). Laughton was hailed for his performance. In 1933 a raucous naval comedy called *Sailor, Beware!* made critics blush and ran for 500 laugh-provoking performances. The glittering Ina Claire returned to the Lyceum in 1934 with Walter Slezak in *Ode to Liberty*; Jessie Royce Landis had a hit in *Pre-Honeymoon* (1936); Maurice Evans was an admired Napoleon in *St. Helena* (1936); Arthur Kober's charmingly ethnic *Having Wonderful Time*, starring Jules Garfield (later, John) and Katherine Locke, was a huge hit in 1937; a British hit, *Bachelor Born*, moved here from the Morosco and played for many months in 1938; and the decade ended with J.B. Priestley's *When We Are Married*.

Kaufman and Hart's *George Washington Slept Here* was one of their lesser hits in 1940; Saroyan had a fanciful fling with *The Beautiful People* (1941); and a marvelous comedy called *Junior Miss*, about adolescence, was expertly staged by Moss Hart and romped for 710 performances.

The authors of *Junior Miss*—Jerome Chodorov and Joseph Fields—came up with another winner for the Lyceum in 1942 when their wartime comedy *The Doughgirls* opened. Arlene Francis was the hit of the show as a Russian guerrilla fighter sharing a Washington apartment with two other women. It was good for 671 performances, thanks to George S. Kaufman's dazzling direction.

Kaufman also cowrote, with John P. Marquand, and directed *The Late George Apley*, based on Marquand's Pulitzer Prize novel of the same name. The play, a warm chronicle about a Boston Brahmin (brilliantly played by Leo G. Carroll) and his family, opened on November 21, 1944, and stayed for 384 performances.

A Sound of Hunting (1945) was not a hit, but it served as the Broadway debut of Burt Lancaster (billed as "Burton"), who promptly went to Hollywood and made a fortune. In 1946 Garson Kanin wrote a comedy called *Born Yesterday* about a dumb blonde and her uncouth keeper, a loudmouth junk dealer, and the morning after it opened at the Lyceum, the blonde —Judy Holliday—and the junk dealer—Paul

⚑ LEFT: Leslie Howard travels back in time in the memorable *Berkeley Square* (1929). BELOW: a set for this fantasy, by Sir Edward Lutyens.

LEFT: Patricia Peardon, Lenore Lonergan, and their boyfriends in *Junior Miss* (1941). RIGHT: Paul Douglas and Judy Holliday battle over gin rummy in *Born Yesterday* (1946).

Douglas—were famous. It was the Lyceum's longest-running show, chalking up 1,642 performances.

The Lyceum's next hit occurred in 1950 when Clifford Odets returned to Broadway with *The Country Girl*, starring Uta Hagen as the courageous wife of an alcoholic actor (Paul Kelly) who has to contend with a tough stage director (Steven Hill). Mr. Odets directed his successful drama.

Melvyn Douglas starred in two fluffy comedies at this theatre: *Glad Tidings* (1951), with Signe Hasso, and *Time Out for Ginger* (1952), with Nancy Malone as his daughter, Ginger, who tries out for her high school's football team. Another light comedy, *King of Hearts* (1954), by Jean Kerr and Eleanor Brooke and directed by Mrs. Kerr's husband, critic Walter Kerr, starred Jackie Cooper and Donald Cook and featured Cloris Leachman.

Anastasia (1954), a fascinating drama about a woman who claims to be the daughter of the last Russian czar and to have survived the family's massacre, was brilliantly acted by Viveca Lindfors as the claimant and by Eugenie Leontovich as the dowager empress. Another powerful drama, *A Hatful of Rain* (1955), by

actor Michael V. Gazzo, dramatized the anguish of a wife (Shelley Winters) married to a drug addict (Ben Gazzara). Harry Guardino and Anthony Franciosa were also in the cast.

Comedy returned to the Lyceum in 1956 when Walter Pidgeon arrived as *The Happiest Millionaire*, based on the life of millionaire Anthony J. Drexel Biddle. In sharp contrast to this high society romp was a 1957 drama from England, John Osborne's *Look Back in Anger*, starring Kenneth Haigh, Alan Bates, and Mary Ure. This lashing protest at the genteel Britain of yesteryear started a new school of playwriting called "kitchen sink drama." Its vitriolic antihero, Jimmy Porter (Mr. Haigh), became the dramatic symbol for the "angry young man."

Another fine drama from Britain, *A Taste of Honey*, by young playwright Shelagh Delaney, started the Lyceum off with a hit in 1960. It starred Angela Lansbury as the mother of a pregnant, unmarried daughter and it was written in the "kitchen sink" style of playwriting. Britain sent still another excellent play in 1961 called *The Caretaker* by Harold Pinter, starring Alan Bates and Robert Shaw as brothers who make the charitable error of taking in a homeless, ominous stranger (Donald Pleasence).

After a number of short runs, the Lyceum had a mild hit in *Nobody Loves an Albatross* (1963), a comedy about an overpowering TV personality (said to be inspired by Lucille Ball) and her coworkers. It starred Robert Preston and Constance Ford.

From 1965 to 1969, the Lyceum became the home for the Phoenix Theatre and the APA Repertory Company with Ellis Rabb as artistic director. During these years, the combined companies staged a rich variety of theatre, including a highly successful revival of *You Can't Take It with You, War and Peace,* Helen Hayes in George Kelly's *The Show-off, The Cherry Orchard, The Cocktail Party, The Misanthrope,* and *Hamlet.*

In the 1970s the Lyceum housed a number of productions, none of which ran very long, except for the gospel musical *Your Arms Too Short to Box with God.* Worthy of mention is *Borstal Boy,* Frank McMahon's adaptation of Brendan Behan's book about his early years in prison. Although the play only ran a few months, it won a Tony Award and a New York Drama Critics Circle Award. Also admired in the 1970s was *Cold Storage,* with Len Cariou and Martin Balsam as patients in a hospital terminal ward, and Arthur Kopit's *Wings,* a harrowing study of a woman who suffered a stroke. Constance Cummings's performance won her a Tony Award.

In 1980 an event occurred at the Lyceum. A play called *Morning's at Seven* by Paul Osborn, which had flopped on Broadway in 1939, was beautifully revived with an all-star cast and turned into a belated hit. It won a Tony as the season's best revival and additional Tonys for its director, Vivian Matalon, and David Rounds for best featured actor.

The Lyceum's most recent tenants have been Jules Feiffer's *Grown Ups* (1981), with Bob Dishy, Frances Sternhagen, and Harold Gould, and Athol Fugard's powerful racial drama *'Mas-*

ABOVE: Shelley Winters and her junkie husband (Ben Gazzara) in *A Hatful of Rain* (1955). BELOW: Alan Bates, Mary Ure, and Kenneth Haigh clash in *Look Back in Anger* (1957).

ABOVE: *Your Arms Too Short to Box with God* (1976). LEFT (from left): Nancy Marchand, Elizabeth Wilson, Maureen O'Sullivan, and Teresa Wright in *Morning's at Seven* (1980).

ter Harold'... and the boys (1982).

In recent years, the Shubert Organization, current owners of the Lyceum, has restored the theatre and decorated its beautiful lobby with memorabilia of famous shows that played there. The Lyceum holds a special place in theatregoers' memories, and Brooks Atkinson paid proper tribute to it in his book *Broadway* when he wrote: "The Lyceum Theatre still has the warmth and hospitality of a cordial era. In the wall above the theatre, it retains a peephole where Dan Frohman, sitting in his office, was able to keep one eye on his business affairs and the other on his actors."

⚓ BELASCO THEATRE ⚓

The history of the Belasco Theatre on Forty-fourth Street, between Broadway and Sixth Avenue, can be very confusing. David Belasco, the flamboyant playwright/actor/producer/director and set designer, who was called "the bishop of Broadway" because he always dressed in priestly garments, had two Belasco Theatres. The first, located on Forty-second Street, was Oscar Hammerstein's Republic Theatre until Belasco named it for himself.

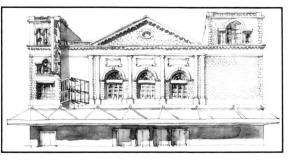

On October 16, 1907, the impresario opened his own theatre, but he called it the Stuyvesant. In 1910, when the Forty-second Street theatre reclaimed its Republic name, Belasco renamed his Forty-fourth Street theatre the Belasco and that name has remained ever since.

Since Belasco was more interested in spectacular, realistic stage sets than in great plays, he made certain that his theatre, designed by architect George Keister, was a marvel of technical wizardry. It cost $750,000 and had a permanent dimmer board with sixty-five dimmers, an elevator stage that could be lowered for set changes, space for set and lighting studios, and a private backstage elevator that ascended to his sumptuous apartments for himself and his leading ladies. Belasco may have worn clerical garments, but there is no evidence that he practiced celibacy.

Our Theatres Today and Yesterday, by Ruth Crosby Dimmick, published in 1913, had this description of the Belasco Theatre: "This was the first theatre to be built in an enclosed rectangular court. It is broad and shallow, seats about 1,100 persons and allows each a clear view of the stage at such close range that opera glasses are superfluous. The decorations are artistic to the Belasco degree. No chandeliers or brackets are visible, the lights being enclosed between the roof and almost flat ground glass globes. A feature of the house is the absence of an orchestra and the unique manner in which the rising of the curtain is announced by the sounding of a muffled gong."

The Stuyvesant Theatre's opening bill was a new play by Belasco and two collaborators —Pauline Phelps and Marion Short—entitled *A Grand Army Man* (1907) and the interesting cast included David Warfield, Jane Cowl, and Antoinette Perry (the actress for whom the Tony Awards are named).

In September 1908 Belasco had a big hit in

BELASCO
THEATRE
44th STREET, near B'WAY, New York

"HIT
THE
DECK"

Under the *solo* management of
DAVID BELASCO

Program cover for the Belasco's first musical success, Vincent Youman's buoyant *Hit the Deck* (1927).

The Fighting Hope, starring Blanche Bates. But in 1909 he topped this with a shocker called *The Easiest Way*, by Eugene Walter. As critic Brooks Atkinson said years later, "*The Easiest Way* was a scandal, a sensation, and a success —the three bright 'S's' of show business." Frances Starr played a mediocre actress of loose morals who tries to reform but finds virtue dull and vice exciting. Her famous curtain line to her maid, "Dress up my body and paint my face. I'm going back to Rector's to make a hit and to hell with the rest," caused women in the audience to faint and priests to denounce the play from their pulpits.

On September 17, 1910, when the Belasco Theatre on Forty-second Street became the Republic again, Belasco changed the name of his Stuyvesant Theatre to the Belasco, as we know it today. On October 4 he had another success with a German play, *The Concert*. Leo Ditrichstein, who translated the play, also starred as a violinist whose wife cures him of his amorous adventures. The hit ran for 264 performances.

Belasco wrote his own next hit, *The Return of Peter Grimm*, starring David Warfield as a man who returns from the dead. The fantasy ran for 231 performances, but Warfield almost drove the cast insane with his onstage practical jokes. One night he secreted Limburger cheese in a bowl of tulips, and when actress Janet Dunbar buried her face in the flowers during the play's climax, she almost passed out.

During these early years of the Belasco Theatre, its owner was celebrated for his development of such stars as Blanche Bates, Frances Starr, Lenore Ulric, Ina Claire, Katharine Cornell, and Jeanne Eagels. He was also famed for his insistence that if a play called for a scene in a laundry, the set designer had better provide a real laundry where people could actually take clothes to be washed and ironed. For one play he duplicated a Child's Restaurant.

David Belasco always wore priestly garb but was not known to practice celibacy.

In 1917 Ina Claire scored a tremendous success in a Cinderella play, *Polly with a Past*, that ran for 315 performances; Jeanne Eagles, who would later achieve immortality as Sadie Thompson in *Rain*, proved an instant hit in *Daddies* (1918), with George Abbott (who, in 1984, is still alive, well, and dancing), and played for 340 performances; and the sexy Lenore Ulric was good for 223 performances in *The Son-Daughter* (1919), a play about China by Belasco and George Scarborough.

Lenore Ulric became a big Belasco star in the 1920s, starring in such seamy dramas as *Kiki* (1921), *The Harem* (1924), *Lulu Belle* (1926), and *Mima* (1928). Other celebrated stars who played the Belasco at this time were Lio-

Melvyn Douglas and Helen Gahagan married after appearing in Belasco's last production, *Tonight or Never* (1930).

nel Barrymore in *Laugh, Clown, Laugh!* (1923) and Katharine Cornell in *Tiger Cats* (1924).

Surprisingly, the Belasco Theatre booked a musical in 1927 and it was one of the theatrical highlights of the 1920s. *Hit the Deck* had a captivating score by Vincent Youmans and it brightened the Belasco for 352 performances. Louise Groody, Charles King, and Brian Donlevy were in the cast.

Two more hits played the house before the end of the decade: *The Bachelor Father*, with C. Aubrey Smith and June Walker, and *It's a Wise Child*, starring Humphrey Bogart, a bright comedy that amused for 378 performances.

David Belasco's last production at his theatre was a success. In November 1930 he presented Melvyn Douglas and Helen Gahagan in a continental romance called *Tonight or Never*. The stars fell in love not only onstage, but offstage as well. They married and remained husband and wife for the rest of their lives.

David Belasco died in New York on May 14, 1931, at age seventy-one. His theatre was then leased to Katharine Cornell Productions, Inc., and her husband, Guthrie McClintic, produced and directed the first play under the new management. It was S. N. Behrman's witty comedy *Brief Moment*, but it must have caused the ghost of David Belasco (often seen in the theatre) unrest because it numbered among its cast the vitriolic critic Alexander Woollcott, who had panned many of his plays. Woollcott played himself in *Brief Moment*—a fat, lazy, snippy dilettante—and one of the biggest laughs in the show occurred when an actress had this line to say to him: "If you were a woman what a bitch you would have made."

Miss Cornell appeared in two plays under her own management at this theatre: *Lucrece*, translated from the French by Thornton Wilder (1932), and Sidney Howard's *Alien Corn* (1933). The Belasco was next leased to Mrs. Hazel L. Rice, wife of playwright Elmer Rice, who pro-

LEFT: Luther Adler, Elia Kazan, Roman Bohnen, and Frances Farmer in the Group Theatre's *Golden Boy* (1937). RIGHT: Jules (John) Garfield and Morris Carnovsky in Odet's *Awake and Sing* (1935).

vided the theatre with two plays: *Judgment Day* (1934) and *Between Two Worlds* (1934), neither of which succeeded.

The famous Group Theatre's association with the Belasco began in December 1934, when it moved its production of *Gold Eagle Guy* there from the Morosco. Some of the Group's illustrious members who appeared in this play included Clifford Odets, Morris Carnovsky, Luther and Stella Adler, Sanford Meisner, and J. Edward Bromberg. On February 19, 1935, the Group Theatre made theatrical history with its production of Odets's *Awake and Sing*, featuring its acting company (including Jules Garfield). The Odets sting was at its sharpest in this chronicle of the volcanic life of a Jewish family living in the Bronx.

On the evening of October 28, 1935, a play opened at the Belasco that would have delighted David Belasco. It was Sidney Kingsley's

Dead End and it ran for 684 performances, the longest-running play in the Belasco's history to this day. Produced and designed by the famed Norman Bel Geddes, it featured a realistic set of a dead-end street on Manhattan's East River that Belasco himself would have cheered. The Dead End Kids, unknown young actors who became famous overnight and later made endless films in Hollywood, actually dove into the orchestra pit, where the East River flowed. The play, which was a social tract on how dead-end boys grow up to be gangsters, featured a short, haunting performance by Marjorie Main as a notorious gangster's mother and she repeated her role in the superb movie version of the play.

Another memorable play came to this theatre in 1937 when the Group Theatre presented Clifford Odets's *Golden Boy*, starring Luther Adler as the boxer/violinist and Frances Farmer as his unlucky girlfriend. Expertly directed by

🎭 Baby Face Martin is gunned down in Norman Bel Geddes's massive waterfront set for Sidney Kingsley's *Dead End* (1935).

Harold Clurman, the play ran for 248 performances. Two more Group Theatre productions followed: Odets's *Rocket to the Moon* (1938) and Irwin Shaw's *The Gentle People*, starring Sylvia Sidney, Franchot Tone, Lee J. Cobb, Sam Jaffe, Karl Malden, and Elia Kazan.

A sorry spectacle in 1940 was a comedy called *My Dear Children*, starring a weary and shamelessly ad-libbing John Barrymore in his last Broadway appearance. A more rewarding play was *Johnny Belinda* (1940), with Helen Craig giving a moving performance as a deaf mute. Amusement was provided by *Mr. and Mrs. North* (1941), about a husband/wife detective team, and by *Dark Eyes* (1943), a comedy about Russian expatriates by Eugenie Leontovich and Elena Miramova, who also starred in the hit play.

A cause célèbre occurred at the Belasco in 1944. A play called *Trio*, with Richard Widmark, Lois Wheeler, and Lydia St. Clair, dealt with lesbianism. For some bizarre reason, no thea-

tre wanted this drama, although it was written with taste. It finally opened at the Belasco on December 29, 1944, but its troubles were not over. The critics did not think it was a very good play, but they agreed that it was not lurid in its approach and that it deserved to have a hearing. Unfortunately, public officials disagreed and *Trio* was forced to close after two months when the owners of the Belasco refused to renew the producer's lease.

Kiss Them for Me in 1945 was notable as the first play in which the great talents of Judy Holliday were noticed. Her performance of a tramp with an honest approach to her profession helped to land her the lead in *Born Yesterday* (1946) that would make her a star. Other 1940s highlights included Arthur Laurents's *Home of the Brave* (1945); a rollicking revival of *Burlesque* (1946), starring Bert Lahr and Jean Parker; Gertrude Berg in *Me and Molly* (1948); and Alfred de Liagre, Jr.'s mesmerizing production of *The Madwoman of Chaillot* (1948), with gloriously loony performances by Martita Hunt and Estelle Winwood.

From mid-1949 until November 1953, the Belasco Theatre was leased to NBC as a radio playhouse. On November 5, 1953, it returned to legitimacy with a glittering hit, George S. Kaufman and Howard Teichmann's comedy *The Solid Gold Cadillac*, starring the incomparable Josephine Hull as a small stockholder who causes a big ruckus at a shareholders' meeting. The satire ran for 526 performances.

Shows worthy of mention in the 1950s include Clifford Odets's *The Flowering Peach* (1954), with Menasha Skulnik as Noah; *Will Success Spoil Rock Hunter?* (1955), starring Jayne Mansfield, Orson Bean, Martin Gabel, and Walter Matthau; Noel Coward's return to Broadway in a thin play of his own, *Nude with Violin*

Dorothy Chansky and John Hammil in their *Oh! Calcutta!* duet (1971).

🦋 Tad Mosel's play caught on after it won a Pulitzer Prize.

(1957–58), alternating with some performances of *Present Laughter* to relieve the tedium.

In November 1960 a beautiful play came to the Belasco. Tad Mosel's *All the Way Home*, adapted from James Agee's novel *A Death in the Family*, starred Arthur Hill, Lillian Gish, Colleen Dewhurst, and Aline MacMahon and etched with feeling the impact of a young father's death on his family. It was awarded the Pulitzer Prize and the New York Drama Critics Circle Award as the best play of the season.

Write Me a Murder (1961), by Frederick Knott, was an off-beat thriller with Denholm Elliott, Ethel Griffies, and Kim Hunter; Sam Levene was his Seventh Avenue best in a popular comedy, *Seidman and Son* (1962); Nicol Williamson gave a lacerating performance in John Osborne's *Inadmissable Evidence* (1965);

♯ The original cast of *Ain't Misbehavin'*, which moved from another theatre to the Belasco in 1981.

The Killing of Sister George (1966), which was much more explicit about lesbians than *Trio*, which had been forced to close at the Belasco, ran for 205 performances unmolested; and *Does a Tiger Wear a Necktie?* (1969) offered the Broadway debut of Al Pacino as a drug addict and his electrifying performance won him a Tony Award.

Oh! Calcutta!, which moved to the Belasco in 1971 from the downtown Eden Theatre, had the entire cast in the nude and also featured the most explicitly sexual revue sketches and dances ever performed in the legitimate theatre.

In recent years, the Belasco's most successful tenants have been long-run musicals that moved there from other theatres. In 1980, *Your Arms Too Short to Box with God* moved in from the Ambassador; and in 1981 *Ain't Misbehavin'* transferred from the Plymouth to run for an additional year at the Belasco.

For years, actors who appeared at this theatre and backstage personnel claimed that they saw the ghost of David Belasco in his priestly garb, usually sitting in an unoccupied box at opening nights. A caretaker at the theatre also told newspapers that he sometimes heard the creaky elevator chains rattling backstage, although Mr. Belasco's private elevator hasn't worked for years. But according to an article that appeared in the New York *Times* some years ago, the Belasco ghost has never been seen in the theatre since *Oh! Calcutta!* played there. This nude show may have been too much realism, even for Belasco.

⚑ LUNT-FONTANNE THEATRE ⚑

This beautiful theatre opened on January 10, 1910, as the Globe, named after Shakespeare's theatre in England. It was built by the illustrious producer Charles B. Dillingham and originally had its entrance on Broadway between Forty-sixth and Forty-seventh streets. Dillingham, who spared no expense on his projects, hired the famed architects Carrère and Hastings to design his theatre. They came up with a fan-shape plan that afforded every seat a close view of the stage.

According to a report in the New York *Dramatic Mirror* on January 22, 1910, the new theatre had a large stage, a compact auditorium, Italian Renaissance decor with draperies of Rose du Barry and walls of old gold, blue, and ivory white. One feature of the theatre that attracted much attention was a large oval panel in the ceiling that could be opened when the weather permitted. The *Mirror* called this "a complete novelty in American theatrical design."

Another unusual feature was the theatre's principal façade on West Forty-sixth Street (which today is used as the entrance). The Globe used this side entrance for its carriage patrons. Above the entrance was an outdoor balcony that

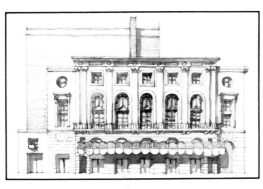

theatregoers could visit during intermissions, weather permitting.

For his premiere attraction, Dillingham wisely chose a lavish musical for two of that era's most popular musical comedy stars, Dave Montgomery and Fred Stone. It was called *The Old Town* and had a book by George Ade and music by Gustav Luders. The two comics won raves and the hit show got the new Globe theatre off to a rousing start.

In 1911 the popular Elsie Janis amused audiences in a sappy musical called *The Slim Princess* in which she played a princess too slim to attract suitors, often stepping out of character to do her famous impersonations of Sarah Bernhardt, Ethel Barrymore, Eddie Foy, and George M. Cohan. In recent years, it has been discovered that Victor Herbert wrote some of the music for this show.

Elsie Janis teamed up with Montgomery and Stone in *The Lady of the Slipper* (1912), and the Victor Herbert musical proved to be a smash.

Montgomery and Stone scored still another triumph in 1914 when they opened in *Chin-Chin*, a Chinese fantasy about Aladdin and his

CHARLES DILLINGHAM'S GLOBE THEATRE

Standard program cover for Globe Theatre shows in the 1920s.

Manners. The New York *Dramatic Mirror* reported that Miss Taylor "has made a triumphant return to her native stage." Also in the cast: young Lynn Fontanne.

One of the Globe's favorite performers, Dave Montgomery, died in the spring of 1917, but his partner, Fred Stone, returned to the theatre on his own and scored a triumph in the musical *Jack o' Lantern* in October of that year. Written by the same team that had created *Chin-Chin*, and produced by Dillingham, the show had sumptuous sets by Joseph Urban of *Ziegfeld Follies* fame and a perfect role for Stone as a loving man who saves two children from a wicked uncle.

The most interesting thing about *The Canary* (1918) was that it had songs by Irving Berlin, Jerome Kern, Harry Tierney, and Ivan Caryll. It starred the beautiful Julia Sanderson and comic Joseph Cawthorn and it was about a man who swallowed a diamond.

Jerome Kern had his own show, *She's a Good Fellow*, written with Anne Caldwell, in 1919, with Joseph Santley playing in drag and the Duncan Sisters doing their vaudeville act. The musical ran for 120 performances and would have continued except for the famed actors' strike, which forced it to close.

The Roaring Twenties at the Globe brought a very mixed bag of material. In June 1920 George White presented his second edition of *George White's Scandals*. It had a score by George Gershwin, lyrics by Arthur Jackson, and sketches by George White and Andy Rice. The headliners were Mr. White, tapping furiously, Ann Pennington as a mechanical piano doll, and Lou Holtz providing the low comedy.

In sharp contrast to the worldly outlook of the *Scandals* was the return of Fred Stone in still another innocent musical involving children, a fantasy fairyland and "family" entertainment. This one was called *Tip Top* (October 5, 1920) and it was written by Globe veterans Anne

two slaves, played by the comedy team. The musical was a sellout for 295 performances.

Irving Berlin's *Stop! Look! Listen!* brought ragtime to the Globe in 1915, plus *Ziegfeld Follies* beauty Justine Johnstone, comic Joseph Santley, and Harland Dixon in a popular show.

In 1916 the Globe had a dramatic change of pace. The great American actress Laurette Taylor, who had been acting in England, returned to Broadway in a play called *The Harp of Life*, written by her husband, J. Hartley

Caldwell and composer Ivan Caryll. Fred Stone's popularity triggered the musical's run of 241 performances.

Since Ziegfeld's New Amsterdam Theatre was occupied by one of his greatest hits, *Sally*, he presented his *Ziegfeld Follies of 1921* at the Globe. It had much to recommend it. Joseph Urban's sets and James Reynolds's costumes were so extravagant that this was Flo's most expensive *Follies*, costing over a quarter of a million dollars. The cast was stupendous.

Fanny Brice sang two of her most memorable numbers: "Second Hand Rose" and "My Man," a radical departure for her. And the great comics W.C. Fields, Raymond Hitchcock, and Ray Dooley joined Miss Brice in sketches that became immortal.

The end of 1921 brought an endearing Jerome Kern show to the Globe, *Good Morning, Dearie*, starring Louise Groody and Oscar Shaw.

George White staged his 1922 *Scandals* at the Globe and it is still remembered today

LEFT: Raymond Hitchcock and Betty Carsdale in the 1921 edition of the *Ziegfeld Follies*. ABOVE: Sheet-music cover for the Jerome Kern hit *The Stepping Stones*, starring Fred Stone (1923).

🎭 Ona Munson in the 1925 smash *No, No, Nanette.*

for George Gershwin's "I'll Build a Stairway to Paradise" and for "Blue Monday Blues," a twenty-five-minute jazz opera that was cut after the opening. It was a work that would influence Gershwin to write his full-scale opera *Porgy and Bess.* W.C. Fields and Paul Whiteman and his orchestra were among the luminaries in the cast. In June of 1923 another *Scandals* with a Gershwin score opened at the Globe, but it was one of the least successful in the series.

In 1923 Fred Stone returned to the Globe in *Stepping Stones*, and this time he brought his stunning, dancing daughter Dorothy along to make her Broadway debut. Dad and daughter were a hit. The memorable score was by Je-

rome Kern and Anne Caldwell and the plot was an adaptation of *Little Red Riding Hood*, allowing Fred Stone to play his usual role of a good man who saves a little girl from the big bad wolf.

Ed Wynn, the lisping comic billed as "The Perfect Fool," brought one of his ingenious shows—*The Grab Bag*—to the Globe in 1924. The Wynn formula was to present a revue in which he would barge in on other acts and amuse the audience with his ludicrous comments and insane inventions—such as a typewriterlike device for eating corn on the cob without getting his fingers full of butter. The revue was a hit and ran for 184 performances.

On the evening of September 16, 1925, the audience attending the opening night of a new musical at the Globe entered the theatre humming two of the show's hits—"Tea for Two" and "I Want to Be Happy"—*before* they even heard the overture. The show was *No, No, Nanette* and it had a curious history. It had already played in London (although it was strictly an American musical), had played for one year in Chicago, and had several road companies touring the country before the Broadway opening. The musical was a hit.

The Globe's next tenant also had a strange history. It was supposed to be the *Ziegfeld Follies of 1926*, but because Flo had ended his partnership with Klaw and Erlanger, he was not permitted, by court decision, to use the *Follies* name. Therefore, he called this edition *No Foolin'* for its Globe opening, but very quickly changed the title to *Ziegfeld's American Revue of 1926.* It was not one of his best revues, but it had young Paulette Goddard and Louise Brooks in the chorus and featured the beautiful Claire Luce (the dancer, not the playwright).

Incredible as it may seem, Fred Stone and his daughter Dorothy appeared in *Cris Cross* at the Globe in 1926 and the musical had practically the same plot as Stone's 1917 musical

Jack o' Lantern. In this one, he saves a child (his daughter) from being swindled out of her inheritance. It was another Jerome Kern/Anne Caldwell show, with Otto Harbach collaborating on book and lyrics. This was to be Fred Stone's last show at the Globe. He and his daughter were supposed to appear in another Globe musical in 1928 called *Three Cheers*, but he was not well, and was replaced by Will Rogers. At the opening night performance, Rogers said to the audience: "I don't know one thing that Fred does that I can do." Dorothy Stone was featured in the cast and she drew raves for her singing and dancing.

In December 1926 Beatrice Lillie starred in Vincent Youmans's musical *Oh, Please,* but it failed. The only thing that survived was the hit song "I Know That You Know."

The last legitimate show to play the Globe Theatre was the memorable musical *The Cat and the Fiddle*. Jerome Kern provided one of his best scores (including "The Night Was Made for Love," "Try to Forget," and "She Didn't Say Yes"). Book and lyrics were by Otto Harbach. The leads in this Brussels operetta were played by Georges Metaxa, Odette Myrtil, Bettina Hall, and Eddie Foy, Jr. It ran for 395 performances.

The stock market crash in 1929, which caused some Broadway theatres to remain dark during the depression years, had a tragic effect on producer Charles B. Dillingham. He was wiped out financially and lost the Globe Theatre. When *The Cat and the Fiddle* closed in mid-1932, his theatre, like so many on West Forty-second Street, was converted to a movie house and showed films until 1957.

Fortunately, Roger Stevens and Robert W. Dowling of the City Investing Company rescued the old house by buying it and spending a fortune to reconstruct it. Dowling chose to redo the theatre in an elegant eighteenth-century style. A new stage was built, the second balcony removed, and a cantilevered mezzanine

Georges Metaxa and Bettina Hall in the memorable musical *The Cat and the Fiddle* (1929).

TOP LEFT: Alfred Lunt and Lynn Fontanne in *The Visit,* their last Broadway appearance (1958). TOP RIGHT: Mary Martin in Rodgers and Hammerstein's last show, *The Sound of Music* (1959). RIGHT: Sandy Duncan flying high in the 1979 revival of the musical *Peter Pan.*

RIGHT:PLAYBILL covers for the Richard Rodgers musical *Rex* (1976) and the long-running revue *Sophisticated Ladies* (1981).

added. Blue damask walls, crystal chandeliers, and a 100-foot mural on the ceiling depicting the theatrical muses added to the house's new opulence, and, most impressive of all, it was renamed the Lunt-Fontanne in honor of America's foremost husband/wife acting couple.

Appropriately, on May 5, 1958, the Lunts opened their new house with one of their best plays, *The Visit*, a stark, harrowing drama of revenge by Friedrich Duerrenmatt. It was a gala occasion. The opening-night tickets were printed in gold, and the celebrity-studded audience gave the Lunt-Fontanne Theatre and the Lunts a clamorous welcome. The critics also loved the new house and the new play, which, unfortunately, was the last show the Lunts would appear in on Broadway.

Since 1958 the Lunt-Fontanne has had a parade of hits. Some highlights: John Gielgud and Margaret Leighton in *Much Ado About Nothing*(1959); the last Rodgers and Hammerstein musical, *The Sound of Music*, starring Mary Martin, which played for 1,443 performances at the Lunt-Fontanne and Mark Hellinger and won six Tony Awards, including best musical, best score, and best performance in a musical (Mary Martin).

The 1960s brought Sid Caesar in a marvelous musical, *Little Me* (1962), that should have run longer but was hampered by a newspaper strike; Martha Graham and her Dance Company (1963); Richard Burton as a commendable Hamlet, attended at each performance by his then wife, Elizabeth Taylor (1964); Julie Harris in her first musical, *Skyscraper* (1965); the British comic Norman Wisdom in *Walking Happy* (1966), a musical version of the novel *Hobson's Choice*; Marlene Dietrich making her Broadway debut in dazzling fashion, singing her famous songs and backed by Burt Bacharach and his huge orchestra (1967); a musical about Wall Street called *How Now, Dow Jones* (1967); and Nicol Williamson as another Hamlet (1969).

The Rothschilds (1970) was a musical suc-

 Elizabeth Taylor and Richard Burton in the 1983 revival of Noel Coward's durable drawing-room comedy *Private Lives*.

cess about the famed Jewish banking family. Hal Linden won a Tony as best actor in a musical, and Keene Curtis won the same award as best featured actor.

Several famous musicals were revived at the Lunt-Fontanne during the 1970s, including *A Funny Thing Happened on the Way to the Forum* (1972), starring Phil Silvers; an all-black production of *The Pajama Game* (1973); the lavish twentieth-anniversary production of *My Fair Lady*, which moved to the Lunt-Fontanne from the St. James in December 1976; and Carol Channing in still another revival of *Hello, Dolly!* (1978). In the middle of all these revivals, a Richard Rodgers/Sheldon Harnick/Sherman Yellen musical about King Henry VIII, called *Rex* (1976), was beheaded by the critics. Nicol Williamson starred as the king.

In 1979 Sandy Duncan brightened the Lunt-Fontanne by flying all over the house in *Peter Pan*; and in 1981 the elegant Duke Ellington revue, *Sophisticated Ladies*, moved into the Lunt-Fontanne, starring Gregory Hines and Judith Jamison, and thrilled theatregoers for 767 performances with its silken Ellington melodies and sparkling choreography.

The Lunt-Fontanne's most recent tenants have been Zev Bufman's revivals of Noel Coward's *Private Lives* (1983), starring Elizabeth Taylor and Richard Burton, for a limited engagement and *The Corn Is Green* (1983), starring Cicely Tyson. The most recent show was the biographical musical *Peg*, starring Peggy Lee.

Now celebrating its seventy-fourth year, the Lunt-Fontanne Theatre is still one of the prime Broadway houses. It is owned and operated by the Nederlander Organization and it does honor to America's late royal couple of acting.

❧ WINTER GARDEN THEATRE ❧

On the blustery evening of March 20, 1911, the Messrs. Shubert unveiled on Broadway at Fiftieth Street the Winter Garden, a lavish music hall "devoted to novel, international, spectacular and musical entertainments." Built on the

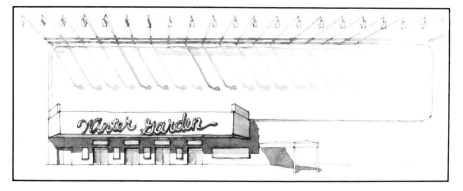

site of the former American Horse Exchange owned by W.K. Vanderbilt, the theatre was designed by architect William Albert Swasey to resemble an English garden with lattice work on the walls and a trellised ceiling.

Unmarred by a marquee, the original Winter Garden had a classical façade with Palladian arches and columns, and contained, besides the auditorium, a "promenoir" in the rear of the house, extending from Broadway to Seventh Avenue for intermission processions "which are joined in by everyone of prominence," an early program proclaimed.

The Winter Garden's opening production, *La Belle Paree* (1911), was composed of two parts. Part one was a one-act Chinese opera called *Bow Sing*; part two was a lively vaude-

ville, *Jumble of Jollity*, with songs by Frank Tours and Jerome Kern. The hit of this segment was singer Al Jolson, who for many years would be the Winter Garden's biggest star.

The Winter Garden was an instant hit ("New York's latest plaything, a very flashy toy, full of life and go and color and with no end of jingle to it!" wrote one critic). Two of the theatre's most talked about features in its early days were a series of Sunday night concerts, in which new talent such as Jolson and Marilynn (later shortened to Marilyn) Miller were brilliantly promoted, and a structural innovation that became a Winter Garden trademark: the "runway." On a European trip, Lee Shubert had met the great German producer/director Max Reinhardt, who broke down the invisible wall between actors and audience by a thrust stage that jutted out into the theatre. The Shuberts borrowed this idea and built a bridge over the tops of orchestra seats from the stage to the rear of the house. On this bridge, Jolson pranced into the audi-

▶ TOP LEFT: Standard Winter Garden program cover before 1930. TOP RIGHT: Eddie Cantor, who appeared in two Winter Garden shows. RIGHT: Al Jolson, who first appeared in blackface at this theatre in *Vera Violetta* (1911).

ence, belting his songs and communicating with his delirious fans. Eighty near-nude show girls also paraded on the runway, which soon became known as "the bridge of thighs."

Just as the New Amsterdam Theatre became identified with the *Follies* and the Apollo with the *Scandals*, the Winter Garden became the home of a rowdy revue series called *The Passing Show*. From 1912 through 1924 there was an annual edition, except in 1920. Among the luminous stars who appeared in these shows were Fred and Adele Astaire, Marilyn Miller, Willie and Eugene Howard, Charlotte Greenwood, Ed Wynn, Frank Fay, John Charles Thomas, Marie Dressler, the Avon Comedy Four, Fred Allen, George Jessel, and James Barton.

The major song contributors were Sigmund Romberg and Jean Schwartz; the gilded sets were mostly by Watson Barratt, and the silken costumes mostly by Cora McGeachey and Homer Conant.

The Passing Show revues were less subtle than those produced by the Shuberts' archrival, Flo Ziegfeld. One wonders what women's lib would have said to a bizarre "Rotisserie" scene in which show girls were roasted on a spit and then placed on tables like well-done chickens. In *The Passing Show of 1924* (the last of the series), a chorus cutie named Lucille Le Seur portrayed a "Beaded Bag" and "Miss Labor Day." The chorine went to Hollywood and became better known as Joan Crawford.

Al Jolson never appeared in a *Passing Show*, but he headlined some of the Winter Garden's biggest hits. He first appeared in "blackface" (which became his specialty) in *Vera Violetta*, a

A sextet of chorines from one of the *Greenwich Village Follies* revues in the 1920s.

1911 musical in which he costarred with the French singer Gaby Deslys and a sexy newcomer named Mae West. He again appeared with Deslys in *The Honeymoon Express* (1913), with a funny girl in the cast named Fanny Brice. In 1918 Jolson took Broadway by storm in *Sinbad*, a fantastic musical in which he belted out some interpolated numbers that were forever identified with him: "My Mammy" (sung on the runway in blackface and white gloves), "Rock-a-Bye Your Baby with a Dixie Melody," and "Chloe." When the show went on tour, Jolson added a song called "Swanee," which made George Gershwin famous overnight. In many of his shows, Jolson played the same character, a blackface servant named Gus. In his last Winter Garden show, *Big Boy* (1925), the singer was Gus, a stableboy.

After *The Passing Show* series was through,

Bert Lahr, Luella Gear, and Ray Bolger clown in the 1934 revue hit *Life Begins at 8:40*.

the Winter Garden staged other revues such as *Artists and Models* and *The Greenwich Village Follies*, studded with tall, medium, and pony-sized show girls and low comics. Eddie Cantor appeared in two Winter Garden shows, *Broadway Brevities of 1920* and *Make It Snappy*, and Martha Graham danced in the 1923 edition of *The Greenwich Village Follies*.

During the 1920s, the Winter Garden was redesigned as it appears today by architect Herbert J. Krapp, and an enormous marquee was added. But to Broadway's dismay, from 1928 to 1933 the theatre was leased by Warner Brothers and converted into a Vitaphone (talking pictures) temple. Aptly, the first movie shown there was Al Jolson in *The Singing Fool*.

After a shaky return to legitimacy with Joe Cook in a mediocre musical, *Hold Your Horses* (1933), the Winter Garden embarked on its golden era of glittering revues, noted for their beauty and sophistication. It all began when the Shuberts and Billie Burke (Ziegfeld's widow) combined to present a posthumous *Ziegfeld Follies* (1934), starring Fanny Brice, Willie and Eugene Howard, Vilma and Buddy Ebsen (who stopped the show with their dancing), and Jane Froman.

In 1934 Ray Bolger, Bert Lahr, Luella Gear, and Frances Williams brightened the house in *Life Begins at 8:40*, a breathtaking revue with mechanical sets and a hit tune—"Let's Take a Walk Around the Block"; this was followed by the *Earl Carroll Sketch Book*, starring Ken Murray.

In 1935 Vincente Minnelli began his splashy tenure as revue master of the Winter Garden and he came up with *At Home Abroad*, a travelogue starring Beatrice Lillie, Ethel Waters, Eleanor Powell, and Reginald Gardiner. Minnelli designed eye-filling sets of foreign ports, Lillie did her hilarious "Dozen Double Damask Dinner Napkins" sketch, Gardiner imitated wallpaper and trains, Powell tapped up a storm, and

👗 ABOVE: Fanny Brice as Baby Snooks pesters Bob Hope in the 1936 edition of the *Ziegfeld Follies*. RIGHT: Barbra Streisand triumphs as Fanny Brice in *Funny Girl* (1964).

Waters sang Dietz and Schwartz gems.

Another *Ziegfeld Follies* arrived in 1936 with Minnelli sets and costumes, Fanny Brice doing Baby Snooks, Bob Hope singing "I Can't Get Started" to Eve Arden, Josephine Baker singing and dancing dressed in strings of bananas.

Late 1936 brought perhaps the Winter Garden's best revue of all time—Vincente Minnelli's *The Show Is On*, a tribute to show business through the ages with Bea Lillie swinging out over the audience on a huge half-moon and dropping garters on bald-headed men, Bert Lahr immortalizing "Song of the Woodman," the Gershwins providing "By Strauss," and Hoagy Carmichael's "Little Old Lady."

In late 1937 Ed Wynn moved in with a marvelous antiwar musical *Hooray for What!* by Harold Arlen and E.Y. Harburg, Howard Lindsay, and Russel Crouse. Wynn played a zany inventor of gases who is pursued by nations that want his concoctions for their wars.

A phenomenon called *Hellzapoppin* opened at the Forty-sixth Street Theatre in 1938 and proved so successful that it was moved to the Winter Garden, where it became the longest-running Broadway musical at that time (1,404 performances). Starring Olsen and Johnson, the revue was a lunatic uproar with all sorts of practical jokes played on the audience. It sparked two more Winter Garden revues—*Sons o' Fun* (1941) and *Laffing Room Only* (1944).

In between the last two Olsen and Johnson shows came two hits: Milton Berle, Ilona Massey, Arthur Treacher, and Jack Cole in the *Ziegfeld Follies of 1943*, and Cole Porter's *Mexican Hayride*, starring Bobby Clark and June Havoc, lavishly produced by Mike Todd.

In the summer of 1945, an operetta called *Marinka* opened at the Winter Garden and proved to be the last legitimate show to play there for several years. Once again, the theatre reverted to a movie house.

In November 1948 the rowdy Bobby Clark brought live theatre back to the Winter Garden in Michael Todd's funny *As the Girls Go*, a fast-paced musical in which Bobby played the husband of the first female president of the United States (Irene Rich). Todd's production was so lush and expensive that he charged a $7.20 top, a record price at that time. Todd continued his association with this theatre by presenting a high-class burlesque, *Michael Todd's Peep Show* (1950).

Phil Silvers, another raucous comic, scored at the Winter Garden in a noisy musical, *Top Banana* (1951), about television, with Silvers impersonating a TV comic said to be inspired by Milton Berle. Then, in 1953, Rosalind Russell triumphed in *Wonderful Town*, a brilliant musical by Leonard Bernstein, Betty Comden, and Adolph Green.

A rarely performed classic, *Tamburlaine the Great*, by Christopher Marlowe, was given a spectacular production in 1956, with Anthony Quayle in the title role and a newcomer named Colleen Dewhurst listed in the cast as "A Virgin of Memphis" in Act One and "A Turkish Concubine" in Act Two. Her fall occurred during the intermission. During the same year, the Old Vic Company from England performed *Richard II, Romeo and Juliet, Macbeth,* and other plays.

The last *Ziegfeld Follies* opened at the Winter Garden in 1957 and starred the illustrious Beatrice Lillie and Billy De Wolfe, but the critics were not enthusiastic and the show closed after 123 performances. In 1958, the landmark musical *West Side Story* blazed across the Winter Garden stage with its jazzy, violent treatment of *Romeo and Juliet* set in the rumble-ridden Bronx. The unusual musical was conceived, choreographed, and directed by Jerome Robbins, had a book by Arthur Laurents, music by Leonard Bernstein, and introduced Stephen Sondheim to Broadway as a lyricist.

The off-beat actress Tammy Grimes proved

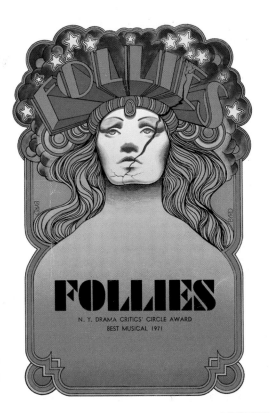

TOP LEFT: Souvenir program for the off-beat musical *Follies* (1971). TOP RIGHT: Souvenir program for the 1974 revival of *Gypsy*, starring Angela Lansbury. RIGHT: Terrence V. Mann and his feline friends in the spectacular success *Cats* (1982).

a sensation in *The Unsinkable Molly Brown* in 1960, playing an actual character from the early 1900s. Harve Presnell was her costar in this popular Meredith Willson musical.

Fanny Brice, who had been a Winter Garden favorite for many decades, was memorably impersonated by Barbra Streisand in the 1964 bonanza *Funny Girl*, with a striking score by Jule Styne and Bob Merrill.

Another musical triumph was scored by Angela Lansbury in the title role of *Mame*, Jerry Herman's musical treatment of the popular play *Auntie Mame*. Angela won a Tony for her spirited performance, and Beatrice Arthur and Jane Connell were her hilarious sidekicks. The hit show ran for 1,508 performances.

Hal Prince brought a most original musical to the Winter Garden in 1971. Called *Follies*, it focused on a reunion of a group of former *Follies* girls and their husbands on the stage of the theatre where they once performed. With an exciting score by Stephen Sondheim and a book by James Goldman, the surrealistic musical starred Alexis Smith, John McMartin, Dorothy Collins, Gene Nelson, and Yvonne De Carlo, and featured old-timers Ethel Shutta and Fifi D'Orsay. *Follies* won seven Tony Awards.

In 1972 and 1973 Neil Diamond and Liza Minnelli made highly successful personal appearances at the Winter Garden. Also praised was the New York Shakespeare Festival's revival of Shakespeare's *Much Ado About Nothing*, imaginatively set in Civil War times in the United States by director A.J. Antoon. Sam Waterston played Benedick, and Kathleen Widdoes was a radiant Beatrice.

Angela Lansbury returned to the Winter Garden in 1974 in a dynamic revival of *Gypsy*; and Hal Prince and Stephen Sondheim came back in 1976 with an original musical called *Pacific Overtures*, about the opening of Japan by Commodore Perry. Boris Aronson won a Tony for his splendid settings, and Florence Klotz won another Tony Award for her colorful costumes.

Zero Mostel, who won a Tony in 1965 for his portrayal of Tevye in the multiaward-winning musical *Fiddler on the Roof*, recreated his performance in a 1976 revival of the famous musical. It played for 167 performances. In 1977 a multimedia show called *Beatlemania* vividly recreated the career of the Beatles in remarkable fashion. It stayed at the Winter Garden until 1979.

A series of shows and personal appearances filled the theatre during 1979 and 1980, including *Zoot Suit*, *Gilda Radner—Live from New York*, and *Twyla Tharp and Dancers*. In August of 1980 David Merrick returned from producing films in Hollywood to bring glamour and excitement to the Winter Garden with an opulent, tap-dancing musical based on the famous 1933 movie *42nd Street*. The brilliant opening night, Broadway's most exciting in years, was marred only by the announcement by Mr. Merrick, at the show's curtain calls, that the musical's choreographer and director, Gower Champion, had died that afternoon.

In 1981 Richard Harris starred in a revival of *Camelot*, and in 1982 Christopher Plummer played a memorable Iago to James Earl Jones's powerful Othello.

In the summer of 1982 the Winter Garden underwent extensive renovation by the Shuberts—indoors and out. One feature that was retained was the block-long billboard over the marquee, which has carried enormous advertisements for each show playing the theatre.

In preparation for the arrival of Andrew Lloyd Webber's British hit *Cats*, set designer John Napier and a battery of workmen transformed the theatre into a "cosmic garbage dump." The effort paid off. Not only has *Cats* won seven Tony Awards, but by the time it completes its run it may well prove to be the most successful show in the Winter Garden's seventy-three-year history.

❧ HELEN HAYES THEATRE ❧

In July 1983, the former Little Theatre at 240 West Forty-fourth Street was officially renamed the Helen Hayes Theatre in honor of one of America's most beloved actresses. The tribute was deemed fitting by the theatrical community since the other theatre bearing the name of Helen Hayes, on West Forty-sixth Street, was torn down in 1982 to make way for a new hotel.

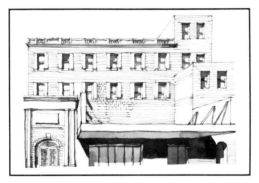

The Little was built by producer Winthrop Ames and opened on March 12, 1912. Ames, an aristocratic New Englander, rebelled against Broadway commercialism and built the Little, with only 299 seats, as an intimate house for the production of noncommercial plays that were too risky to stage in large Broadway theatres.

The New York *Times* admired the theatre's red-brick, green-shuttered exterior, its Colonial-style lobby with a fireplace, the auditorium that had no balcony or boxes and was built on an incline that afforded an unobstructed view of the stage.

The opening play was John Galsworthy's *The Pigeon*, which critic Ward Morehouse described as "a thoughtfully written comedy that brought forth human and delightful characterizations from Frank Reicher and Russ Whytal."

Ames's policy—to produce "the clever, the unusual drama that had a chance of becoming a library classic"—continued to be reflected in the Little Theatre's fare. Among the early productions, all financed solely by Ames, were George Bernard Shaw's *The Philanderer* (1913); *Prunella*, a fantasy by Laurence Houseman and Granville Barker, starring Marguerite Clark and Ernest Glendinning (1913); and Cyril Harcourt's comedy *A Pair of Stockings* (1914).

By 1915 Ames was having financial problems with the Little. Because of his theatre's small seating capacity, the impresario was losing money, even with hits. On March 11, 1915, the New York *Times* reported that Ames was in danger of losing his house. To prevent this, Ames planned to increase the seating capacity to 1,000, add a balcony, and make the stage larger. In 1920 Burns Mantle reported that the Little had been remodeled and the seating capacity was now 450 seats.

Ames, whose money came from his family's manufacturing interests, began leasing the Little to outside producers such as the highly respected John Golden and Oliver Morosco.

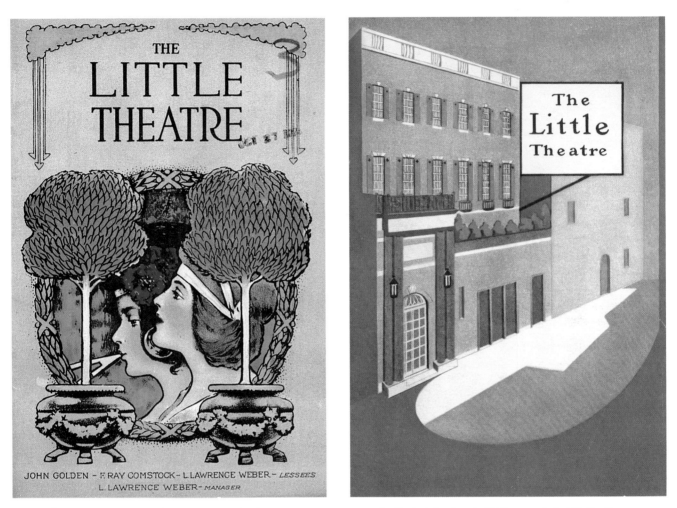

LEFT: Program cover for the 1924 hit *Pigs*. RIGHT: Program cover for Rachel Crothers's 1929 comedy *Let Us Be Gay*.

During the 1918—19 season, Rachel Crothers directed her own comedy, *A Little Journey*, at the Little. It ran for 252 performances. This was followed by another hit, *Please Get Married*, a farce starring Ernest Truex.

The true purpose of the Little Theatre, to present new playwrights and experimental dramas, was fulfilled by its next two bookings. In January 1920 Oliver Morosco presented *Mamma's Affair*, a first play by Rachel Barton Butler that won a prize as the best drama written by a student of Professor George Baker's

famous "English 47" class at Harvard. Morosco presented a cash award to the author and mounted her play successfully with Effie Shannon. The other drama was Eugene O'Neill's first full-length play, *Beyond the Horizon*, which had been playing matinees at other theatres before it was moved to the Little. It starred Richard Bennett and won the Pulitzer Prize.

The Little next housed one of its gold mines. *The First Year*, by actor Frank Craven, who starred in it with Roberta Arnold, proved to be a sensation. It opened on October 20, 1920, was produced by John Golden, and ran for 725 performances.

Producer Golden and playwright Craven thought that lightning might strike twice. In 1922 they tried again with Craven's *Spite Corner*, a small-town play about feuding families and lovers, but the comedy only lasted three months.

Guy Bolton, the prolific playwright who wrote many hit musicals and plays in his long career, had two comedies produced at the Little in 1923. The first, *Polly Preferred*, starring the vivacious blonde Genevieve Tobin and William Harrigan, was a daffy hit about a chorus girl who is sold to promotors like a product in a store window; the other, *Chicken Feed*, subtitled "Wages for Wives," was really ahead of its time. It would have delighted women's lib a half century later. It was about the right of wives to share in their husbands' income.

At this time, Ames still owned the Little, but he leased it to John Golden, F. Ray Comstock, and L. Lawrence Weber, with Weber also managing the theatre.

Brooks Atkinson reports in his book *Broadway* that by 1922 Ames had lost $504,372 on the Little Theatre. His other theatre, the Booth, which he built with Lee Shubert in 1913, was a commercial house and it is still successful today. When Ames died in 1937, his estate had dwindled to $77,000 and his widow was forced to move from the sprawling Ames mansion to a small cottage on their estate.

In 1924 a play oddly titled *Pigs* turned out to be one of the year's best. Produced by John Golden, it starred Wallace Ford as a speculator who bought fifty sick pigs, cured them, and sold them at an enormous profit. He was greatly helped by his girlfriend, played by the refreshing Nydia Westman, who garnered love letters from the critics. The hit ran for 347 performances.

Thomas Mitchell proved popular in a 1926 comedy, *The Wisdom Tooth*, by Marc Connelly; *2 Girls Wanted* was a smash in 1926; *The Grand Street Follies*, a popular annual revue that spoofed the season's plays and players, moved here from the Neighborhood Playhouse in 1927; and Rachel Crothers returned to the Little with *Let Us Be Gay*, a 1929 hit starring Francine Larrimore and Warren William.

In 1930 Edward G. Robinson was praised for his acting in *Mr. Samuel*, and Elmer Rice's *The Left Bank* (1931), about Americans in Paris,

Aline MacMahon and Thomas Chalmers in Eugene O'Neill's Pulitzer Prize play *Beyond the Horizon* (1920).

entertained patrons for 241 performances. A spate of plays with "Honeymoon" in their titles moved in. *Honeymoon* and *One More Honeymoon* were short-lived, but *Pre-Honeymoon*, by Alford Van Ronkel and Anne Nichols (author of *Abie's Irish Rose*), was a big enough hit to move from the Lyceum to the Little and to cause the theatre's name to be changed to Anne Nichols' Little Theatre.

In 1936 Sir Cedric Hardwicke made his U.S. debut in *Promise*; and in 1937, when Cornelia Otis Skinner opened her one-woman show, *Edna His Wife*, the house reverted to being called the Little. A sparkling revue, *Reunion in New York*, opened in 1940 and reunited a group of talented performers from Vienna who had been introduced to New Yorkers previously in another revue, *From Vienna* (1939).

The Little Theatre ceased being a legitimate Broadway theatre for the next two decades. During this hiatus, the house was known as the New York Times Hall from 1942 until 1959, when it became the ABC Television Studio.

The Little returned to the legitimate fold in 1963 with *Tambourines to Glory*, a gospel-music play by Langston Hughes and Jobe Huntley. The Paul Taylor Dance Company appeared there in the same year. In 1964 Habimah, the National Theatre of Israel, staged *The Dybbuk, Children of the Shadows,* and *Each Had Six Wings*. Later that year Paul Newman, Joanne Woodward, and James Costigan appeared in the Actors Studio production of Mr. Costigan's comedy *Baby Want a Kiss*. The critics gave it the kiss of death. In 1964, when the Pulitzer Prize play *The Subject Was Roses* moved to this theatre from the Royale, the theatre's name was changed to the Winthrop Ames.

In March 1965 the name went back to the Little, which it retained until 1983. From late 1964 to mid-1974 the theatre was leased to Westinghouse Broadcasting and hosted the Merv Griffin and David Frost TV shows.

In 1974 the Little went legit again and housed a play called *My Sister, My Sister. The Runner Stumbles* (1976) was a success, but *Unexpected Guests* (1977) was a failure.

In June 1977 Albert Innaurato's comedy *Gemini* moved in, and it epitomized the kind of show Winthrop Ames wanted in his theatre. The play was first done at Playwrights Horizons, then at the PAF Playhouse in Huntington, Long Island, followed by a production at the Circle Repertory Company. Finally, this production was moved to the Little, where it ran for an amazing 1,788 performances, making it the Little's longest-running show and the fifth-longest-running straight play in Broadway history.

The Little's next three shows did not fare well. They were *Ned and Jack* (1981); William Alfred's *Curse of the Aching Heart,* (1982), starring Faye Dunaway; and *Solomon's Child* (1982), an exposé of fanatical religious cults.

In June 1982 another ideal Little Theatre play came to the house. It was *Torch Song Trilogy* by Harvey Fierstein, who starred in his play about the gay life. The comedy originated at LaMama E.T.C., was next done at the Richard Allen Center for Culture, and then at the Actors' Playhouse before it moved to the Little. *Torch Song Trilogy* won the 1983 Tony Award for best play, and a Tony for best performance by an actor went to Mr. Fierstein. At this writing, the play continues at the Helen Hayes.

The Helen Hayes is currently owned by The Little Theatre Group—Martin Markinson and Donald Tick—with Ashton Springer serving as managing director. In 1981 this group spent a considerable amount to restore the house. Its interior was beautifully redesigned by ADCADESIGN: Wayne Adams, John Carlson, and Wolfgang H. Kurth. In its seventy-second year, the house that Winthrop Ames built has proven that a Broadway theatre with a small seating capacity can mount off-beat plays that are too risky for larger houses and make a success of them

🎭 ABOVE: Raphael Klaczkin (with balloons) and Aharon Meskin in *Children of the Shadows* (1964). TOP RIGHT: Danny Aiello, Barbara Coggin, and Kathleen Turner in *Gemini* (1977). RIGHT: Harvey Fierstein gives a Tony Award performance in his Tony Award winning play, *Torch Song Trilogy* (1982).

⚜ CORT THEATRE ⚜

Rarely has a Broadway legitimate theatre opened with as resounding a hit as the Cort had on the night of December 20, 1912. The play was *Peg o' My Heart* by J. Hartley Manners and it starred his illustrious wife, Laurette Taylor. The incandescent actress scored a triumph. As critic Brooks Atkinson reported years later: "J. Hartley Manners wrote a part for Laurette Taylor in 1912 that made her the most generally worshipped star of her time. She opened the new Cort Theatre on 48th Street as Peg and played it for 607 performances—the longest run of any dramatic play up to that time."

The critics also had praise for the new playhouse, located east of Broadway. Built by John Cort, a West Coast theatre impresario who came East, it was designed by architect Edward B. Corey in the style of Louis XVI. It had a marble façade with four Corinthian columns, a lobby of Pavanozza marble with panels of Marie Antoinette plaster work, and an auditorium with a seating capacity of 999. According to the New York *Tribune*, "A distinctive feature of the interior is the proscenium arch, which is of perforated plaster work against a background of art glass capable of illumination during the per-

formance. The sounding board has been decorated with a painting of a minuet during the period made famous in Watteau's drawings of French court life at Versailles."

The article added that instead of an orchestra (most theatres had live orchestras to entertain the patrons) the Cort had a "Wurlitzer Hope-Jones unit orchestra, an electrical instrument capable of operation by one musician."

The Cort's luck continued with its next occupant, *Under Cover*, a play about an undercover customs agent, starring Harry Crosby, Ralph Morgan, and George Stevens. It opened in August 1914 and ran for 349 performances. In 1915 the Cort went musical with Victor Herbert's *The Princess Pat*, which had a hit tune: "Neapolitan Love Song." It ran for 158 performances.

Other successes during this period were a Chinese play called *The Yellow Jacket* (1916); *Flo-Flo* (1917), a musical with some vaudeville headliners; and John Drinkwater's masterly *Abraham Lincoln*, starring Frank McGlyn in the title role. It ran for 244 performances.

The Cort housed a wide variety of fare during the 1920s. A musical comedy called *Jim Jam Jems* featured an incredible collection of

ABOVE: A program cover for the Cort Theatre in 1915. RIGHT: The magnificent Laurette Taylor in the Cort's famed opening show, *Peg o' My Heart* (1912).

comics: Joe E. Brown, Frank Fay, Harry Langdon, Ned Sparks, and Mr. Jokes himself, Joe E. Miller. They provided solid yocks for 105 performances in 1920. The following year brought a farcical comedy, *Captain Applejack*, produced by the estimable Sam H. Harris, and it was funny enough for 366 performances. Then, in 1922, came a classic American comedy: George S. Kaufman and Marc Connelly's *Merton of the Movies*. The critics were unanimous in their praise of this satire in which a shy, movie-crazy grocery clerk, splendidly played by Glenn Hunter, went to Hollywood and became a success because he was such a terrible actor. It was on Burns Mantle's ten-best list and ran for 398 performances.

In contrast to *Merton of the Movies* was the genteel high comedy of Ferenc Molnar's *The Swan* (1923), starring the lovely Eva Le Gallienne as a princess sought by a prince (Philip Merivale) and a humble tutor (Basil Rathbone). The Hungarian romance charmed audiences for 253 performances.

After a number of failures in 1924, the Cort presented Ethel Barrymore, who was praised for her performance in a revival of Sir Arthur Wing Pinero's *The Second Mrs. Tanqueray*, staged by Arthur Hopkins. A comedy called *White Collars* with Cornelia Otis Skinner also found favor in 1925. Six shows followed, none of them successful; then came *The Jazz Singer*, starring George Jessel, which moved here from the Fulton Theatre and ran for 315 performances. This Samson Raphaelson play later became the first talking picture, starring Al Jolson.

A comedy called *The Little Spitfire* played for 201 performances in 1926. A strange drama came to the Cort later that year. It was called *The Ladder*, and before it had run its course (794 performances) it had played in five different Broadway theatres—including two engagements at the Cort. The play was about reincarnation and had Antoinette Perry and Ross Alexander in the cast. The critics called it hokum, and the producer, Brock Pemberton, sometimes let people in for nothing.

George Kelly's *Behold the Bridegroom* (1927), starring Judith Anderson, Mary Servoss, and Lester Vail, was admired, but lasted for only eighty-eight performances. On November 12, 1928, a drama called *These Days* opened with a large cast of young girls playing rich young students in a finishing school. Among them was an actress making her Broadway debut—her name was Katharine Hepburn. The play ran for only eight performances, but launched a spectacular career that is still flourishing a half century later.

Alice Brady appeared at the Cort in *A Most Immoral Lady* in late 1928 and helped the play to run for 160 performances. The Cort's last show of the 1920s was *Your Uncle Dudley*, a homespun comedy by Howard Lindsay and Bertrand Robinson, starring Walter Connolly. It rang out the Roaring Twenties with 96 performances.

In April 1930 Jed Harris, the boy wonder, returned from London and produced and directed an acclaimed revival of Chekov's *Uncle Vanya*, adapted by Mrs. Ben Hecht (Rose Caylor). Harris's direction and the acting of his sterling cast, Lillian Gish, Osgood Perkins, Walter Connolly, Eduardo Ciannelli, Joanna Roos, and others, made the occasion a theatrical event.

The end of 1930 brought a taut, cynical exposé of scandal-mongering newspapers called *Five-Star Final*. It starred Arthur Byron, Frances Fuller, and Berton Churchill, and featured Allen Jenkins. Theatregoers supported it for 176 showings.

Two enterprising producers—Alfred de Liagre, Jr., and Richard Aldrich—brought a screwball family to the Cort in 1933 in a comedy called *Three-Cornered Moon*, making an auspicious producing debut. The excellent cast included Ruth Gordon, Richard Whorf, Brian

riotous *Boy Meets Girl*, by Bella and Samuel Spewack, was a hysterical spoof of Hollywood said to be inspired by the West Coast shenanigans of Ben Hecht and Charles MacArthur when they toiled there as scriptwriters. With Jerome Cowan and Allyn Joslyn as the madcap writers, Joyce Arling as an unwed mother, and Abbott's famous "touch" in direction, *Boy Meets Girl* had Cort audiences in stitches for 669 performances.

On May 19, 1937, Abbott ushered in his production of another raucous farce, *Room Service*, by John P. Murray and Allen Boretz. With such expert farceurs as Sam Levene, Teddy Hart, Philip Loeb, Eddie Albert, and Betty Field,

ABOVE: Lillian Gish in the acclaimed Jed Harris production of *Uncle Vanya* (1930). RIGHT: Laurence Olivier and Jill Esmond in the British shocker *The Green Bay Tree* (1933).

Donlevy, and Cecilia Loftus.

Later in 1933 a sensational drama arrived from Britain. It was Mordaunt Shairp's *The Green Bay Tree* and it starred Laurence Olivier, James Dale, Jill Esmond (Mrs. Olivier at that time), O.P. Heggie, and Leo G. Carroll. Jed Harris's direction was highly praised for its subtlety in depicting a questionable relationship between a wealthy male hedonist and a poor, handsome young boy, played by Olivier.

From October 1935 to July 1938 the Cort had only two bookings, but they were both George Abbott smashes. The first one, the

TOP (from left): PLAYBILL covers for *The Male Animal* (1940), José Ferrer in *Charley's Aunt* (1940), and Wolcott Gibbs's comedy *Season in the Sun* (1950). LEFT: Grace Kelly, making her Broadway debut, with Mady Christians in *The Father* (1949). ABOVE: Katharine Hepburn and William Prince in the 1950 revival of *As You Like It.*

the comedy chronicled the plight of a group of hungry actors and some shoestring producers living in a seedy hotel while trying to get backing for the play they wish to put on. It was a Cort favorite for 496 performances.

The year 1939 witnessed memorable performances by Jessica Tandy and Barry Fitzgerald in Paul Vincent Carroll's *The White Steed.*

The 1940s brought exciting theatre to the Cort. Among the highlights: *The Male Animal* (1940), an intelligent comedy by James Thurber and Elliott Nugent, starring Nugent, Gene Tierney, Ruth Matteson, and Don DeFore; a lively revival of *Charley's Aunt* (1940), staged by Joshua Logan, with José Ferrer and Mrs. Logan (Nedda Harrigan); the warmhearted *Café Crown* (1942), starring Sam Jaffe and Morris Carnovsky as leading actors of the Yiddish Theatre who gather each evening in a popular Second Avenue café; Maxwell Anderson's moving war drama *The Eve of St. Mark* (1942), with William Prince as a farmboy who goes to war and Aline MacMahon as his mother; *A Bell for Adano* (1944), Paul Osborn's faithful adaptation of John Hersey's novel about the American occupation of Italy at war's end, starring Fredric March as an army major; The Theatre Guild Shakespearean Company in *The Winter's Tale* (1946); Katharine Cornell and Cedric Hardwicke in Anouilh's version of *Antigone* (1946), alternating with Shaw's *Candida*, in which Marlon Brando played a rather prissy Marchbanks; Canada Lee in *On Whitman Avenue* (1946), a play about a black family moving into a white neighborhood; Cornelia Otis Skinner, Estelle Winwood, and Cecil Beaton in Wilde's *Lady Windermere's Fan* (1946–47), with sets, costumes, and lighting by Beaton; Meg Mundy's powerful performance in Sartre's *The Respectful Prostitute* (1948), which moved to the Cort from the New Stages Theatre on Bleecker Street; Melvyn Douglas and Jan Sterling in Sam Spewack's political satire *Two Blind Mice* (1949); and a

Katharine Cornell in Anouilh's treatment of *Antigone* (1946).

revival of Strindberg's *The Father* (1949), with Raymond Massey, Mady Christians, and, making her Broadway debut, Grace Kelly.

The Cort continued to house hits in the 1950s, beginning with a leggy Katharine Hepburn in an engaging revival of *As You Like It,* with William Prince as Orlando and Cloris Leachman as Celia. Wolcott Gibbs, drama critic for *The New Yorker,* came up with a hit comedy, *Season in the Sun,* about the straight deni-

ABOVE: Caricatures of José Ferrer and Judith Evelyn in *The Shrike* (1952). BELOW: Susan Strasberg and Joseph Schildkraut in *The Diary of Anne Frank* (1955).

zens of Fire Island (1950). Uta Hagen drew praise for her Joan in Shaw's *Saint Joan* (1951); Joseph Kramm won a Pulitzer Prize for his harrowing drama *The Shrike* (1952), about a husband (José Ferrer) who is committed to a mental institution by his odious wife (Judith Evelyn); Menasha Skulnik entertained in a garment district spoof, *The Fifth Season* (1953); Geraldine Page, Albert Salmi, and Darren McGavin enhanced *The Rainmaker* (1954); Frances Goodrich and Albert Hackett won a Pulitzer Prize, New York Drama Critics Circle Award, and Tony for their moving play *The Diary of Anne Frank* (1955), starring Susan Strasberg as Anne, Joseph Schildkraut and Gusti Huber as her parents, and Lou Jacobi and Jack Gilford as other hideouts in the doomed Frank attic; Siobhan McKenna, Art Carney, and Joan Blondell scored in the tragic drama *The Rope Dancers* (1957); and *Sunrise at Campobello*, Dore Schary's study of FDR's early years, won four Tony Awards, including best play and best male performance (Ralph Bellamy as Roosevelt) in 1958.

The 1960s brought Brendan Behan's rowdy play *The Hostage* (1960), with a cast largely drawn from Joan Littlewood's Theatre Workshop in London. Next came a dramatization of Allen Drury's popular political novel *Advise and Consent*, with a cast that included Richard Kiley, Ed Begley, Kevin McCarthy, and Barnard Hughes. It lasted for 212 performances. This was followed by an engaging black play, *Purlie Victorious*, written by and starring Ossie Davis, with Ruby Dee, Alan Alda, and Godfrey Cambridge. In November 1961 a young Robert Redford trod the Cort stage in Norman Krasna's thin comedy *Sunday in New York*, produced by David Merrick, directed by Garson Kanin, and not very successful.

From mid-1962 until mid-1969 the Cort booked many shows, but few successes. Some of the more interesting exhibits were a brief visit by the Royal Dramatic Theatre of Sweden acting in *The Father*, *Long Day's Journey into Night*, and *Miss Julie* (1962); Kirk Douglas in an unsuccessful adaptation of *One Flew Over the Cuckoo's Nest* (1963); and Louis Gossett and Menasha Skulnik in *The Zulu and the Zayda* (1965).

In 1969, the Cort was leased to television for several years and served as the theatre from which the Merv Griffin Show emanated.

On May 28, 1974, the Cort made a dazzling comeback as a legitimate house. Owned for many years by the Shubert Organization, the theatre was beautifully restored for its return to the theatrical fold. It reopened with *The Magic Show*, a musical that would have died on its opening night if it had not had Doug Henning in the cast. Mr. Henning, one of the world's best and most amiable magicians, created such incredible magic on the Cort's stage that the show ran for 1,920 performances.

The Cort's most recent tenants have run a wide gamut. Al Pacino starred in a disastrous Brooklynese version of Shakespeare's *Richard III* (1979), and Tennessee Williams suffered critical arrows for his play about F. Scott and Zelda Fitzgerald, *Clothes for a Summer Hotel* (1980). An engaging black play, *Home*, won favor that spring; and Glenda Jackson and Jessica Tandy acted grandly in the unsuccessful British play *Rose* (1981). In 1982 there was an engrossing revival of *Medea* starring Zoe Caldwell, whose passionate performance won her a Tony Award, and Judith Anderson, who made the role famous in 1947, playing the Nurse this time.

The Cort's most recent occupants were Murray Schisgal's two one-act plays, collectively called *Twice Around the Park*, starring the husband/wife team of Eli Wallach and Anne Jackson.

The Cort, now enjoying its seventy-second year, is still one of Broadway's most beautiful theatres.

ABOVE: Ralph Bellamy as FDR in *Sunrise at Campobello* (1958). BELOW: Zoe Caldwell and Dame Judith Anderson in the 1982 revival of *Medea*.

⚔ PALACE THEATRE ⚔

"Playing the Palace"—it was the dream of every vaudeville performer. In its heyday, from 1913 until the thirties, the "mecca of migrating minstrels" at Forty-seventh Street and Times Square booked everyone who was anyone—from Sarah Bernhardt to Trixie Friganza and her bag of Trix, from Ethel Barrymore to Dr. Rockwell ("Quack! Quack! Quack!").

The Palace was the dream house of impresario Martin Beck, but by the time it opened, he held only 25 percent controlling interest in the theatre. By complex wheeling and dealing, vaudeville circuit mogul B.F. Keith and E.F. Albee (playwright Edward Albee's adoptive grandfather) stormed the Palace and gained control.

In her book *The Palace*, Marian Spitzer describes the opening of the theatre on Easter Monday, March 24, 1913: "The theatre itself, living up to advance publicity, was spacious, handsome and lavishly decorated in crimson and gold. But nothing happened that afternoon to suggest the birth of a great theatrical tradition."

On the Palace's opening vaudeville bill, presented twice daily with $1.50 top at matinees and $2.00 at night, were such acts as Ota Gygi ("the court violinist of Spain"); McIntyre and

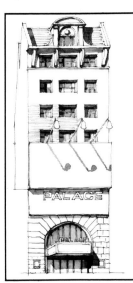

Harty ("a comedy team"); La Napierkowska ("pantomimist and interpretive dancer"); *The Eternal Waltz* ("a condensed Viennese operetta with a cast of 30"); and Ed Wynn ("The King's Jester"). It was the hope of the Palace Theatre management to give competition to its chief rival, Oscar Hammerstein's Victoria Theatre at Broadway and Forty-second Street, but it did not achieve this goal during its opening week. The show was negatively received, especially by *Variety*, the show business Bible, which lamented the poor quality of the acts and the outrageous $2.00 top.

It took the prestige of two major legitimate theatre actresses to put the Palace on the map. In its sixth week, the theatre presented the First Lady of the American Theatre —Ethel Barrymore—in a one-act play by Richard Harding Davis, *Miss Civilization*, and business began to improve. But the turning point came on May 5, when the Divine Sarah Bernhardt brought her French company of actors and her repertoire to the Palace and caused a sensation for almost a month. It was her first appearance in vaudeville in New York. She saved the Palace from disaster and helped turn it into the foremost vaudeville theatre in the world.

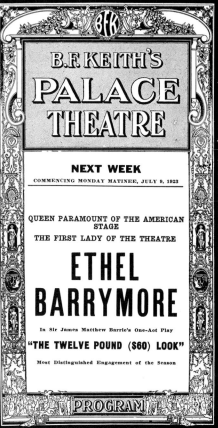

FAR LEFT: Palace program cover for week of May 8, 1922. LEFT: Program for Ethel Barrymore's appearance in 1923. BELOW: The Palace as it looked in 1942.

In the golden era of vaudeville, the Palace stage saw the likes of such great headliners as Harry Houdini, Will Rogers, W.C. Fields, Fanny Brice, Sophie Tucker, Fred Astaire, Ethel Merman, William Gaxton, Eddie Cantor, Jack Benny, Milton Berle, Smith and Dale, the Marx Brothers, Kate Smith, and countless others. Burns and Allen arrived with a new act every season. And then there were other acts like Fink's Mules and Power's Elephants.

The Palace was the queen of Broadway in 1927 when a talking picture called *The Jazz Singer* opened a few blocks uptown. Once the silver screen began to talk, vaudeville was on its way out.

From the thirties on, it was a constant struggle for survival. The Palace tried a little of everything—combination bills of movies and vaudeville shows, then just movies, and finally, in the 1950s, personal appearances by select superstars. The first arrived on the night of October 16, 1951, and her name was Judy Garland. She scored a triumph and played the Palace for nineteen weeks. Next came Betty Hutton, then Danny Kaye (fourteen weeks), fol-

lowed by return engagements of Betty Hutton and Judy Garland. Jerry Lewis was a hit with his personal appearance show, but Liberace failed to draw crowds.

On August 13, 1957, the Palace reverted to showing movies, with no vaudeville, and only interrupted this policy once, on December 15, 1959, when Harry Belafonte made a sensational appearance for more than three months.

On August 19, 1965, a miracle happened. James Nederlander, acting for the Nederlander family, who owned legitimate theatres in Detroit and Chicago, bought the Palace and, at great expense, had it beautifully restored to its original crimson and gold. Crystal chandeliers were removed from storage and rehung in the theatre, stage boxes that had been concealed for decades by false fronts were restored, and the lobby was refurbished and embellished with portraits of Palace greats, loaned by the Museum of the City of New York. The restoration of the Palace was achieved by the famed scene designer Ralph Alswang, and when he and his workers were through, the Palace was ready for its first legitimate show.

OPPOSITE: Portrait of Judy Garland on the cover of the program for her 1951 Palace engagement; program sketch of Danny Kaye for his smash appearance in 1953.

LEFT TO RIGHT: Joel Grey as song-and-dance man George M. Cohan in the musical *George M!* (1968); Gwen Verdon in her hit, *Sweet Charity*, which made the Palace "legitimate" (1966); Lauren Bacall in her Tony Award winning performance in *Woman of the Year* (1981).

LEFT: PLAYBILL covers for Christopher Plummer in the musical *Cyrano* (1973) and Bette Midler in concert (1973). OPPOSITE: PLAYBILL covers for the 1977 revival of *Man of La Mancha* and the huge success *La Cage aux folles* (1983).

The reopening of the Palace as a legitimate theatre on January 29, 1966, was a major news event and was covered by television cameras and the print media. Fortunately, the opening show was *Sweet Charity*, starring the great Gwen Verdon. Both the musical and the restored Palace were a huge hit. With a book by Neil Simon, jaunty score by Cy Coleman and Dorothy Fields, and spectacular choreography by Ms. Verdon's husband, Bob Fosse, the musical, based on Fellini's film *Nights of Cabiria*, brightened the Messrs. Nederlander's Palace for 608 performances.

In July 1967 Judy Garland returned in a production called *At Home at the Palace,* followed later that summer by a double bill of Eddie Fisher and Buddy Hackett.

Don Ameche and Carol Bruce, aided by three talented young girls—Alice Playten, Neva Small, and Robin Wilson—were engaging in a musical called *Henry, Sweet Henry* (1967), but the show only lasted for 80 performances. The Grand Music Hall of Israel paid a visit in the early months of 1968, then, on April 10, *George M!* took over. It is ironic that George M. Cohan was one of the few headliners who never played the Palace. (Al Jolson was another.) But Cohan was skillfully impersonated by Joel Grey in *George M!*; he strutted the Palace stage for 433 performances.

Lauren Bacall, in her first Broadway musical, *Applause,* gave such a cyclonic performance in the spring of 1970 that she was awarded a Tony for her tour de force. The musical, with a book by Betty Comden and Adolph Green and a score by Charles Strouse and Lee Adams, was

based on the celebrated Bette Davis film *All About Eve*. Supported by Len Cariou, Bonnie Franklin, Penny Fuller, and Lee Roy Reams, Bacall flourished at the Palace for eighteen months.

During the 1970s, such superstars as Bette Midler, Josephine Baker, Shirley MacLaine, and Diana Ross made splashy Palace appearances. Legitimate attractions included Christopher Plummer in his Tony Award winning performance in the title role of the musical *Cyrano* (1973); Carol Channing in a revised version of *Gentlemen Prefer Blondes* called *Lorelei* (1974); Richard Kiley in a return engagement of *Man of La Mancha* (1977); Joel Grey in *The Grand Tour* (1979), a musical version of *Jacobowsky and the Colonel*; a lively revival of *Oklahoma!* (1979); a colossal production of *Frankenstein*

(1981), starring John Carradine, that closed on its opening night; and Lauren Bacall, back at the Palace in *Woman of the Year*, a musical version of the popular 1942 film of the same name starring Spencer Tracy and Katharine Hepburn. Bacall's costar in the musical was Harry Guardino. The show won four Tonys: outstanding actress in a musical (Bacall); outstanding featured actress in a musical (Marilyn Cooper); best musical book (Peter Stone); best musical score (John Kander and Fred Ebb).

It is fitting that in its seventy-first year, the Palace is currently housing the musical hit *La Cage aux folles*. After surviving the death of vaudeville, talking pictures, and the television threat, the Palace has carved another niche in theatrical history as a prime musical comedy house in the heart of Times Square.

LONGACRE THEATRE

A colorful character named H.H. Frazee built the Longacre Theatre at 200 West Forty-eighth Street, between Broadway and Eighth Avenue. It was named after Longacre Square, which is now Times Square. Frazee hired architect Henry B. Herts to create a theatre that would specialize in the staging of musical comedies. Herts, who designed some of Broadway's finest theatres, turned out a lovely playhouse that managed to look intimate while seating over 1,400 patrons.

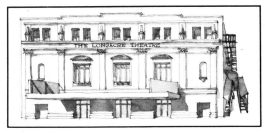

The Longacre opened on the night of May 1, 1913, with an unfunny farce called *Are You a Crook?*, starring Marguerite Clark. It perished after a dozen showings. Frazee did much better with a musical show. On August 28 of that year, his theatre housed a French entertainment called *Adele* and it was the most successful importation of the season. It delighted theatregoers for 196 performances.

A.H. Woods, a producer who thrived on melodramas, presented a play called *Kick In* in 1914. The interesting cast included John Barrymore, Katherine Harris (who became the first Mrs. Barrymore), Jane Gray, and Forrest Winant. The "crook" melodrama stole its way into playgoers' hearts for 188 performances. That year a farce called *A Pair of Sixes* also won favor and ran for 207 mirthful performances.

A number of shows played the Longacre in 1915—Lewis Stone in *Inside the Lines*, May Vokes in *A Full House*—but the most successful was a comedy called *The Great Lover*, starring Leo Ditrichstein, which focused on love among the temperaments of the egocentric opera world.

The Longacre welcomed its biggest hit to date when *Nothing but the Truth* opened on September 14, 1916. Written by James Montgomery, the comedy starred the deadpan William Collier, who convulsed audiences as a man who vowed not to tell lies for one day. He managed to do this for 332 performances.

The kind of intimate, charming musical that Frazee envisioned for his house came to the Longacre in 1917. It was the Jerome Kern/P.G. Wodehouse/Guy Bolton winner *Leave It to Jane*, about a football-crazy college campus. Among the Kern gems were: "The Siren's Song," "The Crickets Are Calling," "Cleopatterer," and the lilting title song. The Longacre had full houses for 167 performances. Guy Bolton and George Middleton provided a palpable hit for the house with *Adam and Eva*, starring Otto Kruger and Ruth Shepley, in 1919.

ABOVE: Standard Longacre program cover in the 1920s. TOP RIGHT: The Longacre's first show, *Are You a Crook?* with Marguerite Clark and Elizabeth Nelson (1913). BOTTOM RIGHT: Dudley Digges, Peter Holden, and Dorothy Stickney in *On Borrowed Time* (1938).

The Group Theatre's stirring production of Clifford Odets's *Waiting for Lefty* (1935).

Some highlights of the 1920s included a musical called *Pitter Patter* (1920), starring William Kent; *The Champion* (1920), with Grant Mitchell; *Little Jesse James* (1923), an intimate musical with only one set, eight chorus girls, a modest cast that included future movie star Miriam Hopkins, one hit song—"I Love You"—and a smash run of 385 performances; *Moonlight* (1924), another intimate musical with tuneful Con Conrad music; *The Dark Angel* (1925), a poignant drama about a woman whose lover returns blind from World War I and pretends that he is dead; *Mercenary Mary* (1925), another Con Conrad musical with a jazz band and a star-and-garter chorus; George S. Kaufman's *The Butter and Egg Man* (1925), a hit "inside" comedy about a hick (memorably played by Gregory Kelly) who comes to Broadway with $20,000 to invest in a show and, after many tribulations, succeeds; a thrilling adaptation of Theodore Dreiser's novel *An American Tragedy* (1926), starring Morgan Farley as the murderer, Katherine Wilson as his victim, and Miriam Hopkins as his rich girlfriend; *The Command to Love* (1927), a surprisingly delightful German high comedy starring Basil Rathbone, Mary Nash, Violet Kemble Cooper, and Anthony Kemble Cooper that lasted for 236 performances; Richard Bennett and his attractive daughter Joan in a shocker about Hollywood low life called *Jarnegan* (1928); Clark Gable in an interesting murder mystery, *Hawk Island* (1929), that only ran for three weeks; and the final play of the twenties, *A Primer for Lovers*, a sex farce with the delightful Alison Skipworth.

After a series of unsuccessful plays in 1930 and 1931, the Longacre finally had a hit in *Blessed Event* (1932), starring Roger Pryor in a thinly disguised impersonation of the egotistical Broadway columnist Walter Winchell, with Isabel Jewell and Allen Jenkins in support. A dramatization of the infamous Lizzie Borden ax murders, *Nine Pine Street*, had a fine performance by Lillian Gish as the neurotic killer, but it only ran a few weeks in 1933. The same fate was accorded to *Wednesday's Child* (1934), a study of a young boy (Frank M. Thomas, Jr.) whose life is ruined when his parents divorce.

During the height of the depression, the Longacre was dark for months on end. Most of the shows that played there were quick flops. A bright spot in 1935, however, was the arrival of the revolutionary Group Theatre at the Longacre with two of Clifford Odets's inflammatory plays, *Waiting for Lefty* and *Till the Day I Die*. Mr. Odets appeared in *Waiting for Lefty*, and both plays had such Group stalwarts as Elia Kazan, Lee J. Cobb, Roman Bohnen, Russell Collins, and Alexander Kirkland. Later in 1935 another Odets play, *Paradise Lost*, with many of the same actors, played the theatre.

Late in 1936 the great actress Nazimova played Ibsen's *Hedda Gabler* for a month; and Vincent Price and the beautiful Elissa Landi starred in a romantic Hungarian play about royal affairs, *The Lady Has a Heart* (1937).

Finally, on February 3, 1938, an enchanting play came to the Longacre. It was Paul Osborn's loving adaptation of a novel called *On Borrowed Time*. Said Brooks Atkinson in the *Times*: "Nothing so original and jovial has turned up on our stages for a long time." The fantasy concerned a grandfather (Dudley Digges) who chases Death (called Mr. Brink) up a tree so that he can have some time to spend with his lovable grandson (Peter Holden). Grandma was played by Dorothy Stickney. Directed by Joshua Logan, the play brought magic to the Longacre for 321 performances.

In late 1939 Paul Osborn returned to this theatre with another endearing play about small-town people—*Morning's at Seven*. Despite Joshua Logan's direction and a superb cast that included Dorothy Gish, Russell Collins, Enid Markey, Effie Shannon, and Jean Adair, this gentle comedy about life among the elderly only lasted for 44 performances. It was clearly ahead of its time. When it was revived on Broadway in 1980, it ran for 564 performances, was hailed as an American classic, and won a Tony Award as the season's best revival.

The critics may have turned up their noses at a comedy called *Three's a Family* (1943), but audiences loved this play about the raising of babies and the care of expectant mothers. It was perfect escapist comedy for World War II

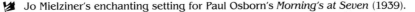

Jo Mielziner's enchanting setting for Paul Osborn's *Morning's at Seven* (1939).

and Arnaud d'Usseau, was staged by Harold Clurman and had in its cast Edna Best, Betty Field, June Walker, Walter Matthau, and Shepperd Strudwick. Unfortunately, its depressing plot about lonely old women who live in hotels did not find a public.

The Longacre's best plays in the 1950s were Lillian Hellman's adaptation of Jean Anouilh's *The Lark* (1955), with Julie Harris as a radiant Saint Joan, also starring Boris Karloff and Christopher Plummer, and a silken comedy of manners, *The Pleasure of His Company* (1958), by Samuel Taylor, starring Cornelia Otis Skinner, Walter Abel, Cyril Ritchard, George Peppard, Charlie Ruggles, and Dolores Hart. In between these two hits there was an amiable comedy about the Seventh Avenue garment district, *Fair Game* (1957), starring the expert comic Sam Levene and a new actress named Ellen McRae, who later changed her name to Ellen Burstyn and became a star.

In 1961 Zero Mostel's powerful performance in *Rhinoceros*, the antic play by Ionesco, won him a Tony Award. The excellent cast also included Eli Wallach, Anne Jackson, Morris Carnovsky, and Jean Stapleton. At the end of the year a popular play about blacks, *Purlie Victorious*, moved to the Longacre from the Cort and stayed for six months.

Highlights of the 1960s included Henry Denker's courtroom drama *A Case of Libel*, based on Quentin Reynolds's libel suit against Westbrook Pegler and starring Van Heflin, Sidney Blackmer, and Larry Gates (1963); Gabriel Dell and Rita Moreno in Lorraine Hansberry's *The Sign in Sidney Brustein's Window* (1964); Margaret Leighton, Zoe Caldwell, and Kate Reid in Tennessee Williams's lunatic *Slapstick Tragedy* (1966); Hal Holbrook in his dazzling one-man show *Mark Twain Tonight* (1966); Holbrook again in Robert Anderson's somber autobiographical drama *I Never Sang for My Father* (1968), also starring Teresa Wright (then Mrs.

theatregoers and it amused them for close to 500 performances. It was to be the Longacre's last legitimate show for a decade. From the spring of 1944 to the fall of 1953 the theatre was leased as a radio and television playhouse.

In November 1953 the Longacre reopened as a legitimate theatre with a promising play. *The Ladies of the Corridor*, by Dorothy Parker

Robert Anderson) and Lillian Gish; and a visit by the National Theatre of the Deaf (1969).

A rollicking hit, *The Ritz* (1975), by Terrence McNally, with Rita Moreno and Jack Weston, caused hysterics for a year, followed by a Tony Award winning performance by Julie Harris in her one-woman show *The Belle of Amherst*, in which she impersonated the poet Emily Dickinson. John Gielgud and Ralph Richardson were hypnotic in Pinter's *No-Man's-Land* (1976); Al Pacino garnered raves in a revival of David Rabe's *The Basic Training of Pavlo Hummel* (1977).

On May 9, 1978, *Ain't Misbehavin'* moved in and proved to be one of this theatre's biggest hits. This revue of Fats Waller's music won a Tony Award, a New York Drama Critics Circle Award, Drama Desk, and Outer Critics Circle Award as the season's best musical. The brilliant performers were Ken Page, Nell Carter, Charlaine Woodard, Andre DeShields, Armelia McQueen, and pianist Luther Henderson. Director Richard Maltby, Jr., won a Tony.

The Longacre's longest-running play, *Children of a Lesser God*, came to the theatre from the Mark Taper Forum in Los Angeles. A sensitive study of a woman with impaired speech and hearing, it won Tony Awards for best play (by Mark Medoff) and outstanding performances by an actress (Phyllis Frelich) and an actor (John Rubinstein). It ran for 887 performances.

The Longacre's most recent plays have been Lanford Wilson's fascinating *Angels Fall* (1983), followed by Peter Nichols's British play *Passion*, starring Frank Langella, Cathryn Damon, Bob Gunton, E. Katherine Kerr, Roxanne Hart, and Stephanie Gordon.

The Shubert Organization is the current owner of the Longacre and has kept the theatre in excellent condition. Although the Longacre was built as a musical comedy house, it has had more success as a playhouse for comedies and dramas.

ABOVE: Armelia McQueen, Nell Carter, and Charlaine Woodard in *Ain't Misbehavin'* (1978). BELOW: John Rubinstein and Phyllis Frelich in *Children of a Lesser God* (1980).

⚜ SHUBERT THEATRE ⚜

The Shubert Theatre occupies a special niche in theatrical history. It was built by the Shubert brothers (Lee and J.J.) in tribute to their brother Sam S. Shubert, who got them started in the theatrical business and who died in a railroad accident when he was just twenty-nine years old.

Occupying a choice location in the heart of the theatre district, on West Forty-fourth Street, between Broadway and Eighth Avenue, it was also enhanced by an alley that separated it from the Hotel Astor. It became famous as Shubert Alley. A private thoroughfare for the Shuberts, the alley was brightened with theatrical posters of current Broadway shows and by Shubert limousines parked between its gates, which were locked at night.

During the depression years, a picket fence divided the alley in two. One side was used as a bus terminal for a New Jersey bus line and the other half served as the alley where the Shubert and Booth theatres had their stage doors. During intermissions, the casts of shows playing at these two theatres would congregate in that part of Shubert Alley for fresh air (theatres were not air conditioned yet), and the audiences could see them buying Popsicles and soda pop.

The Shubert opened on October 2, 1913, and above the auditorium were the offices of the Shubert empire and an apartment where Lee Shubert lived. According to the New York *Tribune* for September 28, 1913, the new theatre had 1,400 seats, making it ideal for housing musicals. The architect was Henry B. Harris, and the elaborate interiors, in a Venetian Renaissance style, were by O.H. Bauer, with mural paintings by Lichtenauer. A portrait of Sam S. Shubert adorned the attractive lobby, overseeing the new house.

The opening attraction, surprisingly, was not a Shubert operetta or musical but the eminent British actor Johnston Forbes-Robertson in his farewell performance as Hamlet. He and his company also acted in other Shakespearean plays.

The Shubert's first musical, *The Belle from Bond Street*, opened on March 18, 1914, and starred the stunning Gaby Deslys and the popular Sam Bernard, but it was not a success. Several other musical failures followed; then there was a well-received revival of George Du Maurier's haunting play *Trilby* (1915), about the hypnotic influence of the sinister Svengali over the singer Trilby O'Farrell. Even the acerbic critic

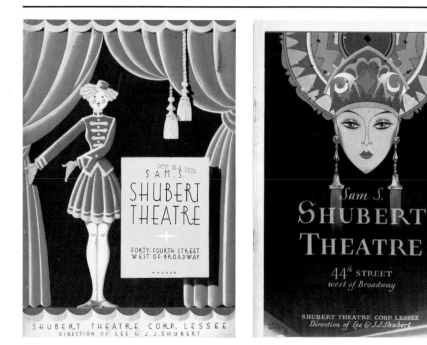

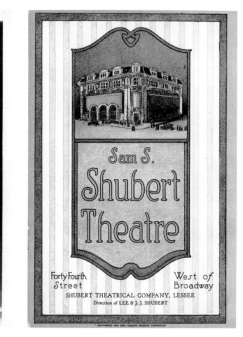

▲ ABOVE (from left): Shubert program covers for 1927, 1928, 1929. LEFT: Lionel Barrymore in the stirring Civil War drama *The Copperhead* (1918). BELOW: Peggy Wood in the beloved Sigmund Romberg operetta *Maytime* (1917).

Alexander Woollcott, who had been barred from Shubert theatres for panning a Shubert show called *Taking Chances,* praised *Trilby.*

The Shubert's first musical hit was *Alone at Last* (1915), a Franz Lehár show starring John Charles Thomas. Jerome Kern had a hit in *Love o' Mike* (1917), with Clifton Webb dancing suavely with Gloria Goodwin. But both of these shows were topped by Sigmund Romberg's lushly romantic operetta *Maytime,* which was so successful that the Shuberts had to open a second company of it right across the street from the Shubert Theatre at the Forty-fourth Street Theatre. The stars at the Shubert were Peggy Wood, Charles Purcell, and Douglas J. Ward, who sang their hearts out for almost 500 performances (1917).

On February 18, 1918, Lionel Barrymore scored one of his greatest successes in *The Copperhead,* a dramatic Civil War drama in which Barrymore had to pretend to be a Dixie sympathizer while supplying military secrets to the Yanks. Despised by his family and friends, he could not reveal his true sympathies until twenty years later.

On October 4, 1918, Mae West and Ed Wynn convulsed Shubert audiences in Rudolf Friml's musical *Sometime.* Mae played a vamp who compromised Ed Wynn and caused his fiancée (Francine Larrimore) to drop him for five years in protest. The musical played only a month at the Shubert, then was transferred to another house where it completed its run of 283 performances. Two 1919 musicals that were moderately successful were *Good Morning, Judge,* a British import that wisely interpolated two George Gershwin numbers: "There's More to the Kiss Than XXX" and "I Was So Young," and Sigmund Romberg's *The Magic Melody,* which was too reminiscent of his *Maytime* plot, even to the employment of its same leading man, Charles Purcell.

Some class returned to the Shubert in the fall of 1919 when E.H. Sothern and Julia Marlowe played their classical repertory at the theatre.

Highlights of the 1920s at this theatre included an appearance by the silent screen siren Theda Bara in a preposterous drama called *The Blue Flame* (1920), in which her dead body is brought back to life by a mad scientist; Margaret Anglin in *The Trial of Joan of Arc* (1921), translated from the French play by Emil Moreau; the luxurious *Greenwich Village Follies* revues, staged by John Murray Anderson, and the *Artists and Models* revues (1921–26), notorious for their nudity, starring such stars as Joe E. Brown, female impersonator Bert Savoy and Jay Brennan (his partner), Ted Lewis, Moran and Mack, and Vincent Lopez and his orchestra; and a revue called *Vogues of 1924,* with expert comics Jimmy Savo and Fred Allen. An interesting failure, *The Magnolia Lady,* starred Ruth Chatterton and Ralph Forbes, performers usually associated with dramas and comedies rather than musicals.

For a change of pace, the Shubert presented Walter Hampden in *Othello* in January 1925, and the actor set a record for that time by playing the Moor of Venice for eight consecutive weeks. Years later, in 1943, at the same theatre, Paul Robeson would also break records with his magnificent portrayal of Shakespeare's tragic Moor.

The homespun comic Chic Sale had a hit with a revue called *Gay Paree* (1925) that had nothing to do with Paris; *Countess Maritza* (1926), an operetta by Emmerich Kálmán, with the popular song "Play Gypsies—Dance Gypsies," was an enormous success; the "rubber legs" Leon Errol had some hilarious drunk scenes in the hit musical *Yours Truly* (1927); the noisy nightclub hostess Texas Guinan, who coined the phrase "Hello, suckers," attracted customers in a revue called *Padlocks of 1927,* supported by Lillian Roth and J.C. Flippen singing some clever lyrics by Billy Rose; not even Laurette Taylor could save Zoe Akins's murder mystery *The Furies* (1928) from rigor mortis; *Ups-a-Daisy* (1928) is a musical worth mentioning only because its cast included a comic butler played by a young man named Bob Hope; *A Night in Venice*, starring Ted Healy, was a minor musical that brought the 1920s to a close at the Shubert.

The 1930s began with sobriety. The Chicago Civic Shakespeare Society, headed by Fritz Leiber, staged nine of Shakespeare's greatest plays in repertory. Nonsense returned with Walter Slezak making his debut in a musical, *Meet My Sister* (1930). Ann Pennington, Oscar Shaw, Frances Williams, and a newcomer named Harriette Lake (later, Ann Sothern of the films) played for 127 performances in a musical called *Everybody's Welcome* (1931), which boasted an immortal song by Herman Hupfeld: "As Time Goes By." Another celebrated song, the theme song of the depression—"Brother, Can You Spare a Dime?"—was first heard in *Americana*, a revue that played the Shubert in 1932.

In January 1933 Fred Astaire in his last Broadway musical, *The Gay Divorce*, moved from the Barrymore to the Shubert and danced "Night and Day" with Claire Luce for six more months. Walter Huston, Fay Bainter, Maria Ouspenskaya, and Nan Sunderland (Mrs. Huston) were the hit of the season in Sidney Howard's *Dodsworth*, a skillful adaptation of the Sinclair Lewis novel of the same name.

The Shubert housed its first Pulitzer Prize play in March 1936. Robert E. Sherwood's anti-war play *Idiot's Delight*, with glittering performances by Alfred Lunt as a seedy hoofer and Lynn Fontanne as the mysterious mistress of a munitions maker, took Broadway by storm and was one of the finest plays that the prestigious Theatre Guild produced in its distinguished history.

In 1937 Maxwell Anderson's *The Masque of*

ABOVE: Al Jolson in his last Broadway show, *Hold On To Your Hats* (1940). BELOW: Fay Bainter and Walter Huston squabble in the 1933 hit *Dodsworth*.

TOP: Ray Heatherton, Mitzi Green, and Alfred Drake in *Babes in Arms* (1937). BELOW: Alfred Lunt and Lynn Fontanne in the heavenly comedy *Amphitryon 38* (1937). OPPOSITE: Katharine Hepburn in her greatest hit, *The Philadelphia Story* (1939).

Kings, a retelling of the Mayerling tragedy, only ran for eighty-nine performances despite the brilliant acting of Dudley Digges (Emperor Franz Joseph) and Margo, Henry Hull, and Leo G. Carroll in other roles. The gloom of this drama was dispelled in April of that year when Rodgers and Hart's *Babes in Arms* opened with a young, largely unknown cast singing such gems as "Where or When," "The Lady Is a Tramp," "My Funny Valentine," "I Wish I Were in Love Again," and "Johnny One Note." George Balanchine supplied the fantastic choreography.

The Lunts returned to the Shubert in S.N. Behrman's elegant adaptation of Jean Giraudoux's *Amphitryon 38* (1937), in which Lunt impersonated Jupiter, who in turn masquerades as Amphitryon in order to woo Amphitryon's wife, Alkmena, blissfully played by Lynn Fontanne. They were excellently supported by Richard Whorf and Sydney Greenstreet. This Olympian frolic was followed by a heavenly musical, *I Married An Angel* (1938), with felicitous Rodgers and Hart songs, angelic dancing by Vera Zorina to Balanchine choreography, glorious singing by Dennis King and Vivienne Segal, clowning by Walter Slezak and Audrey Christie, and lovely Jo Mielziner sets that were whisked on and off on treadmills.

On March 28, 1939, an event occurred at the Shubert: Philip Barry's enchanting high comedy *The Philadelphia Story* opened. It proved a lifesaver for Katharine Hepburn (who had been branded "box office poison" in Hollywood); for Mr. Barry, who hadn't had a hit in years; and for the Theatre Guild, which was on the verge of bankruptcy. Hepburn's company included Shirley Booth, Joseph Cotten, and Van Heflin, and their radiant acting kept the show running for 417 sold-out performances.

During the 1940s, Rodgers and Hart suffered one of their rare flops, *Higher and Higher* (1940), at the Shubert; Al Jolson and Martha Raye drew raves in the musical *Hold On to Your*

Hats (1940), with an entrancing score by Burton Lane and E.Y. Harburg; Katharine Cornell was hailed in her revival of Shaw's *The Doctor's Dilemma* (1941), with Raymond Massey, Bramwell Fletcher, Ralph Forbes, and Clarence Derwent; Mary Boland, Bobby Clark, Walter Hampden, and Helen Ford romped through a revival of Sheridan's *The Rivals* (1942); Rodgers and Hart provided Ray Bolger with one of his best musicals, *By Jupiter* (1942), based on the play *The Warrior's Husband*; Paul Robeson, Uta Hagen, and José Ferrer were cheered in *Othello* (1943), brilliantly directed by Margaret Webster and designed by Robert Edmond Jones; Mae West wiggled her hips in Mike Todd's production of her play *Catherine Was Great* (1944), with Gene Barry as one of Mae's lovers; Celeste Holm became a star as a suffragette in the tuneful musical *Bloomer Girl* (1944); Bobby Clark enlivened Victor Herbert's *Sweethearts* (1947) with Marjorie Gateson for 288 performances; *High Button Shoes* (1947), a charming musical with Jerome Robbins's dances, Nanette Fabray's singing, and Phil Silvers's comedy, moved to the Shubert from the Century Theatre and stayed for almost a year; Maxwell Anderson's *Anne of the Thousand Days* (1948) won Rex Harrison a Tony Award as most outstanding male actor; the Lunts celebrated their twenty-fifth anniversary as America's foremost acting couple in S.N. Behrman's family chronicle play *I Know My Love* (1949); Cole Porter's phenomenal *Kiss Me, Kate* moved from the Century Theatre to the Shubert in 1950 and thrilled musical comedy buffs for a full year.

During the 1950s the Shubert continued its policy of alternating between musicals and straight fare. The Lerner and Loewe show *Paint Your Wagon* (1951), starring James Barton, stayed for 289 performances; Katharine Hepburn and Cyril Ritchard sparkled in Shaw's *The Millionairess* (1952); Rex Harrison and Lili Palmer were their usual urbane selves in Peter

Merrick, all through the run), Walter Pidgeon, Eileen Herlie, Robert Morse, and Una Merkel.

Highlights of the 1960s included Barbra Streisand's Broadway debut in a small but noticeable part in the musical *I Can Get It for You Wholesale* (1962), starring her future husband, Elliott Gould; Anthony Newley starring in *Stop the World—I Want to Get Off* (1962), which he wrote with Leslie Bricusse; Craig Stevens and Janis Paige in Meredith Willson's *Here's Love* (1963), adapted from the popular movie *Miracle on 34th Street*; Barbara Harris, Alan Alda, Larry Blyden, and Robert Klein in an off-beat musical, *The Apple Tree* (1966), by Jerry Bock and Sheldon Harnick; Steve Lawrence, Eydie Gorme, and

LEFT: Uta Hagen and Paul Robeson in the lauded 1943 revival of *Othello*. BELOW: Judy Holliday and Sydney Chaplin in the popular *Bells Are Ringing* (1956).

Ustinov's *The Love of Four Colonels* (1953); Cole Porter's *Can-Can* was a huge hit for two years (1953–55); Rodgers and Hammerstein's *Pipe Dream* (1955), based on John Steinbeck's novel *Sweet Thursday*, was one of their lesser efforts; Judy Holliday scored one of her major coups in the Comden/Green/Jule Styne musical *Bells Are Ringing* (1956), with Sydney Chaplin; Gertrude Berg and Cedric Hardwicke had a hit in *A Majority of One* (1959); and the last hit of the 1950s at this theatre was *Take Me Along* (1959), a musical adaptation of Eugene O'Neill's comedy *Ah, Wilderness!*, starring Jackie Gleason (who feuded with the show's producer, David

Marilyn Cooper in *Golden Rainbow* (1968), a musical version of the play *A Hole in the Head*; and the last show of the decade, the smash musical *Promises, Promises*, Neil Simon's adaptation of the film *The Apartment*, with a jaunty score by Burt Bacharach and Hal David, starring Jerry Orbach.

Some of the shows that played the Shubert in the 1970s were Hal Prince's production of *A Little Night Music*, with a book by Hugh Wheeler and score by Stephen Sondheim, based on the Ingmar Bergman film *Smiles of a Summer Night* (1973), starring Glynis Johns, Len Cariou, and Hermione Gingold; *Over Here!* (1974), a nostalgic, World War II musical with two of the Andrews Sisters—Maxene and Patty —and, in smaller roles, John Travolta and Treat Williams.

The Shubert's second Pulitzer Prize play, Edward Albee's *Seascape* (1975), starred Deborah Kerr and Barry Nelson, and won a Tony Award for supporting actor Frank Langella. Ingrid Bergman made her last Broadway appearance in a revival of Maugham's *The Constant Wife* in April 1975.

On July 25, 1975, Joseph Papp and the New York Shakespeare Festival moved their sensa-

ABOVE: Alan Alda and Barbara Harris as Adam and Eve in *The Apple Tree* (1966). BELOW: PLAYBILL covers for three musical hits at the Shubert.

tional production of *A Chorus Line*, Michael Bennett's musical conception of what happens when dancers audition for a Broadway musical, from its downtown theatre to the Shubert, where, to date, it is still running. In September 1983 this Pulitzer Prize musical, with a book by James Kirkwood and Nicholas Dante, score by Marvin Hamlisch and Edward Kleban, choreography by Michael Bennett and Bob Avian, and direction by Bennett, became Broadway's longest-running musical to date, and the Shubert Theatre, still owned by the Shubert Organization, which in recent years had the theatre admirably restored, celebrated the longest-running show ever to play in the seventy-one-year-old house.

TOP: The original cast of *A Chorus Line*, Broadway's longest-running musical. RIGHT: PLAYBILL cover for the musical. BELOW: The chorus line auditions for a new musical.

✄ BOOTH THEATRE ✄

This warm, intimate theatre was a joint venture of the aristocratic producer Winthrop Ames, owner of the even smaller Little Theatre, and impresario Lee Shubert. Their aim was to offer theatregoers a cozy house for the viewing of dramas and comedies. It was named the Booth in remembrance of another Booth Theatre in Manhattan (named for actor Edwin Booth), in which Mr. Ames's father had held financial interest.

The 668-seat Booth Theatre on West Forty-fifth Street was back-to-back with the Shubert Theatre and shared Shubert Alley with it. According to newspapers at the time of the Booth's opening, the theatre was designed by architect Henry B. Herts in early Italian Renaissance style "with designs in agrafitto in brown and ivory, colors which harmonize with the exterior of the theatre, which is yellow brick and ivory terra cotta." An unusual feature of the Booth was a wall that partitioned the entrance from the auditorium, preventing street and lobby noises and drafts from coming to the interior of the house. Woodwork and walls were in neutral tints of driftwood gray; draperies, upholstery, carpeting, and the house curtain were in various shades of mulberry. Chandeliers and appliqués along the wall gave the impression of candlelight. The theatre contained many Booth souvenirs, including the actor's favorite armchair, a statue of him, and many handbills and posters of Booth's appearances.

The Booth opened with fanfare on October 16, 1913, with the first American production of Arnold Bennett's play *The Great Adventure*, dramatized by him from his novel *Buried Alive*. The stars were Janet Beecher and Lyn Harding and the fascinating plot dealt with a famous artist who is pronounced dead and who decides to go along with the erroneous obituary. Unfortunately, the play lasted only fifty-two performances.

The Booth's first hit was *Experience*, an allegorical play with music in which William Elliott played a character who symbolized Youth. It ran for 255 performances in 1914–15. This was followed by another success, *The Bubble*, starring Louis Mann, which had a run of 176 showings. On February 5, 1917, the distinguished producer/director Arthur Hopkins piloted a hit called *A Successful Calamity*, by Clare Kummer, starring William Gillette, Estelle Winwood, Roland Young, and William Devereaux. Later that year, *DeLuxe Annie*, with Jane

🎭 Program-cover motif for a 1921 Booth Theatre production.

Grey and Vincent Serrano, proved to be another good show.

The year 1918 started out with a huge hit for the Booth. Ruth Gordon, Gregory Kelly, Paul Kelly, and Neil Martin appeared in a delightful adaptation of Booth Tarkington's *Seventeen*. There were two hits the following year: Janet Beecher and Lowell Sherman in a mystery called *The Woman in Room 13*, and a comedy called *Too Many Husbands*.

The Roaring Twenties at the Booth began rousingly with a lively melodrama, *The Purple*

Mask, with Leo Ditrichstein, Brandon Tynan, and Lily Cahill in one of those cloak-and-dagger masquerades set in Napoleon's time. Alexander Woollcott loved it and wrote in the New York *Times* that so would Tom Sawyer and Penrod. This swashbuckler was followed by a charming play, *Not So Long Ago*, a nostalgic Cinderella tale set in early New York, with Eva Le Gallienne giving an enchanting performance as a poor girl who marries a rich boy. She was supported by Sidney Blackmer and Thomas Mitchell. Back to melodrama went the Booth in November 1920 with a rousing adaptation of Mark Twain's *The Prince and the Pauper*, with actress Ruth Findlay playing the dual roles of the title and William Faversham and Clare Eames in other choice parts.

Highlights of the 1920s at the Booth included George Arliss as the Raja of Ruka in a lush adventure play, *The Green Goddess* (1921), set in the Himalayas, that ran for 440 performances; A.A. Milne's engrossing play *The Truth About Blayds* (1922), with O.P. Heggie as Blayds, a famed poet who reveals that someone else wrote all his poems, with Leslie Howard, Frieda Inescort, and Ferdinand Gottschalk helping to keep his secret; Austin Strong's unforgettable *Seventh Heaven* (1922), with Helen Menken and George Gaul as the poor lovers in a Parisian garret, which ran for 683 performances; *Dancing Mothers* (1924), a daring play in which a mother (played by Mary Young) rebels against her flapper daughter (Helen Hayes) and philandering husband (Henry Stephenson) by going wild herself and walking out on them; Edna Ferber and George S. Kaufman's *Minick* (1924), a gentle study of an old man going to live with his son and daughter-in-law; Alfred Lunt and Lynn Fontanne in their third play together, Molnar's *The Guardsman* (1924), which was so successful that it moved from the Garrick Theatre to the Booth and delighted Theatre Guild audiences; publisher Horace Liveright's startling modern-dress production of *Hamlet* (1925), with Basil Sydney as the Melancholy Dane in a dinner suit, King Claudius (Charles Waldron) in flannels, and Ophelia (Helen Chandler) in flapper frocks; *The Patsy* (1925), a winning comedy starring Claiborne Foster ; Winthrop Ames's 1926 production of a fanciful Philip Barry comedy, *White Wings* (a fancy term for street cleaners), which should have lasted longer than 27 performances; Ruth Gordon, Roger Pryor, and Beulah Bondi in Maxwell Anderson's timely comedy about youth, *Saturday's Children* (1927); Leslie Howard and Frieda Inescort in John Galsworthy's excellent drama *Escape* (1927–28), brilliantly produced

BELOW: Alfred Lunt and Lynn Fontanne in their joyous hit *The Guardsman* (1924). RIGHT: Leslie Howard in John Galsworthy's engrossing drama *Escape* (1927).

and staged by Winthrop Ames; *The Grand Street Follies of 1928*, an annual topical revue that spoofed current plays and players, with James Cagney tapping and Dorothy Sands stopping the show with her impression of Mae West playing Shakespeare; *The Grand Street Follies of 1929*, again with Cagney, Sands, and others doing parodies; and the last show of the 1920s at the Booth, a contemporary comedy of ill-manners called *Jenny* (1929), starring Jane Cowl as an actress who tries to straighten out a wayward family but ends up running off with the father of the house, capitally played by Guy Standing.

During the 1930s some fifty shows played the Booth, many of them quick failures and a number of them transferred from other theatres. Among the most noteworthy tenants were: Margaret Sullavan in her Broadway debut, in a shabby play called *A Modern Virgin* (1931); Rose Franken's drama about family tyranny, *Another Language* (1932), splendidly acted by Margaret Wycherly, Margaret Hamilton, Glenn Anders, Dorothy Stickney, and John Beal; *No More Ladies* (1934), an intelligent comedy about infidelity by A.E. Thomas, starring Lucile Watson and Melvyn Douglas; Gladys Cooper making her Broadway debut with Raymond Massey and Adrianne Allen in Keith Winter's *The Shining Hour* (1934), another play about infidelity; John Van Druten's "comedy of women," called *The Distaff Side* (1934), superbly acted by Sybil Thorndike, Mildred Natwick, Estelle Winwood, and Viola Roache; J.B. Priestley's *Laburnum Grove* (1935), in which Edmund Gwenn pretended to be a counterfeiter in order to get rid of sponging relatives who wished to borrow money from him; Melvyn Douglas, Cora Wither-

spoon, Claudia Morgan, Violet Heming, Elsa Maxwell, Blanche Ring, and Tom Ewell—a million-dollar cast—all wasted in a maudlin play called *De Luxe* (1935), by novelist Louis Bromfield and John Gearon; the radiant Grace George in a chilling drama, *Kind Lady* (1935), about a rich old lady held captive in her own home by a gang of clever thieves headed by Henry Daniell; *Blind Alley* (1935), another thriller, with Roy Hargrave as a gangster who is destroyed when a psychologist (George Coulouris) he is holding captive delves into his mind; a classical Chinese drama, *Lady Precious Stream* (1936), starring Helen Chandler, Bramwell Fletcher, and Clarence Derwent; *Sweet Aloes* (1936), a British play by Joyce Carey, with Miss Carey, Evelyn Laye, and Rex Harrison making his Broadway debut; a rowdy farce about wrestling, *Swing Your Lady* (1936); Kaufman and Hart's Pulitzer Prize comedy *You Can't Take It with You* (1936), with Henry Travers and Josephine Hull heading an insane family of lovable eccentrics, which ran almost two years at the Booth; Montgomery Clift, Jessie Royce Landis, Morgan

▄ Kaufman and Hart's 1936 Pulitzer Prize comedy, *You Can't Take It with You*.

James, and Onslow Stevens in *Dame Nature* (1938), a sexual drama adapted from the French by actress Patricia Collinge; Philip Barry's arresting drama *Here Come the Clowns* (1938), with Eddie Dowling, Madge Evans, Doris Dudley, and Russell Collins; a bright, richly designed revue, *One for the Money* (1939), by Nancy Hamilton and Morgan Lewis, with Alfred Drake, Gene Kelly, Keenan Wynn, Grace McDonald, Brenda Forbes, and Nancy Hamilton; and bringing the 1930s to a close at the Booth, another Pulitzer Prize play, William Saroyan's daffy comedy *The Time of Your Life*, with Eddie Dowling, Julie Haydon, Gene Kelly, William Bendix, Edward Andrews, and Celeste Holm (who spelled it Holme in those days).

In the 1940s, the Booth had fewer plays than in the preceding decade, but more long-running hits. The decade started out with a sequel to the revue *One for the Money* called, aptly, *Two for the Show*, by the same authors. This edition boasted a memorable song, "How High the Moon," and comic and tuneful performances by Alfred Drake, Betty Hutton, Eve Arden, Keenan Wynn, Richard Haydn, Brenda Forbes, Tommy Wonder, Eunice Healey, and Nadine Gae. On February 12, 1941, a genuine hit called *Claudia* came to the Booth and stayed for a little over a year. Written by Rose Franken, the touching play about a childlike wife made a star out of Dorothy McGuire and brought back to the stage the famed Belasco actress Frances Starr to play Claudia's mother, with Donald Cook as her husband.

Noel Coward's blissful comedy *Blithe Spirit* moved from the Morosco to the Booth in 1942, with Clifton Webb, Peggy Wood, Leonora Corbett, and Mildred Natwick, and the merry spooks stayed for a year. Another huge hit, *The Two Mrs. Carrolls* (1943–45), starring Elisabeth Bergner, Victor Jory, Vera Allen, and Irene Worth, thrilled Booth audiences with its homicidal plot and stayed for 585 performances.

Souvenir program for Noel Coward's enchanting comedy *Blithe Spirit* (1942).

A war drama, *The Wind Is Ninety*, had a remarkable cast (Kirk Douglas, Wendell Corey, Joyce Van Patten and her brother "Dickie," Blanche Yurka, and Bert Lytell) and played for over 100 performances in 1945. *You Touched Me* (1945), by Tennessee Williams and Donald Windham, had fine performances by Montgomery Clift and Edmund Gwenn, but was a lesser Williams work. Bobby Clark added burlesque touches to Molière's *The Would-Be Gentleman*, with June Knight and Gene Barry; Ben Hecht and Charles MacArthur's psychological murder

ABOVE: Shirley Booth and Sidney Blackmer in William Inge's poignant play *Come Back, Little Sheba* (1950). BELOW: Souvenir program for Beatrice Lillie's hit (1952).

An Evening with
Beatrice Lillie
with Reginald Gardiner

mystery *Swan Song* played for 158 performances; and a revival of Synge's *The Playboy of the Western World* (1946) had Burgess Meredith, Mildred Natwick, J.C. Nugent, Julie Harris, and, making her Broadway debut, Maureen Stapleton.

Additional 1940s hits included: Norman Krasna's farce-comedy *John Loves Mary* (1947), with Nina Foch, Tom Ewell, and William Prince; Gilbert Miller's revival of Molnar's bubbly comedy *The Play's the Thing* (1948), with Louis Calhern, Ernest Cossart, Arthur Margetson, and Faye Emerson making her Broadway debut; James B. Allardice's comedy *At War with the Army* (1949), staged by Ezra Stone, with Gary Merrill giving an excellent performance; and Grace George, Walter Hampden, Jean Dixon, and John Williams in a pleasant religious drama, *The Velvet Glove* (1949).

The 1950s began auspiciously with William Inge's first Broadway play, *Come Back, Little Sheba*, with Shirley Booth and Sidney Blackmer winning Tony Awards for their powerful performances. Beatrice Lillie was the toast of the town in the hilarious revue *An Evening with Beatrice Lillie* (1952), in which she sang some of her most celebrated songs and acted in some of her most outlandish sketches with Reginald Gardiner for 278 performances. A popular comedy called *Anniversary Waltz* (1954–55), directed by Moss Hart and starring his wife, Kitty Carlisle, and Macdonald Carey, moved from the Broadhurst to the Booth and stayed for ten months; *Time Limit* (1956), a taut drama about the Korean War by Henry Denker and Ralph Berkey, starred Richard Kiley, Arthur Kennedy, Allyn McLerie, and Thomas Carlin and played for 127 performances; Gore Vidal's science fiction delight, *Visit to a Small Planet* (1957), starring Cyril Ritchard as a comic extraterrestrial and Eddie Mayehoff as an imbecilic general, ran for a year; William Gibson's *Two for the See-Seesaw* (1958–59), an enchanting two-character love story starring Henry Fonda and Anne Bancroft, ran for almost two years; and Paddy Chayefsky's *The Tenth Man*, about the exorcism of a dybbuk in Mineola, with Gene Saks as a rabbi and Jack Gilford, George Voskovec, Jacob Ben-Ami, and Lou Jacobi giving sublime performances, played 623 times.

Highlights of the 1960s included Julie Harris, Walter Matthau, William Shatner, Gene Saks, and Diana van der Vlis in the continental comedy *A Shot in the Dark* (1961–62); Murray Schisgal's outré comedy *Luv* (1964–66), directed by Mike Nichols, with Eli Wallach, Anne Jackson, and Alan Arkin as three miserable creatures who cavort on a bridge, which lasted for 902 performances; Flanders and Swann, the British comedy team, in *At the Drop of Another Hat* (1966), a follow-up to their popular two-man revue *At the Drop of a Hat*; Harold Pinter's sinister play *The Birthday Party* (1967), his first full-length work; and one of the Booth's most popular tenants, Leonard Gershe's *Butterflies Are Free*, with Blythe Danner making her Broadway debut and winning a Tony Award for her luminous acting, and with Eileen Heckart (later replaced by Gloria Swanson) and Keir Dullea helping the drama about a blind man, his kooky neighbor, and his overprotective mother to run for 1,133 performances.

In 1972 the Booth housed another Pulitzer Prize play, Joseph Papp's production of *That Championship Season* (1972–74), by actor Jason Miller, which moved from the downtown New York Shakespeare Festival and played for almost two years at the Booth. Other attractions of the decade included Terrence McNally's zany *Bad Habits* (1974), two playlets about therapy, which moved uptown from the Astor Place Theatre; Cleavon Little in Murray Schisgal's *All Over Town* (1974), directed by Dustin Hoffman; a revival of Jerome Kern's 1915 musical *Very Good Eddie* (1975–76), from the Goodspeed Opera House in Connecticut;

ABOVE: Alan Arkin, Anne Jackson, and Eli Wallach in *Luv* (1964). BELOW: Keir Dullea, Eileen Heckart, and Blythe Danner in the long-running *Butterflies Are Free* (1969).

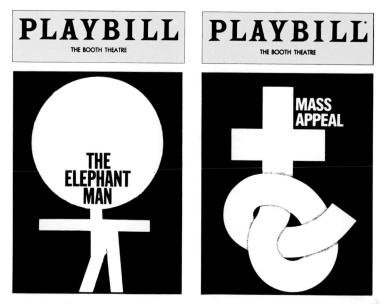

OPPOSITE: Rise Collins and Tarzana Beverley in *For Colored Girls Who Have Considered Suicide When the Rainbow Is Enuf* (1976). RIGHT: Graphic PLAYBILL covers for two Booth Theatre hits.

Ntozake Shange's *For Colored Girls Who Have Considered Suicide When the Rainbow Is Enuf* (1976–78), an exalted program of poetry acted by an extraordinary cast of black artists for 742 performances; and *The Elephant Man* (1979), Bernard Pomerance's enthralling study of a true-life freak of nature, with memorable performances by Philip Anglim, Kevin Conway, and Carole Shelley, which moved from Theatre at Saint Peter's Church to the Booth and won the New York Drama Critics Circle Award for best play and three Tony Awards.

In November 1981 *Mass Appeal,* by Bill C. Davis, directed by Geraldine Fitzgerald, made a successful transference from Off-Broadway to the Booth. This religious drama, first presented at the Circle Repertory Theatre and the Manhattan Theatre Club, featured excellent performances by Milo O'Shea as a luxury-loving priest and Michael O'Keefe as a rebellious young priest. It ran for 212 performances.

The Booth's most recent tenants were the Royal Shakespeare Company's production of *Good,* by the late British playwright C.P. Taylor, starring Alan Howard as an intellectual German in Frankfurt in 1933 who turns into a rabid Nazi;

Total Abandon, a short-lived play by Larry Atlas, starring Richard Dreyfuss as a parent who is guilty of child abuse and murder; and a revival of *American Buffalo* starring Al Pacino in a repeat of his original performance.

The Booth Theatre is owned by the Shubert Organization and is one of the Broadway theatres the Shuberts have renovated. In 1979 the famed interior designer Melanie Kahane, who had redone four of the Shubert theatres, was hired to restore the Booth to its original elegance and grandeur. "What I've tried to do with these old houses is get back to the beginning and then modernize them in some way," she told PLAYBILL at the time. "The Booth was a sad old sack. All in brown. I kept the brown below—to anchor—then put light beige on top. The light color brings your eye up, so you notice the detail." Ms. Kahane characterized the Booth as "very Jacobean." She got rid of the delicate French chandeliers, which she felt didn't belong in that house, and restored the elegant old theatre in the short space of three weeks. The Booth has always been—and still is today—an ideal house for dramas, comedies, and intimate musical shows.

⚼ BROADHURST THEATRE ⚼

George H. Broadhurst, the Anglo-American dramatist (1866–1952), came to America in 1886. In addition to writing popular plays, he managed theatres in Milwaukee, Baltimore, and San Francisco before he opened his own theatre, the Broadhurst, in association with the Shubert brothers.

Located at 235 West Forty-fourth Street, right next door to the Shubert Theatre, the Broadhurst was designed by architect Herbert J. Krapp, one of the major theatre designers of that era. With a

seating capacity of 1,155 and a wide auditorium that offered unobstructed views of the stage, the theatre was constructed to house both musicals and straight fare, which it has done successfully for over sixty years.

The Broadhurst's opening show was George Bernard Shaw's *Misalliance* on September 27, 1917, starring Maclyn Arbuckle. This was the first New York production of Shaw's philosophical 1910 comedy and it ran for only fifty-two performances. It was not performed again on Broadway until the City Center revival in 1953.

In 1918 the Broadhurst had a hit musical in *Ladies First*, starring Nora Bayes and comic William Kent. This suffragette show centered on a woman (Nora Bayes) who dares to run for mayor against her boyfriend. She loses the election but wins the boy. The show had a score by A. Baldwin Sloane. During the run at the Broadhurst, one George Gershwin song, "Some Wonderful Sort of Someone," was interpolated.

The Broadhurst had two hits in 1919. Rachel Crothers's *39 East* was a comedy of manners that starred Alison Skipworth, Henry Hull, and Constance Binney. Later in the run Hull was replaced by Sidney Blackmer and Binney by a striking young actress named Tallulah Bankhead. On December 30 Jane Cowl scored one of her early successes in a romantic drama called *Smilin' Through*, which she coauthored with Allan Langdon Martin. Ms. Cowl played a ghost in some scenes and the ghost's niece in others, serving to confuse critic Alexander Woollcott, who complained that these quick-change tricks belonged more to vaudeville than to the legitimate theatre. But audiences loved *Smilin' Through* for 175 performances.

In September 1921 George Broadhurst brought his American version of the British play *Tarzan of the Apes* to his theatre. The New York *Times* critic labeled the show "rather astonishing." A British actor, Ronald Adair, played Tarzan, and there were real lions and monkeys

The
Broadhurst Theatre

44TH STREET, WEST OF BROADWAY

GEORGE BROADHURST .... DIRECTOR

NOTICE—This Theatre can be emptied in less than three minutes. Choose, now, the exit nearest to your seat. In case of disturbance of any kind, to avoid the dangers of panic, walk (do not run) to that exit.—Fire Commissioner.

WEEK BEGINNING MONDAY EVENING, OCTOBER 22, 1917.

Evenings at 8:20.   TUESDAY and Saturday Matinees at 2:20.

WILLIAM FAVERSHAM

PRESENTS

GEORGE BERNARD SHAW'S

COMEDY

"MISALLIANCE"

Cast of Characters

(In the order of their appearance)

JOHNNY TARLETON .... FREDERICK LLOYD
BENTLEY SUMMERHAYS .... PHILIP LEIGH
HYPATHIA .... MISS ELISABETH RISDON
MRS. JOHN TARLETON............... MRS. EDMUND GURNEY
LORD SUMMERHAYS .... GEORGE FITZGERALD

JOHN TARLETON .... MACLYN ARBUCKLE

JOSEPH PERCIVAL .... WARBURTON GAMBLE

LINA SZCZEPANOWSKA.......... MISS KATHARINE KAELRED

GUNNER .... MALCOLM MORLEY

The
BROADHURST THEATRE

44TH STREET
West of Broadway

ALEX. A. AARONS & VINTON FREEDLEY
Lessees & Managers

Shubert Theatre Corp.—owner

THE
BROADHURST

44TH ST. WEST OF BROADWAY
SHUBERT THEATRE CORPORATION, LESSEE
DIRECTION OF LEE & J. J. SHUBERT

LEFT: Program for the first production at the Broadhurst, in 1917. RIGHT: Program covers for this theatre in 1926.

onstage, but the Ape Man managed to swing from tree to tree for only thirteen performances.

In November 1921 Lionel Barrymore won plaudits for his acting in a French play called *The Claw*, in which he played a politician who is ruined by a conniving woman. Critic Alexander Woollcott reported in the *Times* that the play was attended by "the most bronchial audience of the season that coughed competitively through each scene and applauded with vehemence at its conclusion."

One of the most popular themes of this era —that of two generations of lovers from the same family—cropped up again in the musical *Marjolaine*, starring Peggy Wood. It ran for 136 performances in 1922. In 1923 *The Dancers*, the London play by Sir Gerald Du Maurier in which Tallulah Bankhead had made her dazzling British debut, came to the Broadhurst with Richard Bennett and Florence Eldridge. It was a hit. Later in the year a revue called *Topics of 1923*, with Alice Delysia, frolicked for 143 performances.

On February 12, 1924 (the same day that George Gershwin's famous *Rhapsody in Blue* had its Manhattan premiere), the Broadhurst celebrated Lincoln's birthday with a distinguished hit, *Beggar on Horseback*, by George S. Kaufman and Marc Connelly. This expressionistic play, focusing on a composer (Roland Young) who almost marries into a stuffy rich family but is saved from this fate by an extended surrealistic dream about how life would be with them, caused a sensation. It ran for 224 performances and is still regarded as a classic of its genre.

Another sensation was caused by Katharine Cornell in *The Green Hat* (1925), by Michael Arlen. Based on Mr. Arlen's shocking novel of the same name, the play was considered extremely daring. It dealt with a bride (Cornell) whose husband commits suicide on their honeymoon. The audience does not learn until later that the husband threw himself out of a hotel window because he had a venereal disease. The excellent cast included Leslie Howard, Margalo Gillmore, Eugene Powers, and Paul Guilfoyle. The play was staged by Ms. Cornell's husband, Guthrie McClintic.

One of the theatre's greatest entertainments opened on September 16, 1926. Jed Harris, the boy wonder, brought his production of *Broadway* to the Broadhurst and it hit Times Square like a thunderbolt. Written by Philip Dunning and George Abbott, it mesmerized first-nighters and subsequent audiences with its kaleidoscopic view of life in a New York night-spot called the Paradise Club. A jazz band, dancing girls, a fast-talking hoofer perfectly played by Lee Tracy, gangsters, bootleggers, murderers, and nightclub habitués thronged the Broadhurst stage and electrified theatregoers for 603 performances. Winston Churchill once declared that this was his favorite show of all time.

Winthrop Ames brought his production of *The Merchant of Venice* to the theatre in 1928. With George Arliss as Shylock and Peggy Wood as Portia, it managed to run for a respectable seventy-two performances.

On October 10, 1928, Bert Lahr achieved immortality in a raucous musical, *Hold Everything*, by DeSylva, Brown, and Henderson. Lahr played a punch-drunk boxer named Gink Schiner who was given to making strange sounds like "Gnong, gnong, gnong"; these utterances later became his trademark. The cast also included the beloved Victor Moore, Jack Whiting, Ona Munson, and Betty Compton, but it was Lahr who got the raves and who kept the musical running for 413 performances. The hit song was "You're the Cream in My Coffee."

The Broadhurst had another winner in 1929, *June Moon*. A satire on Tin Pan Alley's song writers, the play was written by George S. Kaufman and Ring Lardner and it kept the Broadhurst shaking with laughter for 272 perform-

OPPOSITE: Katharine Cornell as Iris March in the sensational Michael Arlen play, *The Green Hat*. ABOVE: Lee Tracy and Sylvia Field in the classic Jed Harris production, *Broadway* (1926).

ances. Norman Foster played a lyricist who writes an imbecilic hit tune, "June Moon," and the tart Jean Dixon, Philip Loeb, and Linda Watkins gave comic support to this tuneful cartoon.

Rodgers and Hart came back from Hollywood in 1931 with a new musical, *America's Sweetheart*, that naturally spoofed the movie capital. The two young hopefuls who go to Hollywood were played by beautiful Harriette Lake (who really went to Hollywood and became Ann Sothern) and Jack Whiting. There was one hit song, the infectious depression lament "I've Got Five Dollars," and acerbic performances by Jeanne Aubert and Inez Courtney, but the book by Herbert Fields was proclaimed dull and dirty and the show ran for only 135 performances.

Norman Bel Geddes, set designer extraordinaire, tackled Shakespeare's *Hamlet* at the Broadhurst in 1931. He adapted the play, designed its sets, costumes, and lighting, and directed it. Raymond Massey was the Melancholy Dane, Mary Servoss was Gertrude, Celia Johnson was Ophelia, and Colin Keith-Johnston was Laertes. Wrote Brooks Atkinson in the *Times*: "Mr. Bel Geddes has hacked and transposed until no idle philosophy is left to trip up his scenery. What he has left is, to this department, an incoherent, flat and unprofitable narrative." The production expired after twenty-eight performances.

Philip Barry restored art to the Broadhurst with his finely written high comedy *The Animal Kingdom* in 1932. Leslie Howard gave one of his most ingratiating performances as a man who marries the wrong woman. The blue-chip cast included Frances Fuller, Ilka Chase, and William Gargan. It was Barry at his best.

Claude Rains and the fetching Jean Arthur could not save a drama called *The Man Who Reclaimed His Head* in 1932. Also in the cast, as a maid, was Lucille Lortel, who now has an Off-Broadway theatre named after her.

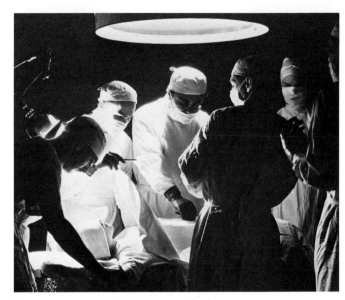

The tense operating scene in Sidney Kingsley's Pulitzer Prize play, *Men in White* (1933).

George Abbott and Philip Dunning, whose play *Broadway* was one of the Broadhurst's biggest hits, produced another hit in 1932, but not of their authorship. They presented Hecht and MacArthur's rambunctious farce *20th Century*, which took place on board the Twentieth-Century Limited en route from Chicago to New York. Moffat Johnston played an egomaniacal Broadway producer (said to be inspired by Jed Harris) trying to get a famous actress (Eugenie Leontovich) to sign a contract with him. Directed with express-train speed by Abbott, the comedy delighted for 154 performances.

Another highlight of the 1930s included the Group Theatre's realistic production of Sidney Kingsley's hospital drama *Men in White*, which won the Pulitzer Prize for the 1933–34 season. Starring Alexander Kirkland, Luther Adler, J. Edward Bromberg, Morris Carnovsky, and Russell Collins, it also featured such Group luminaries as Clifford Odets and Elia Kazan. Staged by Lee Strasberg, the play contained an operation scene that held audiences spellbound with its chilling realism.

Eva Le Gallienne brought her Civic Repertory Company to the Broadhurst in 1934 and performed with Ethel Barrymore (and Barrymore's children, Ethel and Samuel Colt) in Rostand's costume play *L'Aiglon*. Without Ethel, Ms. Le Gallienne also presented and acted in *Hedda Gabler* and *The Cradle Song*.

On January 7, 1935, Leslie Howard returned to the Broadhurst in Robert E. Sherwood's *The Petrified Forest* and enthralled audiences with his portrayal of an intellectual wanderer who allows a gangster to kill him so that he may leave his insurance money to a lovely young woman who wishes to study art in Paris. The gangster was played so vividly by Humphrey Bogart that Leslie Howard brought him to Hollywood to repeat his performance in the film version and made him a star.

Helen Hayes scored perhaps her greatest triumph in *Victoria Regina* in 1935, playing the queen from a young girl to an aged monarch with remarkable physical changes. Gilbert Miller's lavish production and staging, and the enormous cast, including Vincent Price as

ABOVE: Helen Hayes in her triumphant *Victoria Regina* (1935). LEFT: Humphrey Bogart achieves fame as the killer in *The Petrified Forest* (1935).

Prince Albert, made this one of the Broadhurst's most memorable events.

The remainder of the 1930s included Ruth Gordon's brilliant Nora in *A Doll's House*, which moved from the Morosco in 1938; Dodie Smith's charming family-reunion play *Dear Octopus* (1939); the great Bill Robinson in Mike Todd's splashy production of *The Hot Mikado* (1939); and Carmen Miranda's cyclonic Broadway debut in *The Streets of Paris* (1939), a lusty revue starring Bobby Clark, Abbott and Costello, Luella Gear, Gower (Champion) and Jeanne, and Jean Sablon.

During the 1940s musicals, revues, and comedies brightened the Broadhurst. Ed Wynn convulsed his fans in *Boys and Girls Together* (1940), with Jane Pickens and the DeMarcos; George Jessel, Bert Kalmar, and Harry Ruby created a lively musical about a burlesque troupe, *High Kickers* (1941), and Jessel, Sophie Tucker, Betty Bruce, and a cast of burlesque comics turned it into a hit; Eva Le Gallienne and Joseph Schildkraut sent shivers down the spine in the mystery melodrama *Uncle Harry* (1942); Dorothy Kilgallen's husband, Richard Kollmar, produced and starred in *Early to Bed* (1943), a Fats Waller musical about a track team that mistakes a bordello for a hotel, and it ran for 380 performances despite bad reviews; Agatha Christie's *Ten Little Indians*, with practically the entire cast ending as stiffs, enjoyed success in 1944; *Follow the Girls* (1945–46), a noisy musical with Jackie Gleason and Gertrude Niesen, moved from the New Century to the Broadhurst and stayed for almost a year; *Three to Make Ready* (1946), the third and last of the revue series by Nancy Hamilton and Morgan Lewis, starred Ray Bolger, Gordon MacRae, Brenda Forbes, Arthur Godfrey, Harold Lang, and Carleton Carpenter and ran five months after it moved to the Broadhurst from the Adelphi; Helen Hayes returned in *Happy Birthday* (1946–48), a comedy by Anita Loos about a shy Newark, New Jersey, librarian, and the sentimental play ran for 564 performances.

From 1948 to 1950, four revues played the Broadhurst. They were *Make Mine Manhattan*, with Sid Caesar, David Burns, Sheila Bond, Joshua Shelley, and Kyle MacDonnell; Nancy Walker, Jackie Gleason, Hank Ladd, and Carol Bruce in *Along Fifth Avenue*; Charles Gaynor's delirious *Lend an Ear* (which moved here from the National Theatre), with Carol Channing, Yvonne Adair, William Eythe, Gene Nelson, and Jenny Lou Law; and Jean and Walter Kerr's *Touch and Go*, with Nancy Andrews, Peggy Cass,

Dick Sykes, Kyle MacDonnell, Helen Gallagher, and Jonathan Lucas.

The 1950s brought some long-running hits to the Broadhurst, but *Romeo and Juliet*, with Olivia de Havilland and Douglas Watson, was not one of them. It only achieved 49 performances in 1951. An interesting musical, *Flahooley*, with Barbara Cook, Ernest Truex, Jerome Courtland, Irwin Corey, Yma Sumac, and the Bill Baird Marionettes, managed only 40 performances in 1951; a musical version of *Seventeen* (1951) fared much better, playing for 180 performances; a revival of the 1940 Rodgers and Hart musical *Pal Joey* (1952–53), with Vivienne Segal repeating her role as the lusty Vera, who keeps the young Joey (Harold Lang) in a luxurious love nest, was even more successful than the original production, running for 540 performances; Katharine Cornell starred in a fair melodrama, *The Prescott Proposals* (1953), by Howard Lindsay and Russel Crouse; Kitty Carlisle and Macdonald Carey had a long run in a vapid comedy, *Anniversary Waltz* (1954); Sidney Kingsley turned comic with a madcap play, *Lunatics and Lovers* (1954–55), starring Buddy Hackett, Dennis King, Sheila Bond, and Vicki Cummings, which had a healthy run; Shirley Booth found a suitable vehicle in William Marchant's *The Desk Set* (1955); Rosalind Russell made *Auntie Mame* immortal (1956–58); *The World of Suzie Wong* (1958–59), a claptrap Oriental romance starring William Shatner and France Nuyen, managed to last for 508 performances; and the last show of the 1950s—the musical *Fiorello!*—by Jerome Weidman, George Abbott, Sheldon Harnick, and Jerry Bock, brought another Pulitzer Prize winner to this theatre. Tom Bosley played the beloved Mayor La Guardia and won a Tony for his performance. The show also won Tony Awards for best musical, for direction (George Abbott), for best book (Jerome Weidman and George Abbott), best music (Jerry Bock), best

🎵 Harold Lang and Vivienne Segal in the superlative 1952 revival of *Pal Joey*, which ran longer than the original production.

lyrics (Sheldon Harnick), best producers of a musical (Robert Griffith and Harold Prince).

In 1962 Noel Coward's musical *Sail Away* sailed into the Broadhurst, with Elaine Stritch as a hostess on a luxury liner, but it was all too dated and chichi for 1960s audiences and it departed for London after 167 performances. Richard Rodgers fared better with *No Strings*, the first musical for which he wrote both music and lyrics, with a book by Samuel Taylor. The show moved here from the Fifty-fourth Street Theatre and starred Richard Kiley and Diahann Carroll. They made beautiful music together for 580 performances.

Other interesting Broadhurst bookings in the 1960s included the Tom Jones–Harvey Schmidt musical *110 in the Shade* (1963); the British import *Oh, What a Lovely War* (1964); another British musical, *Half a Sixpence* (1965–66) starring Tommy Steele; Ingrid Bergman, Colleen Dewhurst, and Arthur Hill in Eugene O'Neill's *More Stately Mansions* (1967–68) staged by José Quintero; and Woody Allen's *Play It Again, Sam*, starring Mr. Allen, Anthony Roberts, and Diane Keaton.

By the 1970s the revue genre was dead and the Broadhurst fare veered from dramas and comedies to musicals. Highlights included Sada

ABOVE: Colleen Dewhurst, Arthur Hill, and Ingrid Bergman in O'Neill's *More Stately Mansions* (1967). BELOW: Ellen March and cast members of the record-breaking musical *Grease* (1972).

Thompson's brilliant portrayal of three sisters and their mother in *Twigs* (1971), by George Furth; *Grease*, a rock musical about high school students in the 1950s, which moved from the downtown Eden Theatre to the Broadhurst and became the second-longest-running musical in Broadway history (*A Chorus Line* surpassed it in September 1983); Neil Simon's uproarious comedy about two veteran comics, *The Sunshine Boys* (1972); John Wood in a marvelous revival of William Gillette's *Sherlock Holmes* (1974); Katharine Hepburn and Christopher Reeve in Enid Bagnold's curious comedy *A Matter of Gravity* (1976); the wonderful musical *Godspell* (1976), based on the Gospel According to St. Matthew, which moved from Off-Broadway to the Broadhurst; Preston Jones's ambitious work *A Texas Trilogy* (1976), which was not as successful in New York as it had been in Washington, D.C.; Larry Gelbart's wild adaptation of Ben Johnson's *Volpone* (1976), with George C. Scott and Bob Dishy giving bravura performances; Bob Fosse's dance explosion *Dancin'* (1978), a revue spotlighting Fosse's flashy choreography danced by Broadway's best dancers, which ran at the Broadhurst for almost three years before moving to the Ambassador Theatre.

Dancin', the Broadhurst's longest-running show up to that time, was followed by another triumph. On December 17, 1980, Peter Shaffer's acclaimed London play *Amadeus* opened at the theatre, with Ian McKellen as Salieri, Tim Curry as a comic Mozart, and Jane Seymour as the composer's wife. It was the season's most distinguished offering. It won the Tony Award for best play and Ian McKellen won as most outstanding actor. This drama was followed by the musical *The Tap Dance Kid*.

The Broadhurst Theatre, a prime house of the Shubert Organization, has always been one of the most sought-after theatres by producers. It is in its sixty-seventh year.

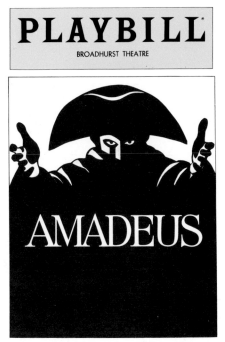

AMADEUS

LEFT: Dan Stone as Jesus in *Godspell*, the long-running musical that moved from Off-Broadway to the Broadhurst (1976). ABOVE: *PLAYBILL* cover for *Amadeus* (1980). Peter Shaffer's prize-winning play. BELOW: One of the dazzling numbers from Bob Fosse's *Dancin'* (1978).

⚜ PLYMOUTH THEATRE ⚜

By the time the Shuberts built the Plymouth Theatre in 1917, the New York *Times* reported: "It is a dull week when no new theatre opens." The Shuberts now had a block of theatres— the Plymouth and Booth on West Forty-fifth Street and the Shubert and Broadhurst, back-to-back with these, on West Forty-fourth Street.

The Shuberts leased their new Plymouth Theatre to the distinguished producer/director Arthur Hopkins. It was designed by architect Herbert J. Krapp, and the *Times* reported that it was simple in decor, was decorated in shades of brown, blue, and gold, and had a seating capacity of about 1,000, with only one balcony.

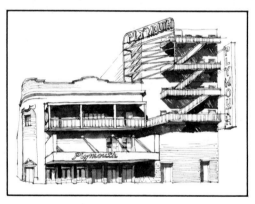

An unusual aspect of the opening bill on the night of October 10, 1917, was that it was not a new show. Clare Kummer's comedy *A Successful Calamity*, starring William Gillette, had been a hit the previous year at the Booth next door and it was revived with virtually the same cast at the Plymouth when it opened.

Producer Hopkins brought John Barrymore to the Plymouth in 1918 to play one of his most successful parts—Fedya in a dramatization of Tolstoy's *Redemption*. Hopkins directed the play, and Robert Edmond Jones designed a sumptuous production. Barrymore and the huge cast gave splendid performances. The producer even invited Tolstoy's son to attend a dress rehearsal, but the Russian's only comment afterward was "Where's Fedya's beard?"

Later in 1918 Walter Hampden played Hamlet at the Plymouth in a revival of Shakespeare's tragedy. On April 9, 1919, Hopkins jolted the town with his superlative production of *The Jest*, an Italian play by Sem Benelli, starring John Barrymore as an effete painter and Lionel Barrymore as an odious Captain of the Mercenaries. The brilliant acting of the Barrymore brothers as deadly enemies, Robert Edmond Jones's magnificent Renaissance sets, and Hopkins's direction made this one of the milestones in American theatre.

On December 22, 1919, Hopkins tried again with a Russian classic—Maxim Gorki's *The Lower Depths*, retitled *Night Lodging*. But despite excellent performances by Edward G. Robinson and Pauline Lord, it lasted only fourteen performances.

The Roaring Twenties started auspiciously at the Plymouth with *Little Old New York*, a hit

🦋 Maude Hanaford, Lionel Barrymore, John Barrymore, and Arthur Forrest in the unforgettable drama *The Jest* (1919).

comedy by Rida Johnson Young that took place in New York of 1910, when, as Burns Mantle noted, "John Jacob Astor spoke with a German accent and Cornelius Vanderbilt ran a ferry." The play concerned an Irish girl, played by Genevieve Tobin, who has to masquerade as a boy in order to inherit a vast fortune. But she falls in love with the boy who is the rightful heir and gives up her inheritance to win him (and his inheritance). This bit of Irish blarney was good for 311 performances.

Other highlights of the 1920s included Zoe Akins's serious study of a marriage gone wrong, *Daddy's Gone A-Hunting* (1921), with fine act-

ing by Marjorie Rambeau, Frank Conroy, and Lee Baker; Arthur Hopkins's production of *The Old Soak* (1922), a lovable comedy about an alcoholic (Harry Beresford) and his wife, Matilda (Minnie Dupree), that was named one of the ten best plays of the season by Burns Mantle; another family comedy, *The Potters*, by J.P. McEvoy, starring Donald Meek as Pa Potter, Catharine Calhoun Doucet as Ma, Raymond Guion (later Gene Raymond of the movies) as Bill Potter, and Mary Carroll as Mamie Potter. *The Potters* amused for 245 performances.

One of the American theatre's most significant plays, *What Price Glory?*, by Maxwell An-

ABOVE: In the foreground, Leyla Georgie, Louis Wolheim, and William Boyd in the rousing *What Price Glory?* (1924). RIGHT: Zita Johann and Clark Gable as illicit lovers in the surrealistic *Machinal* (1928).

derson and Laurence Stallings, detonated at the Plymouth on September 5, 1924. The drama, produced and directed by Arthur Hopkins, was the first war play to use the profane speech of soldiers. The program carried this puzzling note by Mr. Hopkins: "I am presenting *What Price Glory?* exactly as it has been given at the Plymouth Theatre for every performance, except for the elimination of three expressions that are used in the best families and by our noblest public officials." The play focused on battling army buddies, First Sergeant Quirt (William Boyd) and Captain Flagg (Louis Wolheim), and the characters became so memorable that a number of films were made about them. *What Price Glory?* ran for 435 performances.

Laurette Taylor, Frank Conroy, and Louis Calhern tried to make a success of Philip Barry's metaphysical play *In a Garden* (1925), but it was a bit too murky for theatregoers. Winthrop Ames presented several Gilbert and Sullivan operettas during 1927; and on September 1 of that year, another huge hit came to this theatre. It was a lively comedy called *Burlesque*, by Arthur Hopkins and George Manker Watters, and it starred Hal Skelly as a burlesque comic and Barbara Stanwyck as his wife, who performs in a seedy act with him. Burns Mantle named it one of the year's ten best plays and it had a healthy run of 372 performances.

The sensational Snyder-Gray murder case (Ruth Snyder was the first woman electrocuted in America, for plotting to murder her husband) inspired an interesting surrealistic play, *Machinal* (1928), by Sophie Treadwell. Arthur Hopkins staged the drama and it was superbly played by Zita Johann in the Snyder role and by a young actor named Clark Gable as the lover who murders her husband.

On November 26, 1928, playwright Philip Barry returned to the Plymouth, this time in triumph. Arthur Hopkins produced and staged his felicitous comedy *Holiday*, and it became one of the theatre's most prized high comedies.

Written specifically for Hope Williams, the socialite turned actress, the play dealt with a young man, Johnny Case (Ben Smith), who has made some money and wants to take a holiday and enjoy it while he is still young. His socialite fiancée and her stuffy father oppose this, so he takes his joyous holiday with his fiancée's rebellious sister, played by Miss Williams. The star was understudied by Katharine Hepburn, who never got to play the role on Broadway but starred in the excellent movie version.

Hope Williams returned to the Plymouth in 1930 in *Rebound*, a comedy about divorce written especially for her by Donald Ogden Stewart, who had appeared with her at the Plymouth in *Holiday*. Burns Mantle selected it for his ten-best-plays volume.

Highlights of the 1930s at the Plymouth included: Paul Muni at his finest in Elmer Rice's *Counsellor-at-Law* (1931); Roland Young, Laura Hope Crews, and Frances Fuller in Clare Kummer's hilarious comedy *Her Master's Voice* (1933), voted one of the year's ten best plays by Burns Mantle; Tallulah Bankhead suffering a brain tumor in *Dark Victory* (1934); Constance Cummings giving a memorable performance in Samson Raphaelson's comedy *Accent on Youth* (1934); Sidney Howard's *Paths of Glory* (1935), an impassioned play about a true, un-

ABOVE: Donald Ogden Stewart, Hope Williams, Ben Smith, and Barbara White in the charming Philip Barry comedy *Holiday* (1928). BELOW: Paul Muni in Elmer Rice's *Counselor-at-Law* (1931).

Susan and God (1937), another best play of the year; Robert E. Sherwood's *Abe Lincoln in Illinois* (1938), winner of the Pulitzer Prize, starring Raymond Massey as an incredibly realistic Abe, and the first production of the new Playwrights Company; Clare Boothe's anti-Nazi play *Margin for Error* (1939), directed by Otto Preminger, starring Sam Levene as a comic police officer and Mr. Preminger as an odious German consul.

The Plymouth was constantly operating during the 1940s, with new hits, transfers from other theatres, and a few revivals. William Saroyan's *Love's Old Sweet Song* (1940), another screwball comedy about mankind, with Walter Huston, Jessie Royce Landis, and Alan Hewitt, was not as successful as his earlier plays. Alan Dinehart, Glenda Farrell, and Lyle Talbot ran forever in a sleazy comedy, *Separate Rooms* (1940); Mary Anderson was so nasty in *Guest in the House* (1942) that audiences hissed her, while critics raved; Thornton Wilder won another Pulitzer Prize and rattled the-

ABOVE: Gertrude Lawrence and Paul McGrath embrace the Oxford movement in *Susan and God* (1937). RIGHT: PLAYBILL cover for the Pulitzer Prize play *Abe Lincoln in Illinois* (1938).

just incident in World War I, which should have run longer than twenty-four performances; Helen Jerome's faithful adaptation of Jane Austen's *Pride and Prejudice* (1935), which moved to the Plymouth from the Music Box and made the year's ten best list; Robert E. Sherwood's deft adaptation of the French play *Tovarich* (1936), with the famed Italian actress Marta Abba making her Broadway debut, co-starring with the suave John Halliday, another on Mantle's best-play-of-the-year list; Gertrude Lawrence in one of her greatest roles, as a sappy society woman who finds God in the Oxford movement, in Rachel Crothers's scintillating

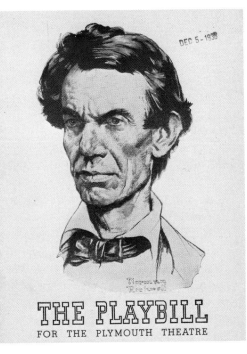

DEC 5-1938

THE PLAYBILL
FOR THE PLYMOUTH THEATRE

LEFT: Tallulah Bankhead and baby dinosaurs in Thornton Wilder's *The Skin of Our Teeth* (1942). RIGHT: Florence Eldridge and Fredric March in Wilder's Pulitzer Prize play.

atregoers with *The Skin of Our Teeth* (1942), a lunatic cartoon about the human race starring Tallulah Bankhead as the eternal temptress, Fredric March as the inventor of the alphabet, the wheel, and adultery, Florence Eldridge as his homespun wife, and Montgomery Clift and Frances Heflin as his children; Katharine Cornell, Raymond Massey, and Henry Daniell had a moderate success in Dodie Smith's *Lovers and Friends* (1943); *Chicken Every Sunday* (1944), a homey comedy by Julius J. and Philip G. Epstein, was a wartime hit; Spencer Tracy returned to Broadway after many years in Robert E. Sherwood's drama *The Rugged Path*, but the idealistic play, directed by Garson Kanin, ran for only 81 performances (1945);

Mary Martin went Chinese in a charming musical, *Lute Song* (1946), adapted from a Chinese classic by Sidney Howard and Will Irwin, with a score by Raymond Scott and two unknowns in the cast (Yul Brynner and Nancy Davis —later Mrs. Ronald Reagan); Clifton Webb returned to Broadway in Noel Coward's light comedy *Present Laughter* (1946), but it was too thin for critics and audiences; Tallulah Bankhead arrived in a dusty drama, *The Eagle Has Two Heads* (1947), by Jean Cocteau, with Helmut Dantine replacing Marlon Brando out of town because Ms. Bankhead claimed Brando was picking his nose and scratching his behind onstage, which would have helped this turkey considerably; Alfred Drake and Marsha Hunt in

🎭 Donald Cook and Tallulah Bankhead during the calm before the storm in *Private Lives* (1948).

Joy to the World (1948), a play about the dangers of liberalism in Hollywood; Tallulah Bankhead and Donald Cook turned Noel Coward's *Private Lives* (1948) into a roughhouse wrestling match, and they succeeded for 248 performances.

The 1950s started out with a huge hit for this theatre. Samuel Taylor's *The Happy Time*, a sentimental comedy about a French Canadian family, starred Claude Dauphin, Kurt Kasznar, Johnny Stewart, and Eva Gabor. The Rodgers and Hammerstein production ran for 614 performances. In April 1952 Paul Gregory's production of Shaw's *Don Juan in Hell*, which had previously played at Carnegie Hall and the Century Theatre, moved to the Plymouth for a two-month run. It starred Charles Boyer, Charles Laughton (who staged it), Cedric Hardwicke, and Agnes Moorehead. On October 29 of the same year, one of the Plymouth's biggest hits opened. It was Frederick Knott's *Dial 'M' for Murder*, one of those thrillers about a husband hiring a hit man to kill his wife. It starred Maurice Evans, Gusti Huber, Richard Derr, and John Williams as an impeccable inspector and it ran for 552 performances.

Highlights of the remainder of the 1950s included *The Caine Mutiny Court-Martial* (1954), staged by Charles Laughton, starring Henry Fonda, Lloyd Nolan and John Hodiak in Herman Wouk's powerful adaptation of his novel *The Caine Mutiny*; Marge and Gower Champion and Harry Belafonte in *3 For Tonight* (1955), a "diversion in song and dance"; Margaret Sullavan in her last Broadway appearance, in Carolyn Green's bubbly comedy *Janus* (1955), with Robert Preston and Claud Dauphin; Maurice Evans, Claudia Morgan, and Signe Hasso in a revival of Shaw's *The Apple Cart* (1956); Arnold Schulman's amusing *A Hole in the Head* (1957), with an expert cast including Paul Douglas, David Burns, Kay Medford, Joyce Van Patten, Lee Grant, and Tom Pedi; Peter Ustinov's satiric *Romanoff and Juliet* (1957), starring Ustinov as a general who plays cupid to a Russian boy and an American girl; Leslie Stevens's sexy comedy *The Marriage-Go-Round* (1958), starring Claudette Colbert, Charles Boyer, Julie Newmar, and Edmon Ryan, which ran into 1960.

The Plymouth greeted the 1960s with a smash musical, *Irma La Douce* (1960), that came by way of France and England. Directed by Peter Brook, it starred Elizabeth Seal, who won a Tony for her performance as a French

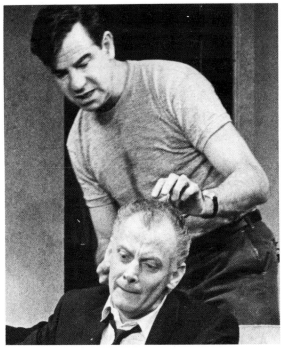

ABOVE: The PLAYBILL cover had to change weekly to satisfy stars' egos (1958). RIGHT: Walter Matthau and Art Carney in *The Odd Couple* (1965). BELOW: Clive Reville, Elizabeth Seal, and Keith Michell in *Irma La Douce* (1960).

hooker, and Keith Michell. Paddy Chayefsky's *Gideon* (1961) starred Fredric March as a debating angel, who is really God; Margaret Leighton and Anthony Quinn brought sparkle to a French/English play, *Tchin-Tchin* (1962); Lillian Hellman had one of her rare failures with a satiric comedy about American materialism, *My Mother, My Father and Me* (1963), directed by Gower Champion and starring Ruth Gordon and Walter Matthau; Arnold Wesker's British hit *Chips with Everything* (1963) amused with the adventures of young recruits in an RAF training unit; Alec Guinness won a Tony Award for his memorable portrayal of the title role in *Dylan* (1964), with Kate Reid as his wife; William Hanley's *Slow Dance on the Killing Ground* (1964) was named one of the best plays of the year, but audiences avoided it; Neil Simon came up with his best and most immortal comedy, *The Odd Couple* (1965), starring Walter Matthau as a sloppy sports announcer who rooms with an incredibly neat divorced man, played to perfection by Art Carney, achieving a run of 965

George C. Scott and Maureen Stapleton in Neil Simon's *Plaza Suite* (1968).

performances; Anthony Perkins, Connie Stevens, and Richard Benjamin starred in Neil Simon's most insipid comedy, *The Star-Spangled Girl* (1966), a stultifying evening of vapidity; Edward Albee also came a cropper with his play *Everything in the Garden* (1967), based on a true incident involving Long Island wives who made extra money as hookers; Neil Simon redeemed himself with a deft trio of playlets called *Plaza Suite* (1968), starring Maureen Stapleton and George C. Scott in vignettes set at New York's celebrated Plaza Hotel, which ran for 1,097 performances.

During the 1970s, the Plymouth continued to reign as one of Broadway's top legitimate theatres. On December 13, 1970, Neil Simon attempted his first serious drama with *The Gingerbread Lady*, a play supposedly inspired by Judy Garland's erratic career. It starred Maureen Stapleton, who won a Tony as the alcohol-drenched singer, but it only ran for 193 performances. In 1973 Jean Kerr came up with *Finishing Touches*, a comedy about a college professor's middle-age problems, but even with Barbara Bel Geddes and James Woods in the leads the play only lingered for five months.

Peter Cook and Dudley Moore brought a sequel to their highly successful revue *Beyond the Fringe*, and they called the show *Good Evening* (1973). They ran for 228 performances. The Plymouth then had another British invader, which turned out to be one of its most illustrious tenants. Peter Shaffer's *Equus*, a London hit based on a true, bizarre case about a young boy blinding a number of horses, became one of the theatre's highlights. It starred Anthony Hopkins as the psychiatrist and Peter Firth as the disturbed youth. Later in the run, Mr. Hopkins was succeeded by Anthony Perkins and Richard Burton. *Equus*, which ran for 781 performances in New York, won the Tony Award as best play of the season and won another Tony for its director, John Dexter.

Another British import, *Otherwise Engaged* (1977), by Simon Gray, starred Tom Courtenay as a British intellectual who tries to play a classical record and keeps getting interrupted by his scabrous friends; Elizabeth Swados's *Runaways* (1978), moved from the downtown New York Shakespeare Festival, ran for 267 performances; *Ain't Misbehavin'* (1979–81), the Tony Award winning revue based on Fats Waller's music, moved from the Longacre and played for two more years; Jane Lapotaire, repeating her triumph from Britain as Edith Piaf in *Piaf*, won a Tony for her interpretation of the famous street singer.

In the fall of 1981, the Royal Shakespeare Company brought its acclaimed production of Dickens's *Nicholas Nickleby* (1981–82), and the Plymouth Theatre had to accommodate its complex scenic design by constructing catwalks all over the house. The eight-hour play (with a din-

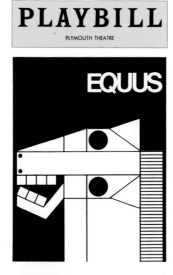

ABOVE: Jane Lapotaire in her Tony Award performance *Piaf* (1981). TOP RIGHT: PLAYBILL cover for the award-winning *Equus* (1974). BELOW: Roger Rees and Emily Richard in the epic *The Life and Adventures of Nicholas Nickleby* (1981).

ner intermission) caused a sensation and won a Tony for best play and for best male performance by an actor—Roger Rees. Directors Trevor Nunn and John Caird were also honored with a Tony for their inspired direction of this extremely complex production.

In 1982 the Circle in the Square offered Colleen Dewhurst in a revival of Ugo Betti's *The Queen and the Rebels*; and in 1983, the New York Shakespeare Festival's production of the British play *Plenty* garnered raves. Written by David Hare, it offered memorable performances by the Canadian actress Kate Nelligan and by American actor Edward Herrmann. This was another case of an Off-Broadway play being transferred to Broadway with gratifying results.

At this writing, the Plymouth is occupied by the all-star revival of Kaufman and Hart's 1936 Pulitzer Prize winning play *You Can't Take It with You*. The next scheduled tenant is Tom Stoppard's British hit *The Real Thing*, starring Jeremy Irons and Glenn Close. This theatre, still owned and operated by the Shubert Organization, has had a distinguished record as a house of hits.

⚜ AMBASSADOR THEATRE ⚜

The Ambassador was the first of six new theatres that the Shuberts built on West Forty-eighth and West Forty-ninth streets in the early 1920s. Located at 215 West Forty-ninth Street and designed by architect Herbert J. Krapp, the theatre was unusual because it had to be built diagonally due to the lack of space on its site. Its auditorium was wide rather than deep, offering an excellent view of the stage from all seats.

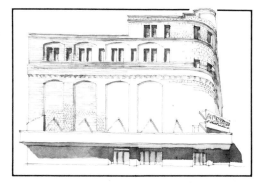

There have been some erroneous reports that this theatre opened with the Shuberts' famous operetta *Blossom Time*. Not so. It opened on February 11, 1921, with a musical called *The Rose Girl*, starring Marjorie Gateson. It was a hit.

In May of 1921, a soldier revue called *Biff! Bing! Bang!* amused theatregoers. Later that year *Blossom Time* did open at the Ambassador and it was this theatre's first smash hit. A musical biography of composer Franz Schubert, it featured melodies adapted from his compositions by Sigmund Romberg. The show stopper was "Serenade." The operetta, which ran for 516 performances, became a perennial Shubert revival.

Operettas were the rage in the 1920s, and the Ambassador had its share of them. After *Blossom Time* came *The Lady in Ermine* (1922), a European import with added numbers by Al Goodman, who conducted the pit orchestras for many Broadway shows, and Sigmund Romberg, whose "When Hearts Are Young" was the hit of the show. This hit was followed by *Caroline* (1923), an American adaptation of a German operetta by Edward Kunneke, starring Tessa Kosta. Next came Victor Herbert's last show, *The Dream Girl* (1924), a fantasy that involved Fay Bainter and Walter Woolf in one of those "dream" plots that take them back to the fifteenth century. There were some Sigmund Romberg interpolations in this operetta, which was produced after Herbert's death.

A change of fare came to the Ambassador in 1925 when a highly successful revival of Shaw's *Candida*, starring Katharine Cornell, who became famed for her interpretation of the leading role, moved from the Eltinge Theatre to this house. More drama arrived when William A. Brady brought in his production of F. Scott Fitzgerald's *The Great Gatsby* (1926), adapted by Owen Davis and starring James Rennie as Gatsby, Florence Eldridge as Daisy,

ABOVE: James Bell and Spencer Tracy in the taut prison drama *The Last Mile* (1930). RIGHT: Olga Cook and Bertram Peacock in the popular operetta *Blossom Time* (1921).

and Elliott Cabot as Tom Buchanan. Directed by George Cukor, the future great film director, the play ran for 113 performances.

The Ambassador returned to musicals with a solid hit, *Queen High*, which ran for almost 400 performances in 1926–27. It starred Charles Ruggles. From September 1927 until December 1929, the Ambassador had a string of quick flops. The few exceptions were an exciting police drama, *The Racket* (1927), starring Edward G. Robinson, Norman Foster, and John Cromwell, which ran for 120 performances and was named one of the year's ten best plays; and *Little Accident*, a play by Floyd Dell and Thomas Mitchell, with Mitchell starring as a man about to marry one woman when he discovers he is the father of another woman's child. This hit comedy moved from the Morosco and played for six months at the Ambassador.

In December 1929 *Street Scene*, Elmer Rice's Pulitzer Prize play that took place in front of a Manhattan tenement house, moved from the Playhouse and completed its run of 601 performances at the Ambassador. *The Last Mile*, a prison drama by John Wexley, starring Spencer Tracy, Joseph Spurin-Calleia, and Henry O'Neill, moved from the Sam H. Harris Theatre

to the Ambassador in October 1930. This lauded drama, one of the year's ten best, served as the springboard for Spencer Tracy's career in Hollywood.

Highlights of the 1930s at this theatre included *Are You Decent?* (1934), a comedy by Crane Wilbur in which Claudia Morgan announced to two suitors that she wished to have a baby without bothering with matrimony; *Kill That Story* (1934), a George Abbott/ Philip Dunning production about a newspaperman whose wife unjustly divorced him because she believed he was having an affair with a stenographer at the newspaper; Lucile Watson and Percy Kilbride in *Post Road* (1935), a comedy about kidnapping that moved here from the Masque Theatre; Ayn Rand's fascinating courtroom drama *The Night of January 16* (1935), starring Doris Nolan and Walter Pidgeon, with a jury selected from the audience at each performance to decide if Ms. Nolan was guilty of murder; The Abbey Theatre Players from Dublin in a season of repertory, including *Katie Roche, The Plough and the Stars, The Playboy of the Western World* and *Juno and the Paycock* (1937); Danny Kaye making his Broadway debut in *The Straw Hat Revue* (1939), with Imogene Coca, Alfred Drake, and Jerome Robbins in the cast spoofing Broadway shows and current trends.

In 1935, the Shuberts had sold their interest in this theatre; they did not buy it back until 1956. During these two decades, the Ambassador did not always function as a legitimate theatre. It was, on different occasions, leased as a movie theatre and a radio and TV studio.

In 1941 the Ambassador returned to legitimacy on November 16 with *Cuckoos on the Hearth*, an insane comedy that moved here from the Mansfield Theatre, with Percy Kilbride, Janet Fox, and Howard St. John. Then two years elapsed before the theatre again housed a play. The Messrs. Shubert brought in a revival of *Blossom Time* in 1943, but it only lasted for forty-seven performances. Edward Chodorov's successful drama *Decision* moved here from

ABOVE LEFT: Sketch of actor David Garrick on Ambassador PLAYBILL cover (1934). BELOW: Pixie Imogene Coca in *The Straw Hat Revue* (1939).

PLAYBILL

a weekly magazine for theatregoers

Feb. 3, 1958

COMPULSION

TOP: Percy Kilbride (far left) and cast members of *Cuckoos on the Hearth* (1941). ABOVE: Roddy McDowall and Dean Stockwell in *Compulsion* (1957).

the Belasco in 1944; and the critically disdained but popular comedy *School for Brides*, starring Roscoe Karns, moved here from the Royale in 1944. For the next twelve years, the Ambassador was leased to radio and television networks. In 1956 the Shuberts once again became the owners and reopened the refurbished house with a comedy, *The Loud Red Patrick*, starring David Wayne and Arthur Kennedy. It was not successful and neither was the next tenant, Tallulah Bankhead in *Eugenia*, adapted from Henry James's *The Europeans*.

In 1957 Meyer Levin's adaptation of his book *Compulsion*, about the famous Leopold/Loeb murder trial in Chicago, played for 140 performances with Dean Stockwell and Roddy McDowall as the murderers and Ina Balin as one of their college classmates. In March 1958 Tyrone Power and Faye Emerson played Adam and Eve and Arnold Moss played George Bernard Shaw in Shaw's *Back to Methuselah* for 29 performances. George C. Scott made his Broadway debut at the Ambassador with Judith Anderson in a drama, *Comes a Day*, and caused an immediate sensation by strangling a bird onstage (a prop, we hope) in 1958. In 1959, Melvyn Douglas, E.G. Marshall, and Jean Dixon appeared in *The Gang's All Here*, a play about the scandalous Harding administration in Washington, D.C.

The 1960s at the Ambassador brought Paddy Chayefsky's *The Tenth Man* (1961) from the Booth Theatre; Gladys Cooper in an interesting adaptation of E.M. Forster's *A Passage to India* (1962); Joseph Cotten, his wife, Patricia Medina, Russell Collins, and John Beal in Joseph Hayes's drama about corruption in big business, *Calculated Risk* (1962); *Stop the World—I Want to Get Off* (1963), the celebrated Anthony Newley/Leslie Bricusse musical transferred from the Shubert Theatre; Ira Wallach's *Absence of a Cello* (1964), with Fred Clark giving a comic performance; appearances by the

THE LION IN WINTER

YOU KNOW I CAN'T
HERE YOU WHEN THE
WATER'S RUNNING

ABOVE: Robert Preston and Rosemary Harris in *The Lion in Winter* (1966). TOP RIGHT: Can you spot the error on this 1967 PLAYBILL cover? BOTTOM RIGHT: Jim Dale in *Scapino*.

PLAYBILL
AMBASSADOR THEATRE

scapino!

Paul Taylor Dance Company and Charles Aznavour (1965); Robert Preston and Rosemary Harris in James Goldman's witty play *The Lion in Winter* (1966), about Henry II and Eleanor of Aquitaine; Robert Anderson's captivating playlets under the collective title of *You Know I Can't Hear You When the Water's Running* (1967), starring Martin Balsam, Eileen Heckart, and George Grizzard; *We Bombed in New Haven* (1968), the unsuccessful Joseph Heller play about men at war, starring Jason Robards, Jr.

The 1970s brought unusual and varied fare to this theatre. A revival of Sandy Wilson's parody of 1920s musicals, *The Boy Friend* (1970), starring Sandy Duncan and Judy Carne, did not

Maurice Hines, Gregory Hines, and Lonnie McNeill in *Eubie* (1978).

Saundra Santiago, Tony Lo Bianco, and James Hayden in the 1983 revival of *A View from the Bridge*.

fare as well as the original; *Paul Sills' Story Theatre* (1970) turned out to be a delightful entertainment that presented children's classic stories with dance, song, narration, and pantomime; Melvin Van Peebles's *Ain't Supposed to Die a Natural Death* (1971) offered an original look at the black experience. Subsequent productions included Jim Dale in a lively revival of *Scapino* (1974); a spirited revival of *Godspell* (1977); Estelle Parsons in a one-woman tour de force, *Miss Margarida's Way* (1977); a marvelous revue of Eubie Blake songs called *Eubie* (1978–79); a revival of the gospel musical *Your Arms Too Short to Box with God* (1980); *Dancin'* (1980–82), the Bob Fosse dance triumph that moved here from the Broadhurst; and the Ambassador's most recent tenant, a revival of Arthur Miller's revised version of *A View from the Bridge*, with potent performances by Tony Lo Bianco, Rose Gregorio, James Hayden, Alan Feinstein, and Robert Prosky.

Now in its sixty-third year, the Ambassador continues to be an ideal theatre for dramas, comedies, and intimate musicals. It is kept in excellent condition by the Shubert Organization.

⚜ RITZ THEATRE ⚜

The restoration of vintage Broadway legitimate theatres admirably continued with the reopening of the Ritz Theatre at 219 West Forty-eighth Street on May 10, 1983. Jujamcyn Theatres, the company that owns the St. James, Martin Beck, Eugene O'Neill, and Virginia theatres, spent $1.5 million in renovating the Ritz and adding it to its growing list of houses.

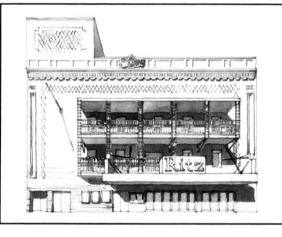

The Ritz was built by the Shuberts as a sister theatre to their Ambassador Theatre on West Forty-ninth Street. It was built in a record sixty-six days in 1921. The architect was Herbert J. Krapp, the eminent theatre designer of that era, and the interior was done in Italian Renaissance with much gold leaf and Italian scrollwork.

On March 21, 1921, the intimate new house (under 1,000 seats) opened with Clare Eames in John Drinkwater's *Mary Stuart*, preceded by a pantomime called *A Man About Town* that included in its cast the future opera composer Deems Taylor.

The Ritz flourished in the 1920s with some distinguished plays and players. A 1921 high-light was an ebullient performance by Ina Claire in *Bluebeard's Eighth Wife*. Roland Young appeared in *Madame Pierre* the following year, and in 1923 Katharine Cornell was admired in *The Enchanted Cottage*, as was Lynn Fontanne in *In Love with Love*. Audiences in 1924 were spellbound by Sutton Vane's eerie *Outward Bound*, starring Alfred Lunt, Leslie Howard, and Margalo Gillmore as dead passengers on a boat that is sailing to the "other world." The same year unveiled *Hassard Short's Ritz Revue*, hailed for its scenic splendors, and John Galsworthy's *Old English*, starring the noted character actor George Arliss.

A saucy Claudette Colbert graced *The Kiss in a Taxi* in 1925, followed by Helen Hayes in *Young Blood*, and Frank Morgan, Ralph Morgan, and Estelle Winwood in *A Weak Woman*. The next year found a young Ruby Keeler tapping in *Bye, Bye, Bonnie*; the beautiful Grace George in *The Legend of Leonora*; and Alice Brady and Lionel Atwill in *The Thief*.

On the day after Christmas 1927 bubbly

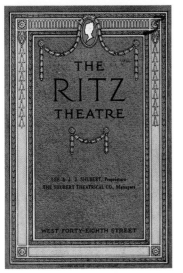

ABOVE: Pixie children in *The Enchanted Cottage* peer out of a window seat (1923). FAR LEFT: Standard Ritz program cover in the 1920s. LEFT: "Herald" for Sutton Vane's mystical play *Outward Bound* (1924). BOTTOM LEFT: Bette Davis and Duncan Penwarden in *Broken Dishes* (1929). BELOW: Claudette Colbert vamps John Williams in *The Kiss in the Taxi* (1925).

Miriam Hopkins and Frank McHugh cheered first-nighters in *Excess Baggage*, followed by another winner, Janet Beecher in *Courage*, which ran until May 1929. The decade came to an end with the successful *Broken Dishes*, with Donald Meek and a young actress named Bette Davis, who was immediately snapped up by Hollywood.

ABOVE (from left): Frank Lawton in *The Wind and the Rain* (1934); standard Ritz program-cover sketch in the 1930s, of British actors Mr. and Mrs. John Wood in *As You Like It*; program art of Ruth Draper in her character sketches (1932). BELOW: The cast of *New Faces of 1943*.

Highlights of the 1930s at the Ritz included the famed comedy team of Smith and Dale in a hit play called *Mendel, Inc.*; noted monologist Ruth Draper in some of her celebrated character sketches; the thriller *Double Door*; Frank Lawton and Mildred Natwick in *The Wind and the Rain*; Dennis King and Leo G. Carroll in Mark Reed's delightful *Petticoat Fever*; Ilka Chase and Peggy Conklin in *Co Respondent Unknown*; the Surry Players (including Shepperd Strudwick, Anne Revere, and Katherine Emery) in a revival of *As You Like It*; and Jessica Tandy and Dame Sybil Thorndike in J.B. Priestly's *Time and the Conways*.

During the late 1930s the Federal Theatre Project (also known as the WPA Theatre) staged some exciting productions at the Ritz. Among them were T.S. Eliot's verse drama *Murder in the Cathedral*; the stirring *Power*, staged by the WPA's Living Newspaper unit, which ran for five months; and a lavish production of *Pinocchio* that ran for 197 performances.

In 1939 the Ritz became the CBS Theatre No. 4, where live radio shows were broadcast, including the programs of the Town Crier, drama critic Alexander Woollcott. On December 22, 1942, the theatre went legit again with

TOP: PLAYBILL cover for the rock musical *Soon* (1971). BOTTOM: Program for *The Flying Karamazov Brothers*, which restored the Ritz to legitimacy in 1983.

Leonard Sillman's *New Faces of 1943*, with the producer onstage to introduce some new faces, including John Lund and Alice Pearce. After that, the long-running *Tobacco Road* moved in from the Forrest Theatre. Toward the end of 1943, NBC took the theatre over; later, so did ABC, for use as a radio and TV studio.

It was not until December 1970 that the Ritz returned to legitimacy, with previews for a new rock opera called *Soon*. The show, which opened on January 12, 1971, marked the Broadway debuts of Peter Allen, Nell Carter, and Richard Gere. Also featured in the cast were Barry Bostwick, Marta Heflin, and Leata Galloway. Unfortunately, it closed after three performances. Later that year, Rip Torn and Viveca Lindfors played a brief run in Strindberg's *Dance of Death*.

Following a major renovation in late 1971, the Ritz reopened on March 7, 1972, with the short-lived thriller *Children, Children*, starring Gwen Verdon. In 1973 it housed a production of the British farce *No Sex, Please, We're British*. Shortly thereafter, the theatre was christened the Robert F. Kennedy Children's Theatre and, for a while, showed films. Now, under the Jujamcyn banner, the Ritz has been restored to its original legitimate splendor.

According to *Interior Design* magazine, the total interior renovation of the Ritz was achieved by Karen Rosen of KMR Designs, Ltd., in Manhattan. Her client, Richard Wolff, president of the Jujamcyn Theatre Corp., requested that the Ritz be made elegant by restoring its classical feeling of the 1920s. Ms. Rosen chose a color scheme of pink/mauve/gray touched with black to reflect the twenties look while appealing to current tastes. She restored ceiling decorations and murals and designed Art Deco-type sconces, chandeliers, balcony, and ceiling lights to achieve illumination without jarring glare.

The restored Ritz reopened on May 10, 1983, with the incredible troupe of jugglers and entertainers known as *The Flying Karamazov Brothers*.

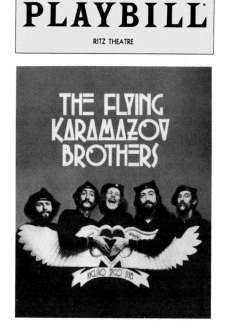

⚓ NEDERLANDER THEATRE ⚓

The Nederlander Theatre has had a long and distinguished history under several different names: the National, the Billy Rose, and the Trafalgar.

Walter C. Jordan, a theatrical agent of note, built the National Theatre at 208 West Forty-first Street. When it opened on September 1, 1921, the New York *Times* reported that the new house cost $950,000 to build, was designed by architect William Neil

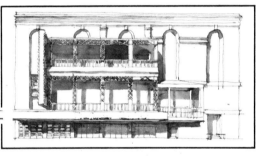

Smith, and contained 1,200 seats, making it capable of housing both dramatic productions and musicals.

The theatre's interior was done in burnished Italian walnut wood, with gold embellishments. "The style is early Renaissance and the carved figures are of lyric and epic subjects, unobtrusive but attractive, and emerging in the half-round from wood like Flemish carvings," wrote the *Times*. The paper went on to praise Mr. Jordan for providing actors with luxurious dressing rooms with baths and the audience with the latest in rest rooms and lounges, making a trip to the new theatre a comfortable and pleasurable experience.

Unfortunately, the National's opening show was *Swords*, Sidney Howard's first play, which only ran for thirty-six performances. Mr. Howard, however, benefited from the play. He married Clare Eames, who played the leading role.

In February 1922 the theatre had a stroke of luck in booking a thriller that would become a classic of its genre: *The Cat and the Canary*. The creeper was written by actor John Willard, and critic Alexander Woollcott wrote in the *Times*: "He has turned out a creepy young thriller, nicely calculated to make every hair on your head rise and remain standing from 8:30 till nearly 11." The play, which took place in a spooky mansion on the Hudson, required an heiress to remain sane, while people were being snuffed out all around her, in order to win her inheritance. Henry Hull was the costar.

In 1923 Walter Hampden revived the Rostand classic *Cyrano de Bergerac* and was rewarded with great notices and a run of 250 performances. The blank verse adaptation of the play was by Brian Hooker. Another hit followed in 1924 when H.B. Warner starred in *Silence*, a melodrama in which a crook (Warner) takes the rap for a crime that his daughter has committed.

The popular movie actress Lila Lee appeared

at the National in 1925 in one of those French farces about a couple who are forced to marry by their parents and then discover that they really love each other. Movie fans bought it for 146 performances. Later in the year *The Gorilla*, a popular spoof of mystery plays, moved here from the Selwyn Theatre. Walter Hampden next moved in from his own house, the Hampden Theatre, with his production of *Hamlet*, and this classic was followed early in 1926 by the great magician Houdini in a spectacular personal appearance.

Fredric March came to the National in 1926 in *The Half-Caste*, subtitled "A story of love and sacrifice in a Land of Forgotten Men," and the *Times* labeled it "a trite and loquacious drama." The National's next offering fared better. It was George M. Cohan's production of a play called *Yellow*, in which Chester Morris played a rotter. (There was a young actor in the supporting cast

named Spencer Tracy.) Some first-nighters felt that the play's author, Margaret Vernon, was a pseudonym for Mr. Cohan. It ran for 132 performances.

John Willard, who had given the National a smash—*The Cat and the Canary*—tried again with a melodrama called *Fog* in 1927, but the critics found it murky and it evaporated after 97 performances. Next came a huge hit and one of the National's fondly remembered shows. It was A.H. Woods's production of Bayard Veiller's *The Trial of Mary Dugan* and it starred Ann Harding as the Mary who was accused of murdering one Edgar Rice. The court remained in session for 437 times.

The 1920s came to a dramatic close at the National with the opening of Martin Flavin's *The Criminal Code*, which jolted theatregoers with its realistic view of life in the big house. Arthur Byron gave a powerful performance as an in-

LEFT: Florence Eldridge as the menaced heiress in *The Cat and the Canary* (1922). BELOW: Walter Hampden in the classic *Cyrano de Bergerac* (1923).

mate who witnessed a murder in the warden's office but chose not to reveal which of his prison mates committed the crime. It thrilled audiences for 174 performances.

Peking's most illustrious actor, Mei Lan-Fang, played a highly successful Broadway engagement with his Chinese company of actors, singers, and musicians in 1930. He opened first at the 49th Street Theatre, then moved to the National for an additional three weeks. On November 13, 1930, a theatrical event occurred at the National: Herman Shumlin opened his production of *Grand Hotel*, a swirling drama based on a play by Vicki Baum, translated from the German by William A. Drake. The opulent production was the first dramatic play on Broadway to use a revolving stage, and it captivated audiences with its portrayal of life in a luxury hotel in Berlin. Eugenie Leontovich played a weary Russian ballerina, Sam Jaffe played a clerk with only a few weeks to live, Henry Hull was a baron who gets murdered in the hotel, and the rest of the enormous cast played employees and guests of the Grand Hotel, with myriad problems. It ran for 444 performances.

The National had a series of failures and quick bookings during 1932 and 1933 and was dark for over a year during those gray depression days. But on October 22, 1934, a distin-guished drama opened at this theatre. It was Sean O'Casey's *Within the Gates*, directed by Melvyn Douglas and starring Lillian Gish as a prostitute, Bramwell Fletcher as a poet, and Moffat Johnston as a bishop. The play took place in Hyde Park, and the very large cast represented the great variety of humanity who spent their days in the park. There was music, dancing, and philosophizing, and Brooks Atkinson in the *Times* pronounced: "Nothing so grand has risen in our impoverished theatre since this reporter first began writing of plays."

A charming, nostalgic play, *Remember the Day*, by Philip Dunning and Philo Higley, came to the National on September 25, 1935. It starred Frankie Thomas as a schoolboy who has a crush on his teacher (Francesca Bruning) until he sees her kissing the school's athletic coach (Russell Hardie). A novelty of the well-received play was that Frank M. Thomas, Sr., played the father of Frankie Thomas.

Another fine drama, *Ethan Frome*, adapted by Owen and Donald Davis from the novel of the same name by Edith Wharton, opened in January 1936. Staged by Guthrie McClintic, the play had magnificent performances by Raymond Massey, Ruth Gordon, and Pauline Lord, but its depressing story and somber atmosphere resulted in a run of only 119 performances.

On November 24, 1936, New York's elite descended upon the National in their finest evening wear and jewels to welcome back Noel Coward and Gertrude Lawrence to the Broadway stage in Coward's collection of nine one-act plays under the collective title of *Tonight at 8:30*. The nine plays were performed in groups of three at three different performances. Coward and Lawrence had not been seen on Broadway together since 1931, when they triumphed in Coward's *Private Lives*, and their return was the social event of the 1936–37 season. At the opening

OPPOSITE, FAR LEFT: Henry Hull and Eugenie Leontovich in *Grand Hotel* (1930). LEFT: Lillian Gish, Moffat Johnson, and Kathryn Collier in *Within the Gates* (1934). BELOW: Program-cover art of British actress Elizabeth Simpson Inchbald. RIGHT: Gertrude Lawrence and Noel Coward in *Tonight at 8:30*.

night, during the first intermission, a lady had her chinchilla coat stolen. At openings in those days, there was always a gray-haired detective stationed in the theatre to keep an eye on the audience. This supersleuth apprehended the thieves and the lady had her coat back by the time the final curtain fell.

In 1938 Orson Welles and John Houseman's celebrated Mercury Theatre had such success with its revivals of Shakespeare's *Julius Caesar* and Thomas Dekker's *The Shoemaker's Holiday* that they moved these productions from the small Mercury Theatre to the larger National. The group was the sensation of the season. They played *Julius Caesar* in black shirts as an indictment of fascism; and *The Shoemaker's Holiday* was turned into a rowdy, lusty prank without an intermission. The Mercury Theatre company for these two productions included such actors as Orson Welles, Joseph Cotten, Martin Gabel, Hiram Sherman, John Hoysradt, George Coulouris, Stefan Schnabel, Vincent Price, Ruth Ford, Edith Barrett, Elliott Reid, and Whitford Kane.

On February 15, 1939, the National housed one of its finest tenants. Lillian Hellman's vitriolic play about greed, *The Little Foxes*, starred Tallulah Bankhead as Regina Giddens, and it was Tallulah's first superior role in the American theatre. Herman Shumlin's direction was praised and so were the supporting cast: Patricia Collinge, Frank Conroy, Dan Duryea, Carl Benton Reid, Charles Dingle, and Florence Williams. It ran for 410 performances.

During the 1940s the National housed some memorable productions. Ethel Barrymore had one of her greatest triumphs in Emlyn Williams's drama *The Corn Is Green*, in which she played a determined schoolteacher in Wales who discovers a literary talent among one of the local miners and exerts all her power to make a success of him. The New York Drama Critics Circle named it the best foreign play of the season, and it ran for 477 performances during the 1940–41 season.

Another notable production came to this theatre in November 1941: Maurice Evans and Judith Anderson in Shakespeare's *Macbeth*. Staged by Margaret Webster, the revival was ac-

claimed as one of the finest productions of this classic ever mounted in the United States. It ran for 131 performances. In 1943 Sidney Kingsley's *The Patriots* opened and won the New York Drama Critics Award as best play of the season. The cast included Raymond E. Johnson as Thomas Jefferson, House Jameson as Alexander Hamilton, and Cecil Humphreys as George Washington. Mrs. Sidney Kingsley, Madge Evans, played a romantic role.

A failure of note was a musical called *What's Up?*, which happened to be Alan Jay Lerner and Frederick Loewe's first Broadway musical. Jimmy Savo had the lead, and the staging and choreography were by George Balanchine, but the critics declared that nothing was up and the show closed after 63 performances in 1943. Early in 1944, Eva Le Gallienne and Joseph Schildkraut acted brilliantly in a revival of Chekhov's *The Cherry Orchard*, staged by Ms. Le Gallienne and Margaret Webster. Later that year Ethel Barrymore returned to this theatre in an adaptation of the Franz Werfel novel *Embezzled Heaven*, but the play was not a success. Lerner and Loewe returned to the National in November 1945 with a delightful musical called *The Day Before Spring,* about a college reunion. Anthony Tudor created the ballets and the cast included Irene Manning, John Archer, Bill Johnson, Estelle Loring, and dancer Hugh Laing. The pleasant musical lasted for 165 performances. This was followed by one of the most entertaining revues ever produced on Broadway —*Call Me Mister*—satirizing the plight of the returning service-man and -woman from World War II. Produced by Melvyn Douglas and Herman Levin, the revue had a beguiling score by Harold Rome and sharp performances by Betty Garrett, Jules Munshin, Danny Scholl, Bill Callahan, Maria Karnilova, and many others and had a gratifying run of 734 performances.

Judith Anderson returned to the National in her shattering performance as Medea in 1947. Assisted by John Gielgud as Jason and Florence Reed as the Nurse, she brought Robinson Jeffers's adaptation of Euripides' tragedy to painful life. It had a record run of 214 performances. John Gielgud was in the National's next production as well, *Crime and Punishment,* costarring with Lillian Gish, but the adaptation of Dostoevsky's novel was not a success. Another failure followed: Gertrude Lawrence attempted to revive Noel Coward's *Tonight at*

OPPOSITE, FAR LEFT: Ethel Barrymore and Richard Waring in *The Corn is Green* (1940). LEFT: Tallulah Bankhead in her biggest hit, *The Little Foxes* (1939). ABOVE: Souvenir program for Judith Anderson in *Medea* (1947). BELOW: The happy military revue *Call Me Mister* (1946).

8:30, with young Graham Payn, but it did not come off in 1948. That spring Michael Redgrave and Flora Robeson revived *Macbeth*, but that, too, failed.

Finally, in December 1948, a delirious revue, *Lend an Ear*, entirely written by Charles Gaynor, set the town on its ear. Carol Channing was an overnight success as a loony, wide-eyed blonde in such numbers as "The Gladiola Girl" and "Opera Without Music," and Yvonne Adair, William Eythe, Gene Nelson, and the rest of the cast made this one of the theatre's best revues of all time.

John Garfield and Nancy Kelly starred in Clifford Odets's *The Big Knife*, an exposé of Hollywood, in 1949, but despite excellent performances and expert direction by Lee Strasberg, the play was only a moderate success. The 1940s at the National came to a scintillating end with Sir Cedric Hardwicke and Lilli Palmer in a shimmering revival of Shaw's *Caesar and Cleopatra*, staged by Hardwicke.

Highlights of the 1950s included an appearance by Les Ballets de Paris and Louis Calhern in *King Lear*, both in 1950; Katharine Cornell, Grace George, and Brian Aherne in a highly successful revival of Somerset Maugham's *The Constant Wife* (1951); Tennessee Williams's fascinating but obscure play, *Camino Real* (1953), with Eli Wallach as Kilroy; Margaret Sullavan, Joseph Cotten, Luella Gear, John Cromwell, and Scott McKay in Samuel Taylor's sterling comedy of manners *Sabrina Fair* (1953).

In 1955 Paul Muni returned to the Broadway stage in one of his finest parts in *Inherit the Wind*, the Jerome Lawrence/Robert E. Lee play about the sensational Scopes monkey trial. Mr. Muni and his costar, Ed Begley, both won Tony Awards for their powerful performances in parts inspired by the great trial lawyer Clarence Darrow (Muni) and William Jennings Bryan (Begley). The enormous cast also included Tony Randall, Bethel Leslie, Muriel Kirkland, and

Staats Cotsworth. Directed by Herman Shumlin, the play ran for 806 performances, the longest-running play in this theatre's history. Mr. Muni was succeeded by Melvyn Douglas during the run.

In 1958 Arlene Francis, Joseph Cotten, and Walter Matthau amused audiences for 263 performances in Harry Kurnitz's *Once More with Feeling*. This comedy was the last show to play the National Theatre before it was bought by Billy Rose and renamed the Billy Rose Theatre. Mr. Rose, songwriter, producer, and millionaire art collector, spent a fortune refurbishing his new theatre in lush red and gold and reopened it on October 18, 1959, with Maurice Evans, Sam Levene, Diane Cilento, Pamela Brown, Diane Wynyard, and Alan Webb in Shaw's *Heartbreak House*. The revival ran for 112 performances.

BELOW: Uta Hagen, Arthur Hill, and George Grizzard trade insults in *Who's Afraid of Virginia Woolf?* (1962). OPPOSITE: Peter Brook's production of *A Midsummer Night's Dream* (1971).

The Billy Rose greeted the 1960s with Katharine Cornell in her final play on Broadway before retirement. It was *Dear Liar*, Jerome Kilty's comedy, with Ms. Cornell and Brian Aherne reading letters adapted for the stage from the correspondence of Mrs. Patrick Campbell and Bernard Shaw. The play ran for only fifty-two performances.

In October 1960 *The Wall*, an adaptation of John Hersey's novel, presented a harrowing play about the Warsaw Ghetto. The cast included George C. Scott, Joseph Buloff, David Opatoshu, and Marian Seldes, and the drama ran for 167 performances.

Edward Albee's first full-length play, *Who's Afraid of Virginia Woolf?*, opened at the Billy Rose on October 14, 1962, and sent shock waves through Times Square. The stinging drama about a self-destructive married couple, brilliantly played by Uta Hagen and Arthur Hill, and their unfortunate guests—George Grizzard and Melinda Dillon—was the sensation of the season and won Tony Awards for its author, director (Alan Schneider), stars (Ms. Hagen and Mr. Hill), and producers (Richard Barr and Clinton Wilder). It ran for 644 performances. Two years later, Mr. Albee tried again at this theatre with a play called *Tiny Alice*, starring John Gielgud and Irene Worth, but not even the actors seemed to understand what this pretentious play was all about. A series of short plays by Albee and Samuel Beckett was presented at the Billy Rose by the Playwrights Repertory Theatre in 1968, followed by the Minnesota

ABOVE: PLAYBILL covers for two British hits, *Whose Life Is It Anyway?* (1979) and *Betrayal* (1980). BELOW, RIGHT: PLAYBILL cover portrait of Lena Horne in her sensational musical autobiography, *Lena Horne: The Lady and Her Music* (1981).

Theatre Company's revivals of *The House of Atreus* and *The Resistable Rise of Arturo Ui.* The decade came to an end with a sleek revival of Noel Coward's *Private Lives*, costarring Brian Bedford and Tammy Grimes, who won a Tony Award for her hoydenish performance as Amanda.

In 1971, the Royal Shakespeare Company's production of *A Midsummer Night's Dream*, directed by Peter Brook, was great fun, and later that year, Harold Pinter's *Old Times* was hailed. In 1974 Brian Bedford and Jill Clayburgh were delightful in Tom Stoppard's buoyant comedy *Jumpers.*

The Billy Rose Theatre closed for a year in 1978, then was bought by James and Joseph Nederlander and the British firm of Cooney-Marsh. It was beautifully refurbished and renamed the Trafalgar. It housed two British hits: *Whose Life Is It Anyway?*, starring Tom Conti, who won a Tony Award for his performance, and Pinter's *Betrayal*, starring Raul Julia, Blythe Danner, and Roy Scheider.

In late 1980 the Trafalgar became the Nederlander Theatre, named in honor of the late theatre owner David Tobias Nederlander, whose sons now operate the Nederlander Organization. On May 12, 1981, this theatre housed one of its most distinguished attractions. The incomparable Lena Horne opened in a spectacular personal appearance called *Lena Horne: The Lady and Her Music*, and the unforgettable occasion won her a special Tony Award and a special citation from the New York Drama Critics Circle for her singing and recounting of the highlights of her brilliant career.

The Nederlander Theatre's most recent tenants have been the charming British import, *84 Charing Cross Road*, by Helene Hanff, starring Ellen Burstyn and Joseph Maher, and a musical version of the James Baldwin play *The Amen Corner.*

The Nederlander has had many memorable plays and musicals in its sixty-three-year history and is still one of the best-constructed playhouses in Manhattan.

❧ MUSIC BOX THEATRE ❧

This lovely theatre on West Forty-fifth Street, which Moss Hart described as everyone's dream of a theatre, celebrated its sixtieth birthday on September 22, 1981. Never once in its six decades has its elegant limestone façade been marred by a movie or burlesque marquee.

The Music Box was built by the late producer Sam H. Harris and composposer Irving Berlin to house a series of lavish *Music Box Revues* to be compos-

ed by Mr. Berlin. The composer now co-owns the theatre with the Shubert Organization.

On September 22, 1921, the resplendent theatre, designed by C. Howard Crane, opened with the first *Music Box Revue*, starring Mr. Berlin, Sam Bernard, Florence Moore, Joseph Santley, and—in the chorus—young Miriam Hopkins. The critics raved about the show and the new theatre, but it was the show's comic, Sam Bernard, who best described the opulent new house: "It stinks from class."

Four editions of the *Music Box Revue*, starring such luminaries as Fanny Brice, Grace Moore, Bobby Clark, Robert Benchley, and Charlotte Greenwood, brought fame to Berlin and the Music Box. In 1925 the theatre departed from its revue-only policy to present a smash hit comedy called *Cradle Snatchers*, starring Mary Boland, Humphrey Bogart, Edna May Oliver, and Raymond Guion (later Gene Raymond of the movies).

Other big Music Box hits in the 1920s include *Chicago* (1926), later made into a successful musical; *The Spider* (1927), a clever thriller that moved here from the 46th Street Theatre; Philip Barry's charming comedy, *Paris Bound* (1927); Cole Porter's *Paris* (1928); and the last Music Box show of the 1920s, the historic intimate revue *The Little Show* (1929), starring Clifton Webb, Fred Allen, and Libby Holman.

The Music Box faced the depression with élan. *Topaze*, a French comedy starring Frank Morgan, was a hit in early 1930, followed by the famed satire *Once in a Lifetime*, the first collaboration of George S. Kaufman and Moss Hart. In 1931, Beatrice Lillie graced the Music Box in *The Third Little Show*, in which she introduced Noel Coward's celebrated song "Mad Dogs and Englishmen" to American audiences.

On December 26, 1931, *Of Thee I Sing*

IRVING BERLIN'S

SECOND ANNUAL
MUSIC BOX REVUE

marched into the Music Box and became the first musical comedy to win a Pulitzer Prize. The musical had a biting book by George S. Kaufman and Morrie Ryskind, memorable music by George Gershwin, and stinging lyrics by his brother Ira. William Gaxton played President John P. Wintergreen, Victor Moore was the mousy Vice-President Alexander Throttlebottom, and George Murphy played a featured role. The show became the longest-running book musical in the 1930s.

George S. Kaufman (with Edna Ferber) brought another hit to the Music Box in 1932. *Dinner at Eight* was a fascinating comedy about a socialite's problems in arranging a dinner for British royalty, who cancel their appearance at the last moment. The play examined the lives of all those invited to the dinner. During its run, the rising star Margaret Sullavan joined the cast

as a replacement. The comedy ran for 232 performances and was later made into a hit MGM classic with an all-star cast.

The Music Box really struck it rich with its next tenant. Irving Berlin and Moss Hart teamed to create a topical revue that would use newspaper headlines to satirize celebrities of that era. The show was called *As Thousands Cheer* and it starred Marilyn Miller, Clifton Webb, Helen Broderick, and Ethel Waters, who stopped the show at every performance with "Heat Wave," "Harlem on My Mind," and "Supper Time." The revue ran for 400 performances at the Music Box and was one of the biggest hits of the depression.

Kaufman and Hart once again joined forces to write the next Music Box show: *Merrily We Roll Along* (1934). This unusual comedy started in the present and went backwards in time.

Five shows played the Music Box in 1935: Tallulah Bankhead in a revival of *Rain*; a hit melodrama about pilots, *Ceiling Zero*, starring Osgood Perkins (Anthony's illustrious father); a prophetic drama, *If This Be Treason*, in which the United States and Japan almost engaged in war; a successful adaptation of Jane Austen's *Pride and Prejudice*; and George S. Kaufman and Katherine Dayton's political comedy *First Lady*, starring the noted actress Jane Cowl playing a role said to be inspired by Alice Longworth Roosevelt.

Margaret Sullavan, now a big Hollywood star, returned to the Music Box in 1936 in *Stage*

OPPOSITE: Souvenir book for the second *Music Box Revue* (1922–1923). BELOW: Lois Moran and William Gaxton in Madison Square Garden on election night in the Pulitzer Prize musical *Of Thee I Sing* (1931).

🎭 LEFT (from left): Marilyn Miller, Clifton Webb and Helen Broderick in the "Easter Parade" finale of the famed revue, *As Thousands Cheer* (1933). RIGHT: Radiant Margaret Sullavan returns from Hollywood stardom to appear in the theatrical comedy *Stage Door* (1936).

Door, by George S. Kaufman and Edna Ferber. Set in the Foot-Lights Club (modeled on the actual Rehearsal Club in Manhattan), the play presented a group of aspiring actresses who live in a popular boarding house for young theatricals. One of the characters—a radical playwright named Keith Burgess—was said to be based on the Group Theatre's Clifford Odets.

Young Madam Conti (1937), starring Constance Cummings, was one of the theatre's lesser tenants, but this melodrama was followed by John Steinbeck's *Of Mice and Men* in 1937, starring Wallace Ford, Broderick Crawford, and Claire Luce and directed by George S. Kaufman. It won the New York Drama Critics Circle Award as best play of the season.

Although George M. Cohan as President Roosevelt in *I'd Rather Be Right* opened at the Alvin Theatre in 1937, it ended its successful run at the Music Box. The satirical political musical by Kaufman and Hart, with a score by Richard Rodgers and Lorenz Hart, dared to portray a living president who was still in the White House when the show opened. Mr. Cohan garnered raves for his good-natured performance and the show was one of the season's top tickets.

In September 1938 Kaufman and Hart came to the Music Box in a new guise. In association with Max Gordon, they presented a topical musical revue called *Sing Out the News*, by Harold Rome and Charles Friedman. The revue perfectly suited the Music Box tradition of topical satire, but was only moderately successful.

In 1939 two more revues graced the house. One of them, *Set to Music*, by Noel Coward and starring Beatrice Lillie, was the type of sophisticated revue for which the Music Box was built and a genre of entertainment that would become almost obsolete after World War II. The opening night was celebrity-studded and was the kind of glittering first night that would become rare in years to come. *Set to Music* was followed by a charming entertainment called *From Vienna* (1939), a revue featuring performers who were Viennese refugees.

It is fitting that the last show to play the Music Box in the 1930s was another satire by Kaufman and Hart. Both were close friends of the obese, waspish, self-promoting critic, author, and radio celebrity Alexander Woollcott, and they wrote a classic comedy about what would happen if someone like him (called Sheridan Whiteside in the play) slipped on the ice while visiting a family and had to stay there with a broken hip. Called *The Man Who Came to Dinner*, this comedy of outrages and insults starred Monty Woolley as Whiteside and also caricatured such luminaries as Noel Coward, Gertrude Lawrence, and Harpo Marx. The comedy proved to be the Music Box's longest-running show at that time, playing for 739 performances.

World War II brought a change in audience tastes on Broadway. The revue form and plays that satirized celebrities soon began to vanish. The last revue to play the Music Box for many years to come was Mike Todd's rowdy *Star and Garter*, starring strippers Gypsy Rose Lee and Georgia Southern and low comics Bobby Clark, Pat Harrington, and Professor Lamberti. The critics were not overjoyed with the burlesque, but audiences loved the show and it ran for 605 performances.

After *Star and Garter* closed at the Music Box, there was a definite change in the house's fare. For the next four decades, only three musicals were housed there: *Lost in the Stars* (1949); *Rainbow Jones* (1974); and *Side by Side by Sondheim* (1977). One of the reasons for the lack of musical bookings was that the theatre's 1,000-seat capacity was no longer considered adequate for an expensive musical show.

During the past four decades, the Music Box has thrived on romantic comedies, usually with small casts, and dramas. *I Remember Mama*

Irene Bordoni glitters in Cole Porter's 1928 musical *Paris*.

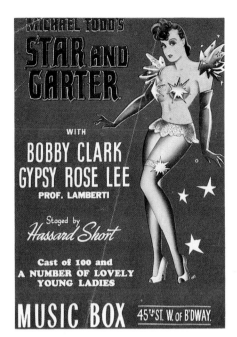

LEFT: Herald for Mike Todd's rowdy burlesque revue *Star and Garter* (1942). RIGHT: Beatrice Lillie sings "I Went to a Marvelous Party" in Noel Coward's revue *Set to Music* (1939). BELOW: Mady Christians (far left) and young Marlon Brando with members of the cast of *I Remember Mama* (1944).

Ritchard, Walter Abel, Charlie Ruggles, and George Peppard in *The Pleasure of His Company* (from the Longacre Theatre); and *Five-Finger Exercise* (1959), with Jessica Tandy and Brian Bedford.

In 1961 *A Far Country* presented Steven Hill as Sigmund Freud and Kim Stanley as his patient in Henry Denker's case study; in 1962, Bert Lahr convulsed theatregoers playing numerous roles in S.J. Perelman's *The Beauty Part*. More laughter followed in 1963 when Gertrude Berg starred in *Dear Me, The Sky Is Falling*. Sandy Duncan, Gene Hackman, Rosemary Murphy, and Don Porter came to the Music Box in February 1964 in *Any Wednesday*, and the comedy stayed for 983 performances, the record holder for this theatre at that time.

LEFT: Ralph Meeker and Janice Rule smolder in William Inge's *Picnic* (1953). BELOW: Paul Rogers and Vivien Merchant (in foreground) under family scrutiny in Harold Pinter's sinister puzzle *The Homecoming* (1967).

(1944) starred Mady Christians and Oscar Homolka, with a young Marlon Brando making his Broadway debut. This was followed by Tennessee Williams's *Summer and Smoke* (1948); *Lost in the Stars*, by Kurt Weill and Maxwell Anderson (1949); and *Affairs of State*, a light comedy starring Celeste Holm that moved from the Royale to the Music Box.

Beginning in 1953 playwright William Inge inaugurated his happy association with this theatre. Over the next five years, he was to have three solid hits in the house: *Picnic* (1953) (Pulitzer Prize, New York Drama Critics Circle Award); *Bus Stop* (1955); and *The Dark at the Top of the Stairs* (1957).

Other 1950s hits included a revival of *The Male Animal*; Josephine Hull in *The Solid Gold Cadillac* (moved from the Belasco); *Separate Tables* (1956), starring Margaret Leighton and Eric Portman; Rod Steiger and Claire Bloom in *Rashomon* (1959); Cornelia Otis Skinner, Cyril

Harold Pinter's *The Homecoming* chilled patrons in 1967, followed by Gig Young in the British comedy *There's a Girl in My Soup*. On November 12, 1970, Anthony Shaffer's *Sleuth* opened with Anthony Quayle and Keith Baxter and played for a record-breaking 1,222 performances. The following year, the Music Box celebrated its fiftieth anniversary, and Irving Berlin was photographed by the New York *Times* proudly standing before the theatre. Mr. Berlin stated that he and the Shubert Organization were constantly refurbishing the theatre.

Absurd Person Singular, the British import,

amused capacity audiences in 1974 with such stars as Geraldine Page, Richard Kiley, Larry Blyden, Carole Shelley, Sandy Dennis, and Tony Roberts. A revival of *Who's Afraid of Virginia Woolf* arrived in 1976, followed by the British play *Comedians* and the delightful portfolio of Sondheim songs *Side by Side by Sondheim* (1977). Then, in 1978, came John Wood and Marian Seldes in Ira Levin's marathon thriller *Deathtrap*. The comedy murder mystery had such an original plot that theatregoers attended it for 1,609 performances, making it the Music Box's champion attraction. Finally, in 1982,

Monty Woolley needles Edith Atwater, Carol Goodner and Theodore Newton in the classic comedy of insults *The Man Who Came to Dinner* (1939).

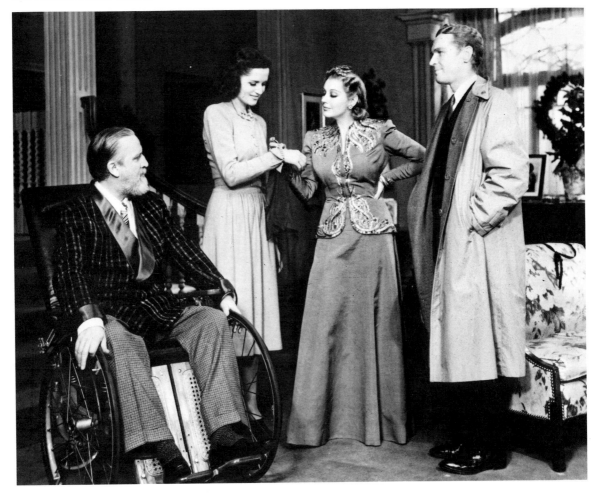

stark drama returned to the Music Box with *Agnes of God*, starring Geraldine Page, Elizabeth Ashley, and Amanda Plummer, who won a Tony Award for her performance. The religious drama played for 599 performances.

Morton Gottlieb, who produced *Sleuth* at the Music Box, summed up Broadway's feeling about this theatre when he said, "It is the best-looking house on Broadway. When you come in—it shines!"

TOP LEFT: Millicent Martin and Julie McKenzie in the song book *Side by Side by Sondheim* (1977). BOTTOM LEFT: Keith Baxter (in disguise) and Anthony Quayle play Anthony Shaffer's complex games in *Sleuth* (1970). BELOW: (from left): Geraldine Page and Amanda Plummer anguish over a baby's murder in the tense drama *Agnes of God* (1982).

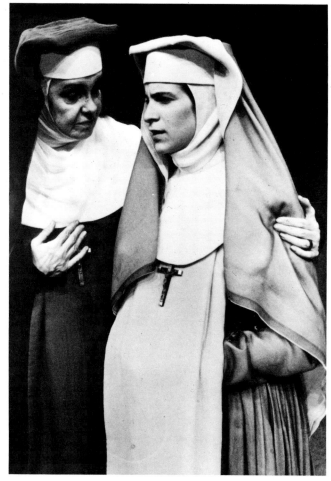

❧ IMPERIAL THEATRE ❧

In 1923 the New York *Times* reported that the new theatre being built at 249 West Forty-fifth Street by the Shuberts was the fiftieth playhouse that the theatrical brothers from Syracuse had built in the New York City area. Their latest theatre was the Imperial and it was obviously designed by Herbert J. Krapp as a musical comedy house, with a large seating capacity of 1,650 seats. The Imperial has been the Shuberts' pride since it opened, housing some of Broadway's most notable and successful musicals.

The theatre's opening show was a hit musical called *Mary Jane McKane*, with Mary Hay in the title role and a jaunty score by Vincent Youmans. It opened on Christmas night 1923 and it ran for 151 performances. In September 1924 this theatre housed one of its most celebrated shows. It was the Rudolf Friml operetta *Rose-Marie*, with a book by Otto Harbach and Oscar Hammerstein II. According to Gerald Bordman in *American Musical Theatre*, this musical was "not only the biggest hit of the season, but the biggest grosser of the decade." Mary Ellis played Rose-Marie, a singer in a hotel located in the Canadian Rockies, and Dennis King was Jim Kenyon, the man she loved, who was unjustly accused of murder. The score included the lilting title song, the sonorous "Indian Love Call," and "The Song of the Mounties." *Rose-Marie* ran for 581 performances on Broadway and there were four road companies touring America at the same time.

The Imperial's next show was a musical called *Sweetheart Time*, with Eddie Buzzell and Mary Milburn, but it was only a moderate hit. The theatre's next bonanza occurred on November 8, 1926, with the opening of *Oh, Kay!*, a musical with a score by George and Ira Gershwin and a book by Guy Bolton and P. G. Wodehouse. Gertrude Lawrence was the star, and her singing of "Someone to Watch Over Me" to a rag doll is one of the musical theatre's most cherished moments. Victor Moore and Oscar Shaw were Lawrence's costars in this merry musical about Long Island bootleggers, and other hit tunes from the score were "Maybe," "Do Do Do," and "Clap Yo' Hands." When Ira Gershwin became ill during the creation of this hit, Howard Dietz wrote some of the lyrics for the show.

On September 19, 1928, another blockbuster came to this house: Sigmund Romberg's glorious operetta *The New Moon*, with a libretto

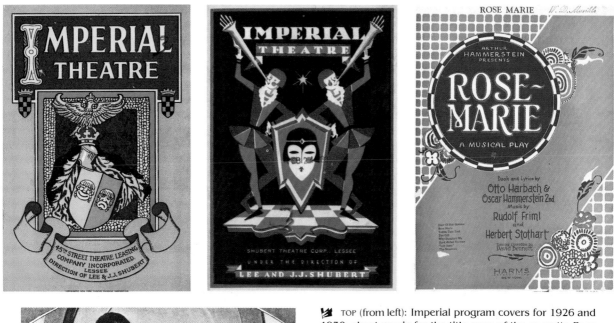

TOP (from left): Imperial program covers for 1926 and 1930; sheet music for the title song of the operetta *Rose Marie* (1924). BOTTOM LEFT: Oscar Shaw and Gertrude Lawrence in this 1926 delight, *Oh, Kay!* RIGHT: Ed Wynn in his sappy revue *The Laugh Parade* (1931).

LEFT: Souvenir program for Sigmund Romberg's *The New Moon* (1928). RIGHT: PLAYBILL cover sketch of Mrs. Hartley of Covent Garden during run of *Jubilee* (1935). OPPOSITE, TOP: Mary Martin and behind her, at left, Gene Kelly in Cole Porter's *Leave It to Me* (1938). BOTTOM: Melville Cooper and Mary Boland in *Jubilee* (1935).

by Oscar Hammerstein II, Frank Mandel, and Laurence Schwab. Set in New Orleans at the time of the French Revolution, the operetta was studded with such gems as "Wanting You," "Lover, Come Back to Me," "Softly, As in a Morning Sunrise," "Stouthearted Men," and "One Kiss." It was the only show of that season to run for over 500 performances.

A snappy World War I musical, *Sons o' Guns*, starring Jack Donahue, Lily Damita, and William Frawley, exploded at the Imperial in November 1929 and, despite the stock market crash, spread mirth for 297 performances. Two hit songs—"Why?" and "Cross Your Fingers" —emerged from the lively score by J. Fred Coots, Arthur Swanstrom, and Benny Davis.

Highlights of the 1930s at the Imperial included Ed Wynn in his joyous vaudeville-type show *The Laugh Parade* (1931), in which he introduced some of his latest zany inventions and interrupted other people's acts with lisping comments; an elaborate revue, *Flying Colors* (1932), with modernistic sets by Norman Bel Geddes, hit songs by Howard Dietz and Arthur Schwartz ("Louisiana Hayride," "Alone Together," "A Shine on Your Shoes"), and a dream cast comprised of Clifton Webb, Tamara

Geva, Patsy Kelly, Charles Butterworth, Imogene Coca, Larry Adler, and Vilma and Buddy Ebsen; *Let 'Em Eat Cake* (1933), a sequel to *Of Thee I Sing* (by the same creators), which reunited William Gaxton, Victor Moore, and Lois Moran, the stars of the latter show, but which was not successful; Bob Hope, Harry Richman, Lillian Emerson, and "Prince" Michael Romanoff in a saucy musical, *Say When* (1934).

Despite the depression, some opening nights on Broadway were the pinnacle of glamour, and such was the case for the glittery opening of the Cole Porter/Moss Hart musical *Jubilee* on October 12, 1935. An opulent satire about the royal holiday of the king and queen of a mythical country (splendidly played by Mary Boland and Melville Cooper), the show drew a bejeweled audience who had heard that some of the characters depicted were really spoofs of Noel Coward, Johnny Weissmuller, Elsa Maxwell, and Britain's Royal Family. Burns Mantle of the Daily News gave the musical his rare four-star rating, and years afterward, two of its Porter songs became classics: "Begin the Beguine" and "Just One of Those Things."

Another memorable musical followed *Jubilee* into the Imperial. It was the Rodgers/Hart/

George Abbott spoof of the Russian ballet craze and it was appropriately called *On Your Toes*. It starred Ray Bolger, Tamara Geva, Luella Gear, and Monty Woolley, and it broke the mold of American musical comedies by using two extended George Balanchine ballets as an integral part of the plot. One of these, *Slaughter on Tenth Avenue*, is the only ballet score from a musical to become popular, and the ballet itself has become part of the repertory of the New York City Ballet.

The battle of the Hamlets raged on Broadway in the fall of 1936. John Gielgud opened first as the Melancholy Dane at the Empire Theatre in October and triumphed. Leslie Howard played the same part at the Imperial in November and came in a poor second. Howard's last Broadway play had been *The Petrified Forest*. When reviewing Howard's Hamlet, critic Robert Benchley wrote in *The New Yorker* that it was "the petrified Hamlet." Gielgud's produc-

tion ran for 132 performances; Howard's only 39.

The Shuberts brought an elaborate operetta, *Frederika*, to the Imperial in February 1937, but even though it had lilting music by Franz Lehár, it ran for only ninety-four performances. The excellent cast included Dennis King, Ernest Truex, Helen Gleason, and Edith King, but as Brooks Atkinson noted in the *Times*, operetta was passé on Broadway. At the end of 1937, Howard Dietz and Arthur Schwartz arrived with a glossy musical about a bigamist who had one wife in London and another in Paris. *Between the Devil* starred three bright British stars, Jack Buchanan, Evelyn Laye, and Adele Dixon, and featured dancers Vilma Ebsen and Charles Walters, but the bigamy theme was distasteful to some and the musical called it quits after ninety-three performances.

The Cole Porter show *Leave It to Me*, which sailed smartly into the Imperial in the fall

of 1938, starred Victor Moore, William Gaxton, Sophie Tucker, and Tamara, but it made Broadway history by introducing a Texas singer named Mary Martin doing a polite strip tease in a Siberian railway station while singing "My Heart Belongs To Daddy." The musical, based on Sam and Bella Spewack's play *Clear All Wires*, was a huge hit and featured some Porter winners, such as "Get Out of Town" and "Most Gentlemen Don't Like Love." One of the chorus boys was named Gene Kelly.

The last musical of the 1930s at this theatre was also a hit. Rodgers and Hart and George Marion, Jr., collaborated on a college campus show, *Too Many Girls*, that took place at Pottawatomie in New Mexico, where the female students wore "beanies" if they were virgins. The only hatless female onstage was Mary Jane Walsh, who played a divorcee. George Abbott directed the show with lightning speed; Robert Alton was highly praised for his swirling dances; and Eddie Bracken, Richard Kollmar, Marcy Wescott, Hal Le Roy, Desi Arnaz, and Ms. Walsh sang and danced such Rodgers and Hart delights as "I Didn't Know What Time It Was," "I'd Like to Recognize the Tune," and "Give It Back to the Indians." One of the chorus boys with a few speaking lines was a newcomer named Van Johnson.

Smash hit musicals continued to populate the Imperial in the 1940s. Irving Berlin and Morrie Ryskind rang the bell with *Louisiana Purchase*, a political musical set in New Orleans, starring Victor Moore, William Gaxton, Vera Zorina, and Irene Bordoni. George Balanchine provided the choreography and Mr. Berlin some fetching songs, such as "It's a Lovely Day Tomorrow," the title song, and some spirited numbers for Carol Bruce. It ran for 444 performances.

Cole Porter returned to the Imperial in 1941 with a rousing wartime musical, *Let's Face It*. Based on the hit 1920s comedy *Cradle Snatchers*, the show focused on three married women (Eve Arden, Edith Meiser, and Vivian Vance) who took up with young soldiers to get even with their philandering husbands. One of the soldiers was Danny Kaye, who stopped the show with specialty numbers, some written by his wife, Sylvia Fine. Porter provided such hits as "Everything I Love," "Farming," "Let's Not Talk About Love," "Ace in the Hole," and "I Hate You Darling."

The enormous success of the operetta *Rosalinda* (1943), Max Reinhardt's version of *Die Fledermaus*, caused it to be moved to the Imperial from the Forty-fourth Street Theatre. Starring Dorothy Sarnoff and Oscar Karlweis, the comic show also featured Shelley Winters and ran for 520 performances.

Mary Martin, who made her debut as an unknown at the Imperial in *Leave It to Me*, returned as a star in *One Touch of Venus* (1943), a musical fantasy with a haunting score by Kurt

Weill and a witty book by S.J. Perelman and Ogden Nash. Ms. Martin played a statue of Venus that comes to life and is pursued by an art gallery owner (John Boles) and a barber (Kenny Baker). Ms. Martin scored a triumph

OPPOSITE: Desi Arnaz and chorus in Rodgers and Hart's college musical *Too Many Girls* (1939). BELOW: Ethel Merman in Irving Berlin's galvanic *Annie Get Your Gun* (1946).

singing "Speak Low," "I'm a Stranger Here Myself," and "That's Him." Paula Lawrence sang the amusing title song and "Very, Very, Very." The show had a smashing run of 567 performances, but not all at the Imperial.

Another successful musical moved to the Imperial from the Winter Garden. It was the *Ziegfeld Follies of 1943* and it starred Milton Berle (who stuck his two cents into everybody's act), the film beauty Ilona Massey, Arthur Treacher, and Jack Cole. The critics praised Berle's highjinks, and this *Follies* still holds the record—553 performances—for the longest run of any *Ziegfeld Follies* ever produced.

On May 16, 1946, one of the Imperial's hallmark shows arrived. Ethel Merman opened in Irving Berlin's *Annie Get Your Gun* and made it one of her most memorable portraits. Jerome Kern was slated to write the score for this show, but he died before he could start it. His successor, Berlin, wrote what many consider his greatest score, with such hits as "They Say It's Wonderful," "There's No Business Like Show Business," "The Girl That I Marry," "Doin' What Comes Natur'lly," "I Got the Sun in the Morning," and many others. Few Broadway musicals have produced as many song hits as this one. It was Merman's longest-running show: 1,147 performances.

The last two shows at the Imperial during the 1940s were minor successes. A revue called *Along Fifth Avenue* moved from the Broadhurst and starred Nancy Walker, Jackie Gleason, Carol Bruce, and Hank Ladd, but it lasted only seven months. Irving Berlin's *Miss Liberty* had a book by Robert E. Sherwood and starred Eddie Albert, Mary McCarthy, and Allyn McLerie, but the critics felt that the project fell flat. It managed to run for 308 performances.

During the 1950s, musicals continued to be the major fare at this theatre. In 1950 there was a successful revival of *Peter Pan*, with new music by Leonard Bernstein. Jean Arthur made a perfect Peter, and Boris Karloff doubled as Mr. Darling and the evil Captain Hook. This was followed by Ethel Merman in another Irving Berlin winner, *Call Me Madam*, in which she played a Pearl Mesta-type character. Howard Lindsay and Russel Crouse wrote the amusing book; Paul Lukas was Ms. Merman's romantic costar; and Merman and a newcomer, Russell Nype, stopped the show with their singing of the contrapuntal melody "You're Just in Love." It ran for 644 performances. In June 1952 *Wish You Were Here*, a fair musical version of Arthur Kober's delightful play *Having Wonderful Time*, opened and managed to run for 598 perform- ances, mainly because Eddie Fisher (who was not in the show) recorded the title song and it became a Hit Parade favorite. The show also had a real pool onstage, which garnered much publicity. In December 1953 one of Broadway's last opulent revues—*John Murray Anderson's Almanac*—arrived, with Hermione Gingold, Billy De Wolfe, Harry Belafonte, Polly Bergen, Orson Bean, Kay Medford, and Carleton Car- penter, but despite some funny sketches and good songs it was a financial failure, proving that TV was killing the revue form on Broadway.

Cole Porter's last musical, *Silk Stockings*, a musical version of Garbo's famous film *Ni- notchka*, was a hit in 1955 with Don Ameche, Hildegarde Neff, and Gretchen Wyler; Frank Loesser was acclaimed for his opera *The Most Happy Fella* (1956), based on Sidney Howard's play *They Knew What They Wanted*; Lena Horne was a popular success in the Harold Arlen/E.Y. Harburg musical *Jamaica* (1957), with Ricardo Montalban; Dolores Gray and Andy Griffith had a hit in *Destry Rides Again* (1959), a musical version of the James Stewart/Marlene Dietrich film, aided by dazzling Michael Kidd choreog- raphy, although a feud betwen Ms. Gray and Mr. Kidd made all the newspapers.

During the 1960s, the Imperial housed some very long running musicals. Ethel Merman

in her triumphant *Gypsy* moved here from the Broadway Theatre in 1960 and was followed by David Merrick's smash *Carnival* (1961), a musical adapted from the film *Lili*, starring Jerry Orbach and Anna Maria Alberghetti, with excellent choreography and staging by Gower Champion. The British import, Lionel Bart's *Oliver!*, based on Dickens's *Oliver Twist*, starred Clive Revill and Georgia Brown and had two song hits: "As Long As He Needs Me" and "Consider Yourself." It played at the Imperial for eighteen months.

On September 22, 1964, *Fiddler on the Roof* opened and stayed at this theatre for over two years before moving to the Majestic. The multi- award-winning musical, written by Joseph Stein, Jerry Bock, and Sheldon Harnick, was based on Sholem Aleichem's tales and starred Zero Mostel in his greatest performance.

Another landmark musical, *Cabaret*, came to the Imperial from the Broadhurst Theatre and continued for a year and half in 1967–68. Kander and Ebb, who wrote the memorable score for *Cabaret*, also wrote the score for the next Imperial tenant, *Zorba* (1968–69), a musical based on the film *Zorba the Greek*, but the stage version did not have the distinction of the film and it ran for a moderately successful nine months. *Minnie's Boys*, a musical about the Marx Brothers, had a short run in 1970. Richard Rodgers also had a minor success with his musical *Two by Two* (1970), a biblical story about Noah and his family based on Clifford Odets's play *The Flowering Peach*. It starred Danny Kaye as Noah, and the comic took to ad-libbing during the show's run, which some in the audience found unprofessional. Two revivals—*On the Town* (1971) and *Lost in the*

OPPOSITE: Jerry Orbach, Pierre Olaf, and Anna Maria Alberghetti in the musical *Carnival* (1961). BELOW: PLAYBILL cover for the British hit *Oliver!* (1963). RIGHT: Zero Mostel talks to God in the multi-award-winning musical *Fiddler on the Roof* (1964).

Imperial Theatre

PLAYBILL

the weekly magazine for theatregoers

OLIVER!

ABOVE: Ben Vereen and chorus in the long-running *Pippin* (1972). OPPOSITE TOP: PLAYBILL covers for two Neil Simon hits (1977, 1979). BOTTOM: Jennifer Holliday, Sheryl Lee Ralph, and Loretta Devine in *Dreamgirls* (1981).

Stars (1972)—struck out before the next gold mine arrived at this theatre.

On October 23, 1972, *Pippin* opened, and it stayed for over four years, making it the Imperial's longest-running show to date. With a score by Stephen Schwartz, this musical about Charlemagne was triggered to success by Bob Fosse's inventive choreography, by Ben Vereen's animated dancing, and by one of the most successful TV commercials ever produced for a Broadway show. It achieved a run of 1,944 performances.

Drama returned to the Imperial with a revival of Eugene O'Neill's *Anna Christie* (1977), starring Liv Ullmann, and Victor Borge returned in a short run of his show *Comedy with Music*

(1977). Two Neil Simon shows next occupied the Imperial and both were long-running hits. *Chapter Two* (1977), a drama about Mr. Simon's personal experience in losing his first wife to cancer, starred Judd Hirsch, Anita Gillette, and Cliff Gorman and ran for 857 performances, the longest-running drama in this theatre's history. The other Simon show, *They're Playing Our Song* (1979), was a musical written with Marvin Hamlisch, about a songwriter (Robert Klein) and his kooky romance with his lyricist (Lucie Arnaz). This ran for a hefty 1,082 performances.

The Imperial's most recent production, and still playing to standing room, is *Dreamgirls* (1981), Michael Bennett's dynamic staging of

PLAYBILL
IMPERIAL THEATRE

chapter two

PLAYBILL
IMPERIAL THEATRE

They're Playing Our Song

a musical about a black singing group said to be patterned on Diana Ross and the Supremes. With book and lyrics by Tom Eyen and music by Henry Krieger, the musical features powerful black performers (the electrifying Jennifer Holliday won a Tony for her titanic performance) in a story that is made memorable by Bennett's original and breathtaking staging. It may well become the longest-running show in this theatre's history.

The Imperial, which was completely refurbished by the Shubert Organization a few years ago, is one of the finest musical comedy houses ever built and has been one of Broadway's most consistently successful houses since it opened.

MARTIN BECK THEATRE

At the time of its opening in 1924, the Martin Beck Theatre at 302 West Forty-fifth Street was described by the New York *Times* as the only theatre in America designed in the Byzantine genre. Martin Beck, the vaudeville mogul who built the house, conceived the building's style and entrusted its design and execution to San Francisco architect G. Albert Alnsburgh. The Martin Beck was also located farther west than any other legitimate theatre at that time, being just west of Eighth Avenue.

With a seating capacity of 1,200 and dressing rooms for 200 actors, the house was ideal for musicals and spectacular productions. Curiously, it has in its sixty years of operation housed many distinguished dramatic plays, some of which were definitely not spectacular. One of the Martin Beck's features has been its unusually large foyer and promenade.

The Martin Beck opened on November 11, 1924, with a Viennese operetta, *Mme. Pompadour*, adapted by playwright Clare Kummer, but the public was weary of schmaltzy operettas at this time and the show ran for a moderate eighty performances.

The theatre had better luck in 1925 when *Captain Jinks* arrived. This was a musical version of Clyde Fitch's play *Captain Jinks of the Horse Marines*, which had made a star of Ethel Barrymore. In this version the marine captain (J. Harold Murray) is in love with a world-famous dancer, Trentoni (Louise Brown). Also in the cast was comedian Joe E. Brown as a hack driver. Five collaborators worked on the musical, and it ran for 167 performances.

One of the most sensational plays ever produced on Broadway, John Colton's *The Shanghai Gesture*, made waves on February 1, 1926. It starred Florence Reed as Mother Goddam, the owner of a notorious Shanghai whorehouse. It was her most famous role. Seeking revenge on a Britisher who once dumped her to marry an English woman, she lures him to her brothel, then sells his own daughter off as a prostitute. Then, discovering that the daughter she had by the Britisher has turned into a dope fiend, she strangles her to death. The critics scoffed at this purple melodrama, but audiences loved it and kept the Martin Beck full for 210 performances.

Next, the Martin Beck booked a comedy and

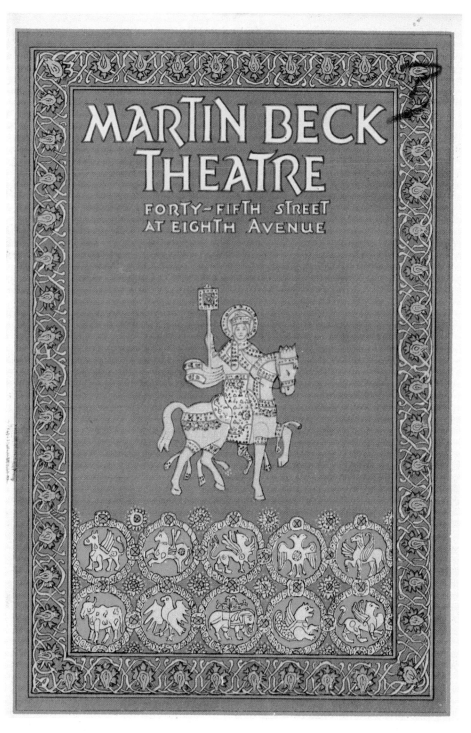

Standard program cover for the Martin Beck Theatre in the 1920s.

it turned out to be its biggest hit so far. It was called *The Shannons of Broadway* and it was written by actor James Gleason, who also starred in it. Playing a vaudevillian, he and his wife (Lucile Webster) have comic adventures when they buy and operate a hotel in New England. The popular comedy ran for 288 performances.

Beginning in December 1928 the prestigious Theatre Guild began producing a number of fascinating plays at the Martin Beck, featuring the famed Theatre Guild Acting Company. Their first production, an anti-war play called *Wings Over Europe*, was chosen by Burns Mantle as one of the year's ten best. Next, in February 1929, they presented Eugene O'Neill's unusual play *Dynamo*, which pitted religion against science and starred Claudette Colbert, Dudley Digges, Glenn Anders, and Helen Westley. Despite its offbeat attraction, the play lasted only 66 performances. More successful was *The Camel Through the Needle's Eye* (1929), a play about an illegitimate girl (Miriam Hopkins) who meets a rich man (Claude Rains) and makes a success out of him by going into the dairy business with him. The excellent cast also included Henry Travers, Helen Westley, and Morris Carnovsky, and the play ran for 195 performances. The 1930 Theatre Guild productions included a Russian play, *Red Rust* (1929), with Lee Strasberg, Luther Adler, and Franchot Tone, who would soon be prominent in the Group Theatre; Philip Barry's metaphysical play *Hotel Universe* (1930), in which a group of guests in a French villa recall incidents from their youth that had a profound influence on their lives, brilliantly acted by Ruth Gordon, Glenn Anders, Katherine Alexander, Morris Carnovsky, and others; and *Roar China!* (1930), a play about a Chinese rebellion in which an enormous British warship occupied the vast reaches of the Martin Beck stage.

In 1931 the Theatre Guild moved its successful production of Maxwell Anderson's *Elizabeth the Queen*, starring the Lunts, from the Guild Theatre to the Martin Beck. The Lunts next appeared at this theatre in one of their acting triumphs, Robert E. Sherwood's romantic comedy *Reunion in Vienna* (1931).

Just before the Lunts' triumph in *Reunion in Vienna*, the Martin Beck housed the first production of the Group Theatre, made up of younger members of the Theatre Guild who had

OPPOSITE TOP: Eva Clark, Wilda Bennett, and Leeta Corder in *Madame Pompadour*, the Martin Beck's first show (1924). BOTTOM: Florence Reed as the sinister Mother Goddam in *The Shanghai Gesture* (1926). THIS PAGE, RIGHT: Glenn Anders and Claudette Colbert in Eugene O'Neill's *Dynamo* (1930). BELOW: A giant battleship and sampans were the highlights of Lee Simonson's epic set for the Theatre Guild's *Roar China!* (1930).

been responsible for the presentation of *Roar China!* The play was Paul Green's *The House of Connelly* and it was produced under the auspices of the Theatre Guild. The play, chosen as one of the year's ten best, was staged by Lee Strasberg and Cheryl Crawford and dealt with the clash of generations in an aristocratic southern family. The critics were very receptive to the production.

In 1932 the Abbey Irish Theatre Players (including Barry Fitzgerald) played a season of repertory, including such Irish classics as *The Far-off Hills, Juno and the Paycock, Playboy of the Western World,* and *The Shadow of a Gunman.*

In December 1933 Broadway waited with great anticipation for the return of Katharine Hepburn to the stage in a British play, *The Lake,* to be directed by Jed Harris. Miss Hepburn had gone to Hollywood and become a superstar in a very short time and so eminent was she that

Mr. Harris forbade the rest of the cast (including many distinguished actors) to speak to her offstage. The play opened, and Hepburn's nervous performance inspired the famed Dorothy Parker crack, "She ran the gamut of emotions —from A to B." The general opinion was that Katharine Hepburn flopped in *The Lake.*

Sidney Howard's documentary play *Yellow Jack* (1934), written with Paul de Kruif and adapted from de Kruif's book *The Microbe Hunters,* opened next. It was based on the true record of Walter Reed and the researchers who located the yellow-fever-breeding mosquito in Cuba. The large cast included James Stewart, Edward Acuff, Myron McCormick, and Sam Levene as marine privates who volunteered to be bitten by the deadly mosquitoes. The play only ran seventy-nine performances but was admired by the critics.

The D'Oyly Carte Opera Company played a four-month season at the Martin Beck in 1934 and was followed by Katharine Cornell as a radiant Juliet in *Romeo and Juliet,* with Basil Rathbone as Romeo, Brian Aherne as Mercutio, Orson Welles as Tybalt, Edith Evans as the Nurse, and John Emery as Benvolio. Cornell was hailed for her luminous performance, and the sumptuous production, with magical sets by Jo Mielziner and dances by Martha Graham, ran for seventy-eight performances. Cornell followed her Juliet with two other productions at the theatre: a revival of her beloved gem *The Barretts of Wimpole Street* (1935), with Brian Aherne, Burgess Meredith, and Brenda Forbes, and John van Druten's antiwar play *Flowers of the Forest* (1935), with Cornell, Burgess Meredith, and Margalo Gillmore.

A major dramatic event occurred at the Martin Beck on September 25, 1935. Maxwell Anderson's *Winterset* opened and proved to be a fascinating and controversial blank-verse drama. Starring Burgess Meredith, Margo, Richard Bennett, and Eduardo Ciannelli, the tragedy

🐱 OPPOSITE: Katharine Hepburn flops in *The Lake* (1933). ABOVE LEFT: Alfred Lunt, Lynn Fontanne, and Henry Travers in *Reunion in Vienna* (1931). RIGHT: Maurice Evans and Katharine Cornell in *Saint Joan* (1936). LEFT: Katharine Cornell and Basil Rathbone in *Romeo and Juliet* (1934). ABOVE: Burgess Meredith and Peggy Ashcroft in *High Tor* (1936).

dealt with a son's quest for his father's murderer. The action took place beneath the Brooklyn Bridge, and Jo Mielziner's majestic set was one of his greatest designs. The play won the first award as best drama of the season conferred by the newly formed New York Drama Critics Circle. It ran for 178 performances.

On March 9, 1936, Katharine Cornell returned in glory to this theatre in her acclaimed revival of Shaw's *Saint Joan*. Brilliantly directed by her husband, Guthrie McClintic, who directed all her plays, the production was hailed as a work of art. Maurice Evans was the Dauphin, and the large cast also included Brian Aherne, Arthur Byron, Eduardo Ciannelli, Kent Smith, George Coulouris, and the future film idol Tyrone Power, Jr.

🔰 Carl Benton Reid, James Barton, Dudley Digges, and Nicholas Joy in Eugene O'Neill's *The Iceman Cometh* (1946).

The D'Oyly Carte Opera Company paid a return visit with their repertory in 1936, followed by another Maxwell Anderson play, a fantasy called *High Tor*, which won the second best-play award conferred by the New York Drama Critics Circle. The fanciful play starred Burgess Meredith, and British actress Peggy Ashcroft, and featured young Hume Cronyn. It was set on top of an actual mountain on the Hudson called High Tor and involved the young man who owned it and who refused to sell it. Ghosts of ancient Dutch sailors waiting for the return of Henry Hudson's boat added comic relief and the refreshing play ran for 171 performances.

The remainder of the 1930s found the Martin Beck occupied by Ina Claire in an unsuccessful adaptation of Trollope's *Barchester Towers* (1937); a revival of *Victoria Regina*, with Helen Hayes repeating her celebrated role (1938); another engagement of the D'Oyly Carte Opera Company (1939); and Helen Hayes again, this time in a modern, murder trial play, *Ladies and Gentlemen* (1939), adapted by her husband, Charles MacArthur, and Ben Hecht from a Hungarian play. It was a moderate success, running for 105 performances.

In 1940, *Lady in Waiting*, a dramatization of Margery Sharp's popular novel *The Nutmeg Tree*, had a sterling comic performance by Gladys George, but ran for only 87 performances. On April 1, 1941, Lillian Hellman's powerful play *Watch on the Rhine*, starring Paul Lukas, Lucile Watson, Mady Christians, and George Coulouris stunned audiences with its antifascist theme. Directed by Herman Shumlin and brilliantly acted, the play won the best American play award conferred by the New York Drama Critics Circle and ran for 378 performances. John Steinbeck's adaptation of his novel *The Moon Is Down* (1942) was next, but did not achieve great success. The popular comedy hit *My Sister Eileen* moved here from the Biltmore and stayed for four months. The Lunts arrived

LEFT: John Forsythe (in striped robe) is harassed in *The Teahouse of the August Moon* (1953). RIGHT: Geraldine Page and Paul Newman in *Sweet Bird of Youth* (1959).

in *The Pirate* in November 1942, S.N. Behrman's colorful adaptation of an idea in a play by Ludwig Fulda. It gave Lunt an opportunity to walk a tightrope and pretend he was a notorious pirate whom Fontanne idolizes. This bizarre burlesque ran for 176 performances.

One of the Martin Beck's biggest hits was S.N. Behrman's adaptation of Franz Werfel's play *Jacobowsky and the Colonel* (1944), starring Louis Calhern, Oscar Karlweis, Annabella, J. Edward Bromberg, and E.G. Marshall. The adventurous story involved a comical and enterprising refugee named Jacobowsky (Karlweis), an aristocratic Polish colonel (Calhern), and a beautiful blonde (Annabella) fleeing together in a car from Nazi-occupied France. The comedy ran for 415 performances.

In March 1945 Tallulah Bankhead and Donald Cook opened in *Foolish Notion*, Philip Barry's most foolish play. This misguided venture was followed by the rollicking musical *On the Town*,

which moved in from the 44th Street Theatre for a stay of five months. Next came the melodious Harold Arlen/Johnny Mercer musical *St. Louis Woman* (1946), with Pearl Bailey, Rex Ingram, Juanita Hall, and the Nicholas Brothers, directed by Rouben Mamoulian; Eugene O'Neill's *The Iceman Cometh* (1946), with James Barton, Dudley Digges, E.G. Marshall, Nicholas Joy, Tom Pedi, and Jeanne Cagney; Nancy Walker in a musical, *Barefoot Boy with Cheek* (1947), adapted from his humorous book of the same name by Max Shulman; Katharine Cornell, Godfrey Tearle, Kent Smith, Eli Wallach, Maureen Stapleton, Charlton Heston, Lenore Ulric, and Douglass Watson in a revival of Shakespeare's *Anthony and Cleopatra* (1949); unsuccessful revivals of Shaw's *You Never Can Tell* and Jerome Kern's *Sally* (1948); Katharine Cornell in one of her poorest productions, *That Lady* (1949), in which she performed with a black patch over her eye.

🎭 Frank Langella as the Count in *Dracula* (1977).

During the 1950s at the Martin Beck, Helen Hayes appeared in *The Wisteria Trees*, Joshua Logan's adaptation of *The Cherry Orchard* (1950), set in America's deep south; Gilbert Miller unveiled his sumptuous production of *Ring Round the Moon* (1950), Christopher Fry's translation of Jean Anouilh's charade with music; Maureen Stapleton, Eli Wallach, Don Murray, and Phyllis Love shined in Tennessee Williams's *The Rose Tattoo* (1951), with Stapleton and Wallach winning Tony Awards for their performances and the play winning a Tony as the best drama of the season; Maxwell Anderson's *Barefoot in Athens* was a failure in 1951, and Truman Capote's *The Grass Harp* also flopped in 1952; Arthur Miller's *The Crucible* (1953), with Arthur Kennedy, Beatrice Straight, E.G. Marshall, Walter Hampden, and Madeleine Sherwood, focused on the Salem witch hunts

and was more successful when it was later revived Off-Broadway.

On October 15, 1953, one of the Martin Beck's most memorable productions opened and stayed for 1,027 performances. It was John Patrick's enchanting comedy *The Teahouse of the August Moon*, and it won five Tony Awards, including best actor (David Wayne) and best play. It also starred John Forsythe and Paul Ford and it delighted with its comical depiction of the American occupation of Okinawa Island.

On October 30, 1956, Shaw's *Major Barbara* was successfully revived. The production, directed by Charles Laughton, also starred Mr. Laughton and Cornelia Otis Skinner, Burgess Meredith, Glynis Johns, and Eli Wallach. It moved to the Morosco to make way for the Beck's next tenant, *Candide*, a musical version of the Voltaire classic with music by Leonard Bernstein, book by Lillian Hellman, lyrics by Richard Wilbur, John Latouche, Leonard Bernstein, and Dorothy Parker. With these geniuses at the helm, the production (directed by Tyrone Guthrie) should have been a triumph, but it was not.

A minor Tennessee Williams's play, *Orpheus Descending*, with Maureen Stapleton, Cliff Robertson, and Lois Smith, lasted only 68 performances in 1957; but a flimsy comedy, *Who Was That Lady I Saw You With?*, with Mary Healy, Peter Lind Hayes, and Ray Walston, managed to last 208 times. The final show of the 1950s at the Beck was a Tennessee Williams winner, *Sweet Bird of Youth*, with Geraldine Page giving an unforgettable performance as a fading movie star who is living with a young hustler (Paul Newman). It ran for 375 performances.

During the 1960s, the Martin Beck housed a number of shows that moved there from other houses. Some highlights that originated at the Beck during this decade included Jerry Herman's *Milk and Honey* (1961), about the new Israel; Anne Bancroft, Barbara Harris, Gene Wilder, and

Zohra Lampert in a revival of Brecht's *Mother Courage and Her Children* (1963), staged by Jerome Robbins; Colleen Dewhurst and Michael Dunn in Edward Albee's adaptation of Carson McCullers's *The Ballad of the Sad Café* (1963); Jessica Tandy, Hume Cronyn, and Robert Shaw in Friedrich Durrenmatt's *The Physicists* (1964), directed by Peter Brook; Buddy Hackett and Richard Kiley in the rowdy musical *I Had a Ball* (1964); the Royal Shakespeare Theatre's mesmerizing production of *The Persecution and Assassination of Marat As Performed by the Inmates of the Asylum of Charenton Under the Direction of the Marquis de Sade* (1965); Jessica Tandy, Hume Cronyn, Rosemary Murphy, and Marian Seldes in Edward Albee's *A Delicate Balance* (1966); Leslie Uggams, Robert Hooks, Lillian Hayman, and Allen Case in the Tony Award winning musical *Hallelujah, Baby!* (1967), by Betty Comden, Adolph Green, and Jule Styne; the long-running musical *Man of La Mancha*, which moved here from the downtown ANTA Theatre (1968).

During the early 1970s the Martin Beck had a run of plays and musicals that did not last very long. The most notable were Edward Albee's *All Over* (1971), with Jessica Tandy, Colleen Dewhurst, Betty Field, and George Voskovec; a musical version of *The Grass Harp* (1971), starring Barbara Cook; and a British import, *Habeas Corpus* (1975), with June Havoc, Rachel Roberts, Richard Gere, Celeste Holm, Jean Marsh, and Paxton Whitehead. On October 20, 1977, Frank Langella opened in the title role of *Dracula*, and the Martin Beck became a happy haven for thrill-seekers for 925 performances. Mr. Langella was succeeded by Raul Julia and David Dukes. The much publicized Broadway debut of Elizabeth Taylor in *The Little Foxes* had a sellout run in 1981.

The Martin Beck's most recent tenants have been a baseball musical, *The First* (1981); *Come Back to the Five and Dime Jimmy Dean, Jimmy Dean* (1981), with Cher making her Broadway debut; Angela Lansbury in *A Little Family Business* (1982); and the Royal Shakespeare Company's splendid revival of Shakespeare's *All's Well That Ends Well* (1983).

The Martin Beck Theatre remained in the Beck family until 1966. The theatre is currently owned and operated by Jujamcyn Theatres, which has kept the house in the finest condition.

Elizabeth Taylor makes her Broadway debut in *The Little Foxes*, with Ann Talman (1981).

46th STREET THEATRE

During the 1920s, two brothers—Irwin S. and Harry I. Chanin—who had a lucrative construction business became interested in show business and constructed six legitimate theatres in the short span of five years. One of these was called Chanin's Forty-sixth Street Theatre, located at 226 West Forty-sixth Street, and today it is simply known as the 46th Street Theatre.

The architect was the very busy Herbert J. Krapp, and this time he came up with a novel notion. Instead of building the orchestra level in the style of other theatres, he had the seats—from Row "L" on—slope upward so that theatregoers in the rear of the orchestra had an excellent view of the stage. The rear section of the orchestra was really as high as a mezzanine, and patrons in that section had to climb stairs to reach their orchestra seats.

According to Brooks Atkinson in his book *Broadway*, the Chanins made critics feel welcome by putting nameplates on the seats they occupied on opening nights. For their opening attraction on Christmas Eve, 1924, the brothers chose the 1924 edition of the *Greenwich Village Follies*, which was not new. It had already played at the Shubert and Winter Garden theatres and it only stayed briefly at the new house.

This theatre was to have a curious history in its early years. It had a policy of booking shows that had played in other theatres first and, on occasion, these shows had interrupted runs. This was the case with the 46th Street Theatre's second booking. The long-running comedy about boxing, *Is Zat So?*, moved in from the 39th Street Theatre in February 1925 and played there until mid-December. On Christmas Eve, the latest edition of the *Greenwich Village Follies* opened and ran until March. Then, on March 15, 1926, *Is Zat So?* reopened at the theatre and stayed until the end of July.

In September 1926 the lurid melodrama *The Shanghai Gesture* moved here from the Shubert and stayed for three months. This was followed by the eminent French team of Sacha Guitry and his wife, Yvonne Printemps, in two plays by Mr. Guitry: *Mozart* and a short piece, *Deburau*. They alternated these plays with another comedy by Guitry, *L'illusioniste*. The French company of actors was highly praised.

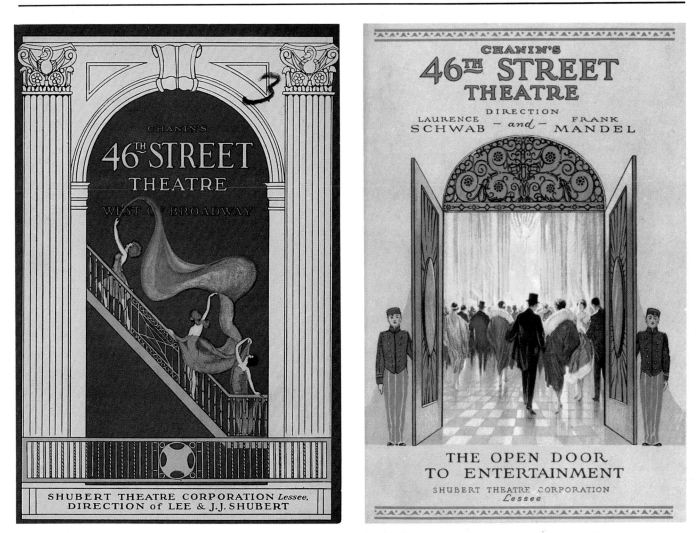

🦃 Two standard covers used for the 46th Street Theatre in the 1920s. Program at left is for the musical *Follow Thru* (1929); program at right is for the revue *Greenwich Village Follies* (1926).

In March 1927 a tingling thriller called *The Spider* excited audiences by a novel device. The scene of the play was a vaudeville house, and the murders took place in the audience, with policemen, detectives, and nurses running up and down the aisles during the performance. A theatregoer could attend this play with the wonderful apprehension that he might be seated next to the murderer in the house.

The 46th Street's next tenant, *Baby Mine* (1927), lasted only twelve performances, but

it attracted publicity because it marked the return to the stage of a famed movie comic whose film career was ruined by a notorious sex murder case. He was Roscoe ("Fatty") Arbuckle, and the New York *Times* reported that the actor was given "an extremely cordial reception."

On September 6, 1927, this theatre's biggest hit to date—and one of the 1920s' most famous musicals—opened. It was the spirited *Good News* by the rah-rah team of DeSylva, Brown, Henderson, and Laurence Schwab. To

🎭 Jack Haley and Zelma O'Neal in the golf musical *Follow Thru* (1929).

get the audience in the mood for this youthful football scrimmage, the ushers wore college jerseys and the musicians in George Olsen's nifty jazz orchestra delivered school cheers before the overture. The sappy plot about a dumb football player who has to be tutored in order to pass an exam and be allowed to play in the season's biggest game was enlivened by such durable musical comedy songs as "The Best Things in Life Are Free," "Lucky in Love," "Just Imagine," and two rousing show-stoppers, "Good News" and "The Varsity Drag," both sung by a fabulous flapper named Zelma O'Neal.

The four creators of *Good News* scored again in 1929 when they brought *Follow Thru* to this theatre. This time the subject was golf, and they paired Zelma O'Neal with the likable comic Jack Haley. Their big number was the infectious "Button Up Your Overcoat." *Good News* ran for 551 performances; *Follow Thru* for 401. The latter show had a sensational tap dancer in the cast: the young Eleanor Powell.

Christmas night, 1929, brought a platinum gift to the 46th Street Theatre: the Broadway debut of Ginger Rogers as Babs Green, a wealthy young thing who stopped the show with a song called "Hot and Bothered." The musical was called *Top Speed* and it ran for 104 performances.

The enterprising songwriter Billy Rose became a producer in November 1930 by putting his illustrious wife, Fannie Brice, into a revue, *Sweet and Low*, to which he also contributed some excellent lyrics. Miss Brice was a standout, assisted by George Jessel and James Barton.

Another college musical, *You Said It*, breezed into the 46th Street Theatre on January 19, 1931, bringing Lou Holtz, Benny Baker, and the Polish sexpot Lyda Roberti. Ms. Roberti stopped the proceedings with her torrid singing of Harold Arlen's "Sweet and Hot."

The radiant Margaret Sullavan appeared briefly in 1932 in a drama called *Happy Landing* and was praised by critic Brooks Atkinson as having fine possibilities as an actress. Two shows from other theatres—*Of Thee I Sing* and *Autumn Crocus* (Richard Nixon's favorite play) —were next, followed by a hit comedy, *She Loves Me Not*, by Howard Lindsay, which took place at Princeton. The lunatic plot involved a nightclub singer (Polly Walters) who hides out in a Princeton dorm because she is wanted as a witness to a murder. Burgess Meredith and John Beal played two students, and the merry campus lark sang for 367 performances.

In October 1934 young actor Henry Fonda finally played a part that attracted attention —Dan Harrow in *The Farmer Takes a Wife*—and his performance whisked him off to Hollywood to repeat his role in the film version of this play about the Erie Canal. Margaret Hamilton went with him to repeat her performance as Lucy Gurget.

The smash musical *Anything Goes* moved here in the summer of 1935 from the Alvin (minus Ethel Merman). For several years after this, the 46th Street Theatre had a series of undistinguished plays.

In September 1938 Olsen and Johnson brought their insane show *Hellzapoppin* to this theatre. The critics hated this rowdy vaudeville revue, but Walter Winchell kept plugging it and turned it into a hit. It was quickly moved to the Winter Garden, where it became Broadway's longest-running musical (1,404 performances) until its record was surpassed by *Oklahoma!*

The 1930s went out in style at this theatre with a ribald Cole Porter triumph called *DuBarry Was a Lady* (1939). The trumpet-voiced Ethel Merman and the baggy-pants clown Bert Lahr played dual roles in this royal fantasy: She was a nightclub singer, May Daly, and DuBarry in the dream sequences; Lahr was Louis Blore, a washroom attendant, and Louis XV, king of France, in the dream scenes. The cast also included Betty Grable, Benny Baker, Ronald Graham, and Charles Walters. Porter's hit songs were "Do I Love You?" and "Friendship."

Porter and Merman struck another lucky vein with their next musical, *Panama Hattie*, at this theatre. It opened in October 1940 and ran for 501 performances. For the first time in her fabulous career, Merman received solo star billing. Her supporting cast included Arthur Treacher, James Dunn, Betty Hutton, Rags Ragland, and little Joan Carroll, who stopped the show with Merman in their charming duet "Let's Be Buddies." The chorus line for this musical featured such forthcoming talents as June Allyson, Betsy Blair, Lucille Bremer, Vera-Ellen, Constance Dowling, and Doris Dowling.

In March 1945 an unusual play, *Dark of the Moon*, called "a legend with music," opened to some negative reviews, but the public found this sexual drama about a witch boy (Richard Hart) who wants to be human so he can marry Barbara (Carol Stone) fascinating and it ran for 318 performances.

In 1945 the successful revival of Victor Herbert's *The Red Mill* moved here from the

Henry Fonda and June Walker in *The Farmer Takes a Wife* (1934), the play that won Fonda a Hollywood contract.

ABOVE LEFT: Ethel Merman and Bert Lahr in the raucous *DuBarry Was a Lady* (1939); RIGHT: Merman, Rags Ragland, Frank Hyers, Pat Harrington in Cole Porter's *Panama Hattie* (1940). BELOW: The whimsical hit *Finian's Rainbow* (1947).

Ziegfeld Theatre and remained for a year. On January 10, 1947, the joyful *Finian's Rainbow* opened and played for 725 performances. This entrancing fantasy about a leprechaun (David Wayne), an Irishman (Albert Sharpe), and his daughter (Ella Logan) was the work of Burton Lane, E.Y. Harburg, and Fred Saidy, and the memorable score included such delights as "How Are Things in Glocca Morra?", "If This Isn't Love," "Old Devil Moon," "Look to the Rainbow," "When I'm Not Near the Girl I Love," and "Something Sort of Grandish."

Alan Jay Lerner and Kurt Weill supplied the next musical at this theatre, but *Love Life* (1948), starring Nanette Fabray and Ray Middleton, was only a moderate success. An opera version of *The Little Foxes* called *Regina*, by Marc Blitzstein, starring Jane Pickens, Brenda Lewis, William Warfield, and Priscilla Gillette, could only muster 56 performances in 1949. *Arms and the Girl* (1950), a musical version of the play *The Pursuit of Happiness*, was more successful, running for 134 performances. It had a score by Morton Gould and Dorothy Fields; book by Herbert and Dorothy Fields; and starred Nanette Fabray, Pearl Bailey, and Georges Guetary.

A landmark musical, *Guys and Dolls*, opened here on November 24, 1950, and stayed put for three years. It was one of Broadway's greatest shows. Based on a story and characters by Damon Runyon, with a book by Jo Swerling and Abe Burrows, a superb score by Frank Loesser, and direction by George S. Kaufman, the show won eight Tony Awards, was named best musical by the New York Drama Critics Circle, and ran for 1,194 performances.

In 1954 the lovely Audrey Hepburn illuminated the theatre as a water sprite in Giraudoux's *Ondine*, staged by Alfred Lunt and costarring Ms. Hepburn's husband, Mel Ferrer. The play won four Tony Awards, including best actress (Hepburn), best director (Lunt), best cos-

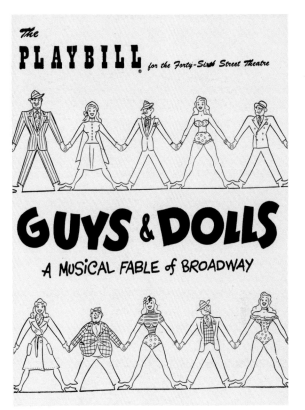

Program cover for Frank Loesser's award-winning musical *Guys and Dolls* (1950).

tume designer (Richard Whorf), and best set designer (Peter Larkin). A revival of the 1936 Rodgers and Hart musical *On Your Toes*, starring Zorina, Bobby Van, and Elaine Stritch, did not wear well in 1954, but Maxwell Anderson's frightening play, *The Bad Seed*, fascinated audiences for 334 performances. Little Patty McCormack as a sweet-as-taffy murderess got rid of some of the cast. Nancy Kelly, who played her mother, won a Tony Award for her bravery.

From May 5, 1955, until mid-March 1960, this theatre could have been renamed the Gwen Verdon Theatre. The great singer/dancer reigned here in three successive musicals: *Damn Yankees*, *New Girl in Town*, and *Redhead*. Ms. Verdon was rewarded for her bravura talents by winning three Tony Awards as best musical actress in all three shows. The hit musicals also won Tonys for the other creative talents involved.

Highlights of the 1960s at the 46th Street Theatre included Maurice Evans in the musical *Tenderloin* (1960); the Pulitzer Prize winning musical *How to Succeed in Business Without Really Trying* (1961), by Frank Loesser, Abe Burrows, Jack Weinstock, and Willie Gilbert, starring Robert Morse and Rudy Vallee, which played for 1,417 performances; *Do I Hear a Waltz?* (1965), the moderately successful musical version of *The Time of the Cuckoo*, by Richard Rodgers, Stephen Sondheim, and Arthur Laurents, starring Sergio Franchi, Elizabeth Allen, and Carol Bruce; Mary Martin and Robert Preston in the two-character musical *I Do! I Do!* (1966), based on the hit play *The Fourposter*, with libretto and score by Tom Jones and Harvey Schmidt; and the last musical of the 1960s at this theatre, *1776*, the Sherman Edwards/ Peter Stone depiction of the signing of the Dec-laration of Independence, which was awarded a Tony for best musical and ran for 1,217 performances.

The happy 1971 revival of the 1925 musical *No, No, Nanette* brought Ruby Keeler back to the stage in triumph. It ran for 861 performances, far surpassing its predecessor, which registered only 329 showings. Ms. Keeler sang and tapped and won many accolades for her comeback. Also in the cast were her old friend Patsy Kelly, Helen Gallagher, Bobby Van, Jack Gilford, and Susan Watson.

A 1973 revival of *The Women* did not win favor, but *Raisin*, a musical adaptation of Lorraine Hansberry's play *A Raisin in the Sun*, fared better, running for 258 performances. Virginia Capers won a Tony for her performance. The 1975 revival of *Private Lives*, starring Maggie Smith and John Standing, directed by John Gielgud, won raves and stayed for three months.

A musical version of the hit 1920s play *Chicago* proved a solid show in 1975 with daz-

Souvenir programs for Gwen Verdon in *Damn Yankees* (1955); Verdon in *Redhead* (1959); and the Richard Rodgers/ Stephen Sondheim musical *Do I Hear A Waltz* (1965).

LEFT: Ronald Holgate, Howard Da Silva, William Daniels in the historical musical *1776* (1969). ABOVE: Saucy Anita Morris in her torrid dance number in *Nine* (1982).

zling choreography and staging by Bob Fosse and an evocative score by John Kander and Fred Ebb. Starring the sensational Gwen Verdon, Chita Rivera, and Jerry Orbach, it ran for 898 performances.

A true blockbuster, *The Best Little Whorehouse in Texas*, moved to this theatre in July 1978 from the Entermedia Theatre and stayed for three years and nine months, making it the 46th Street Theatre's longest-running show. Carlin Glynn and Henderson Forsythe won Tony Awards for their performances.

On May 9, 1982, the off-beat musical *Nine* opened and promptly won Tony Awards for best musical, best score, best direction, best costumes, and best featured actress (Liliane Montevecchi). An adaptation of the Fellini film *8½*,

this unusual musical had an arresting score by Maury Yeston, adaptation from the Italian by Mario Fratti, book by Arthur Kopit, and direction by Tommy Tune. Raul Julia played the Italian film director and lover Guido Contini, a young boy played Guido as a child, and the rest of the cast was mainly composed of the many women in the Don Juan's life. Anita Morris stopped the show with a torrid dance, and Karen Akers, Shelly Burch, Taina Elg, Camille Saviola, and Kathi Moss all had spectacular roles.

In 1932 the Chanins lost the 46th Street Theatre and their name no longer graced the marquee. Today, it is owned by the Messrs. Nederlander and it is still one of Broadway's prime musical comedy houses.

❧ BROADWAY THEATRE ❧

The Broadway Theatre at Broadway and Fifty-third Street is one of the few legitimate theatres that was built as a movie house. B.S. Moss, a mogul who operated a chain of movie houses that also featured vaudeville, built this theatre in 1924. Designed by architect Eugene DeRosa, the house had one of the largest seating capacities (1,765) of any theatre on Broadway, thus making it ideal, in later years, for the staging and performing of musical comedies.

When this movie/vaudeville palace opened on Christmas Eve, 1924, it was called B.F. Moss's Colony Theatre. By 1930 Moss realized that the talkies were killing vaudeville and he converted his house to a legitimate theatre called the Broadway. At this time, he placed an ad in PLAYBILL in which he stated that his new playhouse "embodies an ideal not only for the theatrical profession, but equally for the public it serves. This ideal combines the magnitude, luxury and courtesy of the theatre with the comforts and charm of the drawing room. Every modern device for the production of greater entertainment has been incorporated into the physical perfection of the New Broadway. This insures not only more pretentious productions, but a price scale that is within the reach of every man's pocketbook. It is the aim of the management to make this theatre the last word in theatrical entertainment—the brightest spot on Broadway."

After that credo, Moss had to come up with something glittering for his first legitimate show. He chose *The New Yorkers*, a very sophisticated "sociological" musical by Cole Porter and Herbert Fields in which a Park Avenue woman (played by the true blue-blood Hope Williams) dreams that she's in love with a bootlegger. The show opened on December 8, 1930, and the critics liked it, especially the outlandish clowning of Jimmy Durante. The gold-plated cast also included Fred Waring and his Pennsylvanians, Ann Pennington, Frances Williams, Charles King, and Rags Ragland, who sang a Porter song called "I Happen to Like New York" that Bobby Short popularized years later. Another song from this show, the sensuous "Love for Sale," was banned on the radio as obscene. Despite Moss's claim that his price scale would suit every man's pocketbook, he charged a $5.50 top, which was quite high in 1930. He soon had to lower his prices, but the depression was on, and after twenty weeks *The New Yorkers* closed at a financial loss.

B. S. MOSS'

BROADWAY THEATRE

THE NEW YORKERS

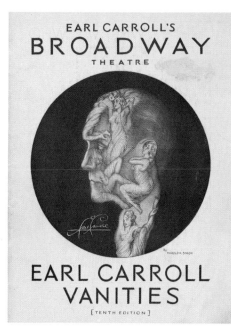

EARL CARROLL'S

BROADWAY
THEATRE

EARL CARROLL
VANITIES

[TENTH EDITION]

LEFT: Peter Arno's program sketch for the "sociological musical satire" *The New Yorkers* (1930). RIGHT: Harold K. Simon's cover sketch of showman Earl Carroll for the tenth edition of the *Earl Carroll Vanities* (1932).

The Broadway's next show was a new edition of the Earl Carroll *Vanities* (1932), with the upcoming comic Milton Berle, deadpan comedienne Helen Broderick, and the beautiful ballerina Harriet Hoctor. An outstanding feature of this revue were the spectacular neon effects by a young genius named Vincente Minnelli, plus a hit tune—"I've Got a Right to Sing the Blues," by Harold Arlen and Ted Koehler—but times were bad and the show ran for only eleven weeks (1932).

After a dud called *The O'Flynn* in 1934, the Broadway went back to showing talkies. Then, in 1940, it went legit again and began a policy that it was to pursue on and off during the rest of its history. It became the last stop for big, hit Broadway musicals that were nearing the end of their runs. They would then move to the huge Broadway Theatre and offer seats at lower prices until their runs came to an end. This began with the Rodgers and Hart musical *Too Many Girls*, which moved here from the Imperial in 1940.

A great theatrical event occurred at the Broadway on July 4, 1942. America was at war, and Irving Berlin, who had written a famed World War I soldier show called *Yip Yip Yaphank*, now came up with another. It was *This Is the Army*, and its opening night at the Broadway was one of the greatest in the history of the theatre. Singer Kate Smith, who had immortalized Berlin's "God Bless America," paid $10,000 for two seats. All proceeds from the show went to Army Emergency Relief. Berlin himself appeared in the revue, repeating his world-famous number "Oh, How I Hate to Get Up in the Morning," from his earlier soldier show. The cast of *This Is the Army* was composed of professional actors who were in the armed services and their wives. Many of these performers later became famous on stage and screen. Berlin's score had such standout numbers as "I Left My Heart at the Stage Door Canteen," "I'm Getting Tired So I Can Sleep," and the rousing title tune.

Later in 1942, the hit comedy *My Sister Eileen* moved in from the Biltmore; and in 1943, Gertrude Lawrence returned from a tour in her

🎭 Irving Berlin and Ezra Stone in Berlin's all-soldier revue *This Is the Army* (1942).

historical musical *Lady in the Dark*, and played for three months at the Broadway in this Moss Hart/Kurt Weill/Ira Gershwin classic. This was followed by a revival of *The Student Prince* and the San Carlo Opera Company in repertory.

On December 2, 1943, Billy Rose brought his production of *Carmen Jones* to this theatre and it flipped the critics. Oscar Hammerstein II, who was back on top with *Oklahoma!*, conceived the off-beat notion of doing an all-black *Carmen* set in a parachute factory in America's South during World War II. The experiment worked and the jazz opera ran for 502 performances.

The policy of moving hit shows to the Broadway continued with Mike Todd's *Up in Central Park*, which moved from the Century Theatre in 1945 and stayed for nine months. The operetta *Song of Norway* moved from the Imperial in 1946, and the propaganda play *A Flag Is Born* transferred from the Music Box.

Late in 1946 Duke Ellington's version of *The Beggar's Opera*, which he called *Beggar's Holiday*, opened, with book and lyrics by John Latouche. It starred Alfred Drake and featured Avon Long and Zero Mostel (who got panned); it was not a success.

The year 1948 brought a revival of *The Cradle Will Rock*, also starring Alfred Drake, which moved from the Mansfield. Leonard Bernstein appeared in this as a clerk. The Habimah Players from Palestine presented a repertory of *The Golem*, *The Dybbuk*, *Oedipus Rex*, and other plays in 1948.

In the summer of 1949 concert impresario Sol Hurok brought a dancing/singing show from Madrid called *Cabalgata* for a three-month engagement.

Olsen and Johnson of *Hellzapoppin* and other zany revues tried a new one out here called *Pardon Our French* in 1950, but even with French beauty Denise Darcel in the show it only ran for 100 performances. *Where's Charley?*, the Ray Bolger smash from the St. James Theatre, ended its run here; then a revival of Marc Connelly's Pulitzer Prize play *The Green Pastures* arrived in 1951, but could only last for 44 performances. Mae West wiggled in with a revival of her play *Diamond Lil* (1951), which didn't fare too well, nor did revivals of the Gertrude Stein/Virgil Thompson opera *Four Saints in Three Acts* (1952) and the black revue *Shuffle Along* (1952). The Pulitzer Prize musical *South Pacific*, from the Majestic, ended its run here, chalking up 1,925 performances.

Les Ballets de Paris and Spanish dancer José Greco played the Broadway in 1954, and there was a premiere engagement of Gian-Carlo Menotti's opera *The Saint of Bleeker Street*, a powerful religious work that ran for 92 performances. More dance companies paid visits —Katherine Dunham, Azuma Kabuki Dancers and Musicians—before Sammy Davis, Jr., and Sr. opened in the popular musical *Mr. Wonderful* in 1956. With comic Jack Carter, Chita Rivera, and Pat Marshall in the cast, the musical recorded 383 performances.

Mel Brooks and Jor Darion made a musical of Don Marquis's *archy and mehitabel*, called *Shinbone Alley*, but Eartha Kitt, Eddie Bracken, and others could not turn it into gold. *The Most Happy Fella* dropped in to end its long run from the Imperial and stayed for three months. A new musical, *The Body Beautiful*, with a score by Jerry Bock and Sheldon Harnick, went nowhere, and closed to make room for Les Ballets de Paris, the Beryozka Russian Dance Company, and the Old Vic, imported by Sol Hurok, doing *Henry V*, *Twelfth Night*, and *Hamlet*.

In May 1959 one of the Broadway Theatre's milestones arrived. It was Ethel Merman in *Gypsy* and it offered the great singer her most memorable part—Rose, the incredibly pushy mother of Gypsy Rose Lee and June Havoc. With a book by Arthur Laurents, soaring score by Jule Styne and Stephen Sondheim, choreography and direction by Jerome Robbins, this tough show about show business has become a classic of the American musical theatre. Merman's 11:00 o'clock spot—"Rose's Turn"—was electrifying, as was her belting of "Everything's Comin' Up Roses." The Broadway Theatre was extensively renovated for this engagement and the house had one of its most impressive bookings.

In 1963 *Tovarich* was notable for offering Vivien Leigh in her musical comedy debut with Jean Pierre Aumont as her costar. Ms. Leigh won a Tony for her delightful performance and the show ran for 264 performances. Noel Coward's *The Girl Who Came to Supper* (1963) was a musical that was almost as boring as the play from which it was adapted (*The Sleeping*

Prince). It starred Florence Henderson and José Ferrer, but it was music hall singer Tessie O'Shea who woke up the audience and was awarded with a Tony for her efforts.

The Obratsov Puppets, the *Folies-Bergere*, and dancer Zizi were booked in the 1960s, and Alexander Cohen opened his lavish musical *Baker Street* in 1965 with Fritz Weaver as Sher-

Ethel Merman doing "Rose's Turn" in the memorable musical *Gypsy* (1959).

lock Holmes, Peter Sallis as Dr. Watson, Martin Gabel as the nefarious Professor Moriarty, and Inga Swenson as the love interest. Hal Prince directed the show, which had a rare four-color PLAYBILL cover and ran for nine months.

The Devils, a dramatization of Aldous Huxley's nightmarish book about diabolism in seventeenth-century France, scared theatregoers away from the box office in 1966, although it starred Jason Robards, Jr., and Anne Bancroft. A musical version of the famed novel How Green Was My Valley, retitled A Time for Singing, was also unsuccessful that year. The Lincoln Center revival of Irving Berlin's Annie Get Your Gun, with its original star, Ethel

Merman, and a new Berlin show-stopper, "Old Fashioned Wedding," was so popular that it moved here in 1966, to be followed by the Winter Garden hit Funny Girl, which ended its long run here.

After the Harkness Ballet played an engagement, a new musical version of the hit comedy The Happy Time (1968) opened and offered a Tony Award winning performance by Robert Goulet. It was brilliantly directed by Gower Champion and attracted much publicity because of an incident that occurred on opening night. Clive Barnes, the critic for the New York Times, was delayed on a plane, and the first-night curtain was held until he arrived. His critical colleagues were highly critical about this excessive favoritism.

Cabaret and Mame moved in from other theatres to finish their long runs (1968–69), and a new black musical, Purlie, based on the hit play Purlie Victorious, opened in 1970 and ran for 690 performances. Cleavon Little and Melba Moore won Tony Awards for their engaging performances. In 1972 Fiddler on the Roof, the multiaward-winning musical, came here to end its run, and on the evening of June 17, 1972, it became the longest-running musical in Broadway history up to that time (3,225 performances). By the time it ended its run, it had reached 3,242 performances.

The creators of Hair, the enormously popular rock (and nude) musical, opened their newest, Dude (1972), which required that the Broadway Theatre be drastically renovated, with tons and tons of dirt (to simulate the earth) brought in, and bleachers constructed to replace theatre seats. It was all for naught. The critics buried this disaster and the Broadway had to be restored to normalcy.

In 1974 Candide, Leonard Bernstein's musical version of Voltaire's classic, which had flopped on Broadway in 1956, came to the Broadway in a revised version. With additional

Mark Baker in the title role of Candide, the musical that won five Tony Awards.

Patti LuPone in her Tony Award-winning performance as Eva Peron in *Evita* (1979).

lyrics by Stephen Sondheim and a new book by Hugh Wheeler, it was tried out first at the Chelsea Theatre Center of Brooklyn, with dynamic, arena-style staging by Harold Prince. It was so successful that it was transferred to the Broadway Theatre, where it triumphed for almost two years. The house was renovated into a labyrinth, with the audience seated on many levels and the action occurring all over the theatre. Mr. Prince won a Tony Award for his galvanic staging.

An all-black revival of *Guys and Dolls*, with new orchestrations, proved popular in 1976–77. This was followed by another hit black musical, *The Wiz*, which transferred here from the Majestic and stayed for over a year and a half. A new musical, *Sarava*, which moved from the Mark Hellinger, played for four months in early 1979 and was followed by the longest-running show in the Broadway's history—the phenomenal *Evita*, by Andrew Lloyd Webber and

Tim Rice, with revolutionary staging by Harold Prince. It won seven Tony Awards and is, at present, this theatre's longest-running show. Its most recent tenant is the revival of the musical *Zorba* starring Anthony Quinn.

When B.S. Moss built this theatre in 1925, he had no idea that its large capacity would ensure its durability through the years. Today, when new theatres are designed, they are geared toward musical comedy proportions, with seating capacities over the 1,500 mark. The Broadway, with 1,765 seats, is still one of the largest legitimate houses in Manhattan, and it has thrived on booking new musicals, musicals from other theatres, dance companies, and other spectacle-type shows. For a brief time in the 1950s it showed Cinerama films, but since then it has adhered to legitimate show bookings. It is currently owned by the Shubert Organization, which has kept it in perfect condition.

✦ VIRGINIA THEATRE ✦

The Virginia Theatre at 245 West Fifty-second Street originated as the Guild Theatre, built by the Theatre Guild to be used as a home base for its own repertory company. The Guild, which began presenting plays on Broadway in 1919, had been using the Garrick Theatre for many of its shows, but after its fourth season it decided to build a theatre of its own so that the Guild's 15,000 subscribers and its acting company and school could prosper in comfort and luxury.

In his book *The Magic Curtain*, Lawrence Langner, the founder of the Guild, wrote that the theatre was built in the then popular "pseudo-Italian style." It was designed by C. Howard Crane, Kenneth Franzheim, and Charles Bettis, in consultation with set designers Norman Bel Geddes and the Guild's Lee Simonson. According to Langner, the Guild Theatre was one of the company's greatest failures. The stage was made so large that there was little room left for dressing rooms or even audience space. "We made the ghastly mistake," he wrote, "of providing a theatre with all the stage space necessary for a repertory of plays without enough seating capacity to pro-vide the income necessary to support the repertory." The theatre had 914 seats.

Nevertheless, the Guild Theatre building was one of the most impressive legitimate houses in Manhattan, and a novel aspect of it was that the auditorium was not on street level but on the second story of the edifice. The Guild Theatre opened with great fanfare on the evening of April 13, 1925. President Coolidge officially opened the theatre by pushing an electric button in Washington, D.C., throwing the lights on a lush production of Shaw's *Caesar and Cleopatra*, starring Helen Hayes as the Egyptian queen and Lionel Atwill as Caesar. The critics were kind, and the revival managed to run for 128 performances.

The Guild Theatre's next production was also a Shaw revival—*Arms and the Man*—but this offering proved far more successful. It starred the Guild's foremost acting couple, Alfred Lunt and Lynn Fontanne, and it prospered for 181 performances.

Ferenc Molnár, one of the Guild's favorite playwrights, provided the theatre's next show, a romantic play called *The Glass Slipper*, starring June Walker, Lee Baker, and Helen Westley, but audiences attended it only for sixty-five performances. Since the Guild had 15,000 subscribers, each play it produced ran a few weeks for the subscribers. If the reviews were good and the show was a hit, it could be moved to another, larger theatre while the Guild continued with its repertory at its own house.

From the mid-twenties on, the Guild presented its company in a great variety of plays, many of them by foreign authors. Stars such as Alfred Lunt, Lynn Fontanne, Edward G. Robinson, Dudley Digges, Helen Westley, Philip Loeb, Armina Marshall (Mrs. Lawrence Langner), Henry Travers, Clare Eames, and many artists who would later establish the Group Theatre, appeared at the Guild Theatre in plays that usually ran for fifty or more performances. The Lunts appeared together at the Guild Theatre in Franz Werfel's bizarre play *Goat Song* (1926), in C.K. Munro's *At Mrs. Beam's* (1926), in Franz Werfel's *Juarez and Maximilian* (1926), in a dramatization of Dostoevski's *The Brothers Karamazov* (1927), in S.N. Behrman's witty comedy *The Second Man* (1927), in Shaw's *The Doctor's Dilemma* (1927), in Sil-Vara's *Caprice* (1928), and in another Behrman comedy, *Meteor* (1929). All of these productions were staged at the Guild from 1926 through 1929.

The Lunts occasionally did not appear together in plays during the 1920s. At the Guild Theatre, Lunt appeared without Lynn as Marco Polo in Eugene O'Neill's *Marco Millions* (1928); and Lynn appeared without Alfred in a revival of Shaw's *Pygmalion* (1926).

Other interesting productions presented at the Guild during the 1920s that did not star the Lunts were Edward G. Robinson in Pirandello's *Right You Are if You Think You Are* (1927); a straight version of *Faust* (1928), with Dudley Digges as Mephistopheles, Helen Chandler as Margaret, and George Gaul as Faust; Alice Brady, Otto Kruger, Frank Conroy, Gale

Helen Hayes as the Egyptian queen in the Guild's opening production of Shaw's *Caesar and Cleopatra* (1925).

Sondergaard, and Claude Rains in *Karl and Anna*; and the same stars (except Sondergaard) in Romain Rolland's *The Game of Love and Death* (both in 1929). During these years, the Theatre Guild practiced "Alternating Repertory," which meant that its actors would perform in

♨ Alfred Lunt and Lynn Fontanne in *The Second Man* (1927) and *Elizabeth the Queen* (1930).

one play for a week (perhaps at the John Golden or Martin Beck theatre), then report to the Guild Theatre the following week and appear in a different production. Lawrence Langner wrote in *The Magic Curtain* that this plan was highly successful and that the 1920s constituted the Guild's golden era.

The 1930s changed the Theatre Guild's operating system. The "Alternating Repertory" became too difficult to manage and the depression did not help the Guild's economic situation. Although it continued to present fine actors in excellent plays, there were also many flops that drained the company's resources.

In 1930 the Guild Theatre housed a revival of Turgenev's *A Month in the Country*, with Nazimova, Dudley Digges, and Henry Travers. It was successful, and during the run Katharine Hepburn joined the cast. It was her first role with the Guild and she was to play an important role in the Guild's survival in years to come.

Some highlights of the 1930s at this theatre included the third edition of the popular revue *The Garrick Gaities* (1930), with Imogene Coca, Cynthia Rodgers, Edith Meiser, and many others, who were joined during the run by the young Rosalind Russell, making her Broadway debit; the Lunts in Maxwell Anderson's verse play *Elizabeth the Queen* (1930), which moved from the Guild to the larger Martin Beck; Lynn Rigg's lovely *Green Grow the Lilacs* (1931), which would save the Guild in 1943 when it became the landmark musical *Oklahoma!*

On October 26, 1931, the Guild Theatre was the scene of one of its greatest triumphs: Eugene O'Neill's five-hour trilogy (with a dinner intermission) called *Mourning Becomes Electra*. O'Neill based his three plays on Aeschylus' *Oresteia*, but changed the locale to New England. The tragedy, which starred Nazimova, Alice Brady, Earle Larimore, and Lee Barker, was hailed by critics as a masterpiece. The eminent critic Joseph Wood Krutch wrote: "It may turn out to be the only permanent contribution yet made by the twentieth century to dramatic literature." The play posed a fashion problem to first-nighters. The performance started at 5:00 P.M. Should they wear evening clothes or afternoon wear? Critic George Jean Nathan wore afternoon clothes, but when he saw financier Otto Kahn arrive in evening clothes, Nathan ran home at intermission to change. Kahn also ran home and changed to afternoon wear.

Other 1930s highlights included Beatrice Lillie and Hope Williams in a revival of Shaw's *Too True to Be Good* (1932); Nazimova, Henry Travers, Claude Rains, Sydney Greenstreet, and Jessie Ralph in an adaptation of Pearl Buck's novel *The Good Earth* (1932); Ina Claire in one

LEFT: Earle Larimore and Alice Brady in Eugene O'Neill's masterly *Mourning Becomes Electra* (1931). RIGHT: Gene Lockhart and George M. Cohan in Eugene O'Neill's *Ah, Wilderness!* (1933).

⚡ Ina Claire and Van Heflin in S.N. Behrman's captivating comedy, *End of Summer* (1936).

of her greatest high comedy performances in S.N. Behrman's *Biography* (1932); Judith Anderson, Humphrey Bogart, Shirley Booth, and Leo G. Carroll in *The Mask and the Face* (1933), translated from an Italian play by Somerset Maugham; George M. Cohan and Gene Lockhart in Eugene O'Neill's only comedy, *Ah, Wilderness!* (1933); Maxwell Anderson's *Valley Forge* (1934), with Philip Merivale as General George Washington; Jimmy Savo, Eve Arden, Charles Walters, and Ezra Stone in a colorful revue, *Parade* (1935); the Lunts, Richard Whorf,

and Sydney Greenstreet in an inspired revival of *The Taming of the Shrew* (1935); Ina Claire, Osgood Perkins, Van Heflin, Mildred Natwick, and Shepperd Strudwick in another Behrman gem, *End of Summer* (1936); and Sylvia Sidney, Leslie Banks, and Evelyn Varden in Ben Hecht's *To Quito and Back* (1937).

Despite brilliant acting, some of the above plays ran barely longer than fifty performances and there were many in-between that ran for less. By the end of 1938, the Guild found itself in such financial straits that it began renting the Guild Theatre to other producers. In October 1938 Gilbert Miller presented J.B. Priestley's *I Have Been Here Before*, but it failed; and in December, Herman Shumlin presented Max Reinhardt's production of Thornton Wilder's *The Merchant of Yonkers*, starring Jane Cowl and featuring Percy Waram, June Walker, and Nydia Westman. This farce was a curious flop. Wilder later rewrote it as *The Matchmaker*, which was a hit; then it was turned into *Hello, Dolly!*

William Saroyan's first Broadway play, with a Group Theatre cast—*My Heart's in the Highlands*—played a brief but acclaimed run in 1939, to be followed in February 1940 by Saroyan's *The Time of Your Life*, which won both the Pulitzer Prize and the New York Drama Critics Circle Award and moved to the Guild Theatre from the Booth. In the early 1940s, the Theatre Guild had a series of short-lived plays at their theatre—a revival of *Ah, Wilderness!*, with Harry Carey; Frederic March and Florence Eldridge in *Hope for a Harvest*; Celeste Holm and Jessie Royce Landis in *Papa Is All*; Paul Muni, Jessica Tandy, and Alfred Drake in *Yesterday's Magic*; Stuart Erwin and Lillian Gish in *Mr. Sycamore*; and finally, a Russian drama called *The Russian People*.

With all these disasters, the Theatre Guild decided to lease its theatre as a radio playhouse in 1943 and it remained so until 1950.

At this time, the federally chartered American National Theatre and Academy bought the theatre and renamed it the ANTA Playhouse. Lawrence Langner observed: "ANTA has now taken it over, and are operating it on a tax-free basis with subsidies and concessions from all the unions, which will make their burden far less than ours; and I wish them better luck with the building than we had." In 1944 the Theatre Guild moved out of the Guild Theatre to an imposing town house on West Fifty-Third Street.

The beautifully renovated ANTA Playhouse opened auspiciously on November 26, 1950, with Judith Anderson, Marian Seldes, and Alfred Ryder in *The Tower Beyond Tragedy*, by Robinson Jeffers. The critics hailed Anderson's acting, but the verse tragedy based on the Electra theme only played for thirty-two performances. On Christmas Eve, 1950, Santa brought a gilt-edged gift to this beleaguered theatre: Gloria Swanson and José Ferrer in a revival of Hecht and MacArthur's comedy *Twentieth Century*. But, as in the past, it was so successful that it was moved to the Fulton Theatre. The ANTA Play Series continued with revivals of *Mary Rose* (1951); Molière's *L'Ecole des Femmes*, performed in French by Louis Jouvet and company; *Desire Under the Elms* (1952), with Karl Malden, Douglas Watson, and Carol Stone, directed by Harold Clurman; and *Golden Boy* (1952), with John Garfield, Lee J. Cobb, and Jack Klugman. During this time, a genuine hit moved to the ANTA—Mary Chase's delightful fantasy *Mrs. McThing* (1952), starring Helen Hayes, Ernest Borgnine, Jules Munshin, and Brandon de Wilde—but it tarried briefly before moving to the Morosco. In 1955 Katharine Cornell, Tyrone Power, and Christopher Plummer appeared in Christopher Fry's "winter comedy" *The Dark Is Light Enough*. The light burned out after sixty-nine performances. A musical version of *Seventh Heaven*, with Chita Rivera, Beatrice Arthur, Gloria DeHaven, Ricardo Montalban, and Kurt Kasznar, only made it to

Helen Hayes as a wealthy-aristocrat-turned-scrubwoman in Mary Chase's comic fairy-tale, *Mrs. McThing* (1952).

forty-four showings. ANTA's star-studded revival of *The Skin of Our Teeth* (1955) had Helen Hayes, Mary Martin, George Abbott, Florence Reed, and Don Murray in the cast. It played successful engagements in Paris, Washington, D.C., and Chicago before coming to the ANTA theatre.

In 1956 the Lunts returned to the theatre where they had performed so often for the Guild. Their vehicle, *The Great Sebastions*, was one of their poorest. A melodramatic comedy

THE DARK IS LIGHT ENOUGH

TOP LEFT: Katharine Cornell and Tyrone Power as they appeared on the PLAYBILL cover for Christopher Fry's *The Dark Is Light Enough* (1955). ABOVE: Raymond Massey and Christopher Plummer in the Pulitzer Prize-winning drama *J.B.* (1958). LEFT: Mona Freeman (in touring cast) and Edward G. Robinson in *Middle of the Night* (1956).

by Howard Lindsay and Russel Crouse in which they played a mind-reading act, the play managed to last for 174 performances.

On February 8, 1956, the ANTA theatre finally housed a play that enjoyed a long run. Edward G. Robinson returned to this theatre, where he had acted for the Guild many times, and garnered superlatives for his performance in Paddy Chayefsky's *Middle of the Night*, a love story about a fifty-three-year-old man who falls in love with a twenty-four-year-old woman, played by Gena Rowlands. June Walker, Anne Jackson, and Martin Balsam were also in the cast. For the first time in its history, this theatre housed a play that ran for 477 performances. Joshua Logan produced and directed.

The success of the Chayefsky play at the ANTA turned the tide for this house. After engagement by the Dancers of Bali and Dancers of India, the house booked several hits that enjoyed substantial runs. *Say, Darling* (1958), a comedy about the troubles encountered when producing a Broadway musical, was satiric fact rather than fiction. It was plainly about the backstage shenanigans in getting *The Pajama Game* produced on Broadway. David Wayne, Vivian Blaine, Johnny Desmond, and Constance Ford were in the cast, but Robert Morse stole the show doing an outrageous impersonation of a flamboyant producer/director said to be inspired by Hal Prince. The comedy ran for 332 performances.

The ANTA's next tenant won the Pulitzer Prize. It was *J.B.* (1958), a verse drama by Archibald MacLeish, with Pat Hingle as J.B. (Job), Raymond Massey as Mr. Zuss (God), and Christopher Plummer as Nickles (Satan). Elia Kazan directed the Biblical drama, which ran for 364 performances.

Critics praised Rex Harrison's acting in Anouilh's comedy *The Fighting Cock* (1959), but audiences supported it for only eighty-seven performances. Next came a healthy hit, *A Thur-*

ber Carnival (1960), described as "a new entertainment patterned after the revue form," by James Thurber, with music by Don Elliott. The show was a series of humorous sketches based on Thurber writings and performed with charm by Tom Ewell, Peggy Cass, Paul Ford, John McGiver, Alice Ghostley, and others.

Highlights of the 1960s included Hugh Wheeler's *Big Fish, Little Fish* (1961), with Jason Robards, Jr., Hume Cronyn, Martin Gabel, Elizabeth Wilson, and George Grizzard, directed by Sir John Gielgud; Robert Bolt's distinguished historical play, *A Man for All Seasons* (1961), which won six Tony Awards, including best play, best actor (Paul Scofield), and best director (Noel Willman), later included Faye Dunaway in the cast and ran for 640 performances; James Baldwin's *Blues for Mister Charlie* (1964), with Diana Sands, Al Freedman, Jr., John McCurry, Rosetta Le Noire, Pat Hingle, and Rip Torn, directed by Burgess Meredith; Diana Sands and Alan Alda in the two-character comedy *The Owl and the Pussycat* (1964), which ran for 421 performances; Peter Shaffer's *The Royal Hunt of the Sun* (1965), starring Christopher Plummer as Pizarro and George Rose as Ruiz, with David Carradine as an Inca leader; engagements by the National Repertory Theatre (1967) and the American Conservatory Theatre (1969); Len Cariou in the American Shakespeare Festival's production of *Henry V* (1969); and a revival of *Our Town* (1969), with Henry Fonda, Ed Begley, Elizabeth Hartman, Harvey Evans, Mildred Natwick, John Beal, and Margaret Hamilton from the Plumstead Playhouse.

The 1970s brought Helen Hayes, James Stewart, and Jesse White in a revival of *Harvey* (1970), jointly produced by ANTA and the Phoenix Theatre; engagements of the dance companies of Alvin Ailey, Louis Falco, Pearl Lang, Paul Taylor, Nikolais, and the Dance Theatre of Harlem (all in 1971); the musical *Purlie*

🔰 Diana Sands and Alan Alda in the 1964 comedy *The Owl and the Pussycat*.

The Suicide, in 1980, for sixty performances; and a musical version of Dickens's *David Copperfield*, shortened to *Copperfield*, had a brief run of thirteen performances in 1981. *Annie* moved in from the Alvin across the street for one month, followed by an unsuccessful musical, *Oh, Brother*, based on Shakespeare's *The Comedy of Errors*, and the Pilobolus Dance Theatre (1981).

In August 1981 the ANTA theatre was acquired by Jujamcyn Theatres and subsequently renamed the Virginia Theatre, in honor of Mrs. Virginia M. Binger, owner of Jujamcyn along with her husband, James Binger. Richard G. Wolff, president of Jujamcyn Theatres, supervised the renovation of the theatre and announced the firm's intention of booking both legitimate attractions and dance companies at the Virginia.

The most recent shows at the Virginia have been a lavish revival of the Eva Le Gallienne/Florida Friebus adaptation of *Alice in Wonderland*, with Ms. Le Gallienne repeating the role of the White Queen, which she played in 1932, and with Kate Burton as Alice. The current attraction at the Virginia is the hit revival of the 1936 Rodgers and Hart musical *On Your Toes*, which won a Tony Award as the best revival of the season and won another Tony for its star, ballet great Natalia Makarova.

The Virginia Theatre has had a unique history. For more than a decade, when it was the Guild Theatre, it was America's finest repertory theatre, with brilliant Guild actors appearing in a variety of plays. Its loyal subscribers not only attended the shows but some even became stockholders in the Guild Theatre when it was built, making it a most unusual project on commercial Broadway. And considering some of the long-run hits the theatre has housed in the last three decades, the limited seating capacity has not been as damaging as it seemed to the founders of the Theatre Guild.

from the Broadway Theatre, which played for seven months in 1971; Julie Harris winning a Tony Award for her performance in *The Last of Mrs. Lincoln* (1972); Elizabeth Ashley, Keir Dullea, Fred Gwynne, and Kate Reid in a revival of *Cat on a Hot Tin Roof* (1974); the exuberant black musical *Bubbling Brown Sugar* (1976–77), which ran for 766 performances; Charles Repole in a revival of Eddie Cantor's 1920s hit *Whoopee!* (1979), from the Goodspeed Opera House; Maggie Smith in Tom Stoppard's *Night and Day* (1979).

Derek Jacobi starred in a Russian drama,

❦ EUGENE O'NEILL THEATRE ❦

The Eugene O'Neill Theatre at 230 West Forty-ninth Street originated as the Forrest Theatre in 1925. It was named after one of America's greatest classical actors, Edwin Forrest, whose bitter feud with the classical British actor William Charles Macready ignited the tragic 1849 riot at the Astor Place Opera House in New York City. In the course of this event twenty-two persons were killed and several hundred wounded.

The Forrest Theatre was built by the Shuberts and designed in the Georgian style by architect Herbert J. Krapp. The capacity was 1,200, making it flexible for the staging of dramas or musical comedies. The theatre officially opened on November 25, 1925, with a musical comedy called *Mayflowers*, starring Ivy Sawyer, Joseph Santley, and a newcomer named Nancy Carroll, who would later become a movie star. The New York *Times* labeled the show "attractive," but it lasted for only eighty-one performances.

Unfortunately, the new theatre began with a string of flops. After *Mayflowers*, it housed such short-lived shows as *The Matinee Girl*, *Mama Loves Papa*, *Rainbow Rose*, and *My Country*.

After six more very short-lived plays in 1927,

the Forrest finally had a hit in a drama called *Women Go on Forever*. Produced by William A. Brady, Jr., and Dwight Deere Wiman, the play featured this impressive cast: Mary Boland, Osgood Perkins, Douglass Montgomery, and James Cagney. A seamy, realistic play that the *Times* found "cheap and malodorous," the show attracted the public for 118 performances.

After that, the Forrest reverted to potboilers whose very titles denoted their doom: *Bless You, Sister; Mirrors; It Is to Laugh; The Skull; Fast Life; The Common Sin; The Squealer;* and *Café de Danse*, all from December of 1927 to December of 1928. Ruth St. Denis and Ted Shawn brought some class to the house with their dancing in 1929 and things brightened a bit when the popular comedy *Bird in Hand*, by John Drinkwater, transferred here from the Masque Theatre in 1930.

The Blue Ghost, a mystery play, managed to run for 112 performances in 1930, possibly because it was the only creepy show in town. Ushers at the Forrest Theatre wore blue hoods over their heads to get the audience in the proper shivery mood, but the New York *Times* declared that after that device they expected the worst—and got it.

A farce called *Stepping Sisters*, about three ex-burlesque queens, moved to the Forrest from the Royale Theatre in August 1930 and stayed for two months. In October of that year, the theatre suddenly became Edgar Wallace's Forrest Theatre when Mr. Wallace's play *On the Spot* opened there. This gangster play, with Anna May Wong and Glenda Farrell, was the theatre's biggest hit thus far, running for 167 performances.

A terrible farce called *In the Best of Fami-*

🖤 Standard program cover for the Forrest Theatre in the 1920s.

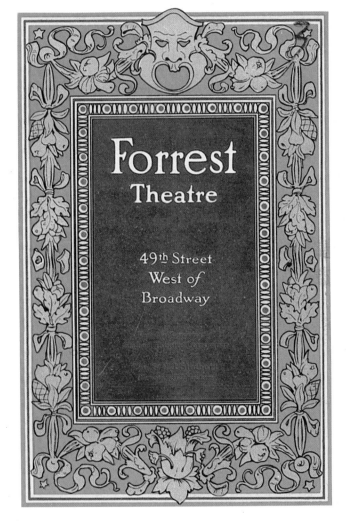

lies was pronounced dull and dirty by Brooks Atkinson of the *Times*, so it ran for 141 performances, moving to the Forrest from the Bijou in March 1931. From October of that year until November of 1932, this theatre housed seven plays of such mediocrity that none of them ran for more than thirty-six performances and four ran for fewer than twelve performances.

Things picked up a bit in 1932 when the Helen Hayes/Walter Connolly hit *The Good Fairy* moved here from Henry Miller's Theatre and stayed for two months. A revival of Rachel Crothers's comedy *As Husbands Go* chalked up 144 performances in 1933. The Ballets Jooss played a gratifying engagement from October to December of 1933.

From January through August 1934 the Forrest had seven flops, including a lavish musical romance, *Caviar*, with dancer Jack Cole in the cast, and a musical revue, *Keep Moving*, starring Tom Howard. Then, in September 1934, a bonanza finally arrived at this theatre. It was *Tobacco Road*, Jack Kirkland's shocking dramatization of Erskine Caldwell's novel of the same name, which had opened at the Masque Theatre on December 5, 1933. Starring Henry Hull as Jeeter Lester, Margaret Wycherly as Ada, and Dean Jagger as Lou, this seamy play, which many critics disliked, stayed at the Forrest from September 1934 until the week of May 25, 1941. When it ended its marathon run at the Forrest, it had played for 3,182 performances, making it the longest-running play in the history of the American theatre. Today, it is second only to *Life with Father*, which ran for 3,224 performances. Henry Hull was succeeded by the following actors during this record run: James Barton, James Bell, Eddie Garr, and Will Geer. *Tobacco Road* came back to the Forrest in 1942, after a long road tour, and then John Barton, son of James, was playing Jeeter Lester. But the return engagement lasted only thirty-four performances. Audiences had had enough

🖋 A formal portrait of the turnip-eating Jeeter Lester family in *Tobacco Road*. From left: Reneice Rehan, Margaret Wycherly, Sam Byrd, James Barton, as Jeeter Lester, and Ruth Hunter.

of squalor, sex, and turnips in this drama about Georgia "crackers." Meanwhile, the mayor of Chicago had deemed the play too dirty to be staged there, and Rhode Island and the American South had made the same decision.

The 1940s at the Forrest reverted to the unfortunate booking of a series of flop shows.

Occasionally, hits from another theatre, such as *Three Men on a Horse* and *Claudia*, played there, but usually it was clinkers like *Bright Lights of 1944; Manhattan Nocturne; Tropical Revue; Listen Professor; Dark Hammock;* and *Hand in Glove.* The last show to play the Forrest before it changed its name was a comedy

✌ LEFT: Betty Field and Wendell Corey in Elmer Rice's bewitching comedy *Dream Girl* (1945). RIGHT: Ed Begley (seated) and Arthur Kennedy in Arthur Miller's first success, *All My Sons* (1947).

called *The Overtons* (1945), which moved in from the Booth. It played for three months at the Forrest before the theatre closed for extensive renovations.

In 1945 City Playhouses Inc., with Louis A. Lotito as managing director, bought the Forrest from the Select Operating Corporation, which was controlled by the Shuberts. The new owners completely renovated this theatre, turning it into a stunning playhouse covered com

pletely with silken gray fabrics. Renamed the Coronet, it became one of the handsomest playhouses in Manhattan. And with this new dressing and new management, its luck changed. The first show to play the Coronet, *Beggars Are Coming to Town*, opened on October 27, 1945. It had an impressive cast: Paul Kelly, Luther Adler, Dorothy Comingore, Herbert Berghof, E.G. Marshall, George Mathews, and Adrienne Ames. Despite excellent acting and expert direction by Harold Clurman, it only ran for 25 performances. But the Coronet's second show turned out to be a winner. Elmer Rice's enchanting fantasy *Dream Girl* was written for his wife, Betty Field, and she gave a captivating performance as a woman who enlivened her dull life with vivid daydreams. She was ably supported by Wendell Corey, Evelyn Varden, and Edmon Ryan, and the cheerful comedy ran for 348 performances.

In January 1947 Arthur Miller's first successful play, *All My Sons*, opened here and stayed for 328 performances. The cast featured Ed Begley, Arthur Kennedy, Karl Malden, and Lois Wheeler, and Brooks Atkinson in the New York *Times* wrote: "With the production of *All My*

Sons at the Coronet . . . the theatre has acquired a new talent . . . Arthur Miller."

For a change of pace, the Coronet next booked a revue, *Angel in the Wings* (1947), and it was one of the season's big hits. Starring the infectious dance satirists, Paul and Grace Hartman, assisted by Hank Ladd, Elaine Stritch, Nadine Gae, Johnny Barnes, and others, the revue cheered audiences for 308 performances. Another bright revue, *Small Wonder* (1948), followed this, and its scintillating cast included Tom Ewell, Alice Pearce, Mary McCarthy, Jack Cassidy, Joan Diener, Jonathan Lucas, and many others. Staged by Burt Shevelove and choreographed by Gower Champion, it pleased revue lovers for 134 performances.

LEFT: Steve Cochran comes up to see Mae West in a revival of her play *Diamond Lil* (1949). ABOVE: PLAYBILL cover for Paul and Grace Hartman's hit revue *Tickets, Please!* (1950).

Patty McCormack and Nancy Kelly in Maxwell Anderson's homicidal thriller *The Bad Seed* (1954).

The indestructible Mae West revived her play *Diamond Lil* with sumptuous sets and gaudy costumes in February 1949, and the public flocked to it for 181 performances.

Maurice Evans starred in Terence Rattigan's two plays in one evening—*The Browning Version* and *A Harlequinade*—costarring with Edna Best, but the Peter Glenville production only lasted for 69 showings. After two unsuccessful plays—*Happy As Larry* and *The Bird Cage*—the Coronet had another hit revue with the Hartmans—*Tickets, Please!* in the spring of 1950. Their cast this time included Jack Albertson, Tommy Wonder, Larry Kert, Dorothy Jarnac, and many others. The Hartmans' formula paid off for 245 performances.

Other 1950s highlights at this theatre included Jessica Tandy, Beulah Bondi, Evelyn Varden, Eileen Heckart, and John Alexander in Samson Raphaelson's *Hilda Crane* (1950), staged by Hume Cronyn; Lillian Hellman's fascinating play about the middle-age crisis, *The Autumn Garden* (1951), with Fredric March, Florence Eldridge, Jane Wyatt, Ethel Griffies, and others, directed by Harold Clurman; Edna Best giving a memorable performance in S.N. Behrman's *Jane* (1952), based on a Somerset Maugham story; a revival of Lillian Hellman's explosive play *The Children's Hour* (1952), with Patricia Neal, Kim Hunter, Robert Pastene, and Iris Mann; Burgess Meredith, Martha Scott, Glenn Anders, and Una Merkel in Liam O'Brien's *The Remarkable Mr. Pennypacker* (1953); Robert Anderson's *All Summer Long* (1954), with John Kerr, Ed Begley, June Walker, and Carroll Baker; Noel Coward's *Quadrille* (1954), starring the Lunts, Brian Aherne, and Edna Best, directed by Lunt, with striking sets and costumes by Cecil Beaton; Maxwell Anderson's hit thriller about a sweet little murderess, *The Bad Seed* (1954), with Nancy Kelly, Patty McCormack, Eileen Heckart, Henry Jones, and Evelyn Varden, which moved here from the 46th Street Theatre; Arthur Miller's *A View from the Bridge*, with Van Heflin, J. Carrol Naish, and Eileen Heckart, in tandem with a shorter play called *A Memory of Two Mondays* (1955); the Lunts again in *The Great Sebastians* (1956), from the ANTA Playhouse; Barbara Bel Geddes, Michael Redgrave, and Cathleen Nesbitt in Terence Rattigan's *The Sleeping Prince* (1956); Siobhan McKenna in *St. Joan* (1956), transferred from the Phoenix Theatre; Sir Ralph Richardson and Mildred Natwick in Jean Anouilh's memorable play *The Waltz of the Toreadors* (1957), directed by Harold Clurman; Katharine Cornell and Anthony Quayle in Christopher Fry's *The Firstborn* (1958), with songs by Leonard Bernstein; Jason Robards, Jr., in his Tony Award winning performance as a writer said to be inspired by F. Scott Fitzgerald in *The Disenchanted* (1958), with Jason Robards, Sr., also in the cast and George Grizzard, Rosemary Harris, and Salome Jens. The last show to play the Coronet before it had a change of name was a revival of Eugene O'Neill's play *The Great God Brown* (1959), with Fritz Weaver, Robert Lansing, and Nan Martin, in a Phoenix Theatre production.

In November 1959 the Coronet was renamed the Eugene O'Neill Theatre, in honor of America's greatest playwright, who had died in 1953. The first play at the O'Neill was William Inge's *A Loss of Roses*, with Betty Field, Warren Beatty, Carol Haney, Robert Webber, and Michael J. Pollard, but the critics found the play dull and it closed after twenty-five performances.

After several quick failures, the theatre housed Carol Channing in Charles Gaynor's revue *Show Girl*, with Jules Munshin and Les Quat' Jeudis, a quartet of singing Frenchmen. It ran for 100 performances. John Mills starred in Terence Rattigan's *Ross* (1961), about Lawrence of Arabia; Jason Robards, Jr., and Sandy Dennis enjoyed a long run in Herb Gardner's comedy *A Thousand Clowns* (1962). Other 1960s shows: Hal Prince's production of the charming musical *She Loves Me* (1963), by Joe Masteroff, Sheldon Harnick, and Jerry Bock, with Barbara Cook, Daniel Massey, and Jack Cassidy; two hits from other theatres—*The Odd Couple* and *Rosencrantz and Guildenstern Are Dead* (1966–67); and the London musical version of *The Canterbury Tales* (1969), with George Rose, Sandy Duncan, Hermione Baddeley, Martyn Green, and Reid Shelton.

In the late 1960s playwright Neil Simon bought this theatre, but did not change its name. A series of Simon plays were then staged here, beginning with the successful comedy *Last of the Red Hot Lovers* (1969), with James Coco, Linda Lavin, Marcia Rodd, and Doris Roberts; *The Prisoner of Second Avenue* (1971), with Peter Falk, Lee Grant, and Vincent Gardenia, who won a Tony Award for his performance; *The Good Doctor* (1973), a series of sketches and songs, which Simon adapted from Chekhov stories, starring Christopher Plummer, Marsha Mason, Rene Auberjonois, Barnard Hughes, and Frances Sternhagen; *God's Favorite* (1974), Simon's comedy version of the Biblical story of Job, with Vincent Gardenia, Charles

From left: Van Heflin, Jack Warden (holding chair), Eileen Heckart, in background, Gloria Marlowe and Richard Davalos in Arthur Miller's *A View from the Bridge* (1955).

From left: Barbara Barrie, Jack Weston, Tammy Grimes, and George Grizzard in Neil Simon's comedy *California Suite* (1976).

Nelson Reilly, and Rosetta LeNoire, staged by Michael Bennett.

The Simon parade was interrupted in 1975 by the arrival of *Yentl*, a play by Isaac Bashevis Singer and Leah Napolin, starring Tovah Feldshuh, which stayed for seven months. Simon returned with *California Suite* (1976), an evening of four short plays, with Tammy Grimes, Jack Weston, and George Grizzard, which ran for 445 performances. Simon's hit play *Chapter Two* moved here from the Imperial in 1979, followed by another of his comedies, *I Ought to Be in Pictures* (1980), with Ron Leibman, Joyce Van Patten, and Dinah Manoff, who won a Tony Award for her performance. Simon's play *Fools*, with John Rubinstein, had a brief run in 1981, followed by *Annie*, which moved in from

another theatre. A revival of Simon's musical, *Little Me*, starring James Coco did not succeed in 1982; and the hit musical *The Best Little Whorehouse In Texas* returned from its tour and played at this theatre for a month.

In 1982 Jujamcyn Theatres bought the Eugene O'Neill from Neil Simon and is currently operating the theatre. Its most recent tenants have been Beth Henley's *The Wake of Jamey Foster*, William Gibson's *Monday After the Miracle*, and the very short-lived *Moose Murders*.

The Eugene O'Neill, with a seating capacity of 1,101 seats, is ideal for dramas and intimate musicals and revues. After some disastrous early years, its luck changed and in the last several decades it has housed some impressive plays.

⚑ BILTMORE THEATRE ⚑

The Chanin Brothers, construction moguls who were bitten by the show biz bug in the 1920s, built six legitimate theatres. The Biltmore, at 261 West Forty-seventh Street, was their second project. When this theatre opened on December 7, 1925, the New York *Times* reported that it was the first theatre to be built on the north side of Forty-seventh Street, just east of Eighth Avenue. The theatre was designed by the busiest architect in town, Herbert J. Krapp, with a single balcony, 1,000 seats, and a color scheme of cerise and brown.

The opening show at the Biltmore was not new. It was an Owen Davis farce called *Easy Come, Easy Go*, which moved here from the George M. Cohan Theatre on Broadway. Otto Kruger and Victor Moore played bank robbers and Edward Arnold was also involved in the fracas. It had a run of 180 performances.

Next came a very steamy drama, *Kongo* (1926), with Walter Huston as "Deadleg Flint," a bitter man in the Belgian "Kongo" who gets even with a man who not only stole his wife but caused his legs to be paralyzed. This jungle rot lasted for 135 performances. A comedy called *Loose Ankles* (1926) followed, with

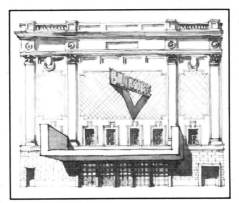

Osgood Perkins, and it was sufficiently foolish to run for 161 performances.

Walter Huston returned to the Biltmore in a solid hit, *The Barker* (1927), a play about carnival life by Kenyon Nicholson. Huston played a tent show barker; Claudette Colbert played a snake charmer who vamps Huston's son, acted by Norman Foster. She vamped him so well that they got married, off-stage. The critics admired Claudette's legs and this lively show ran for 225 performances.

A comedy called *Jimmie's Women* was a hit in 1927, but moved to another theatre after a month. Noel Coward's *The Marquise* was chi-chi nonsense about an errant society woman (Billie Burke) who returns to her family years later just in time to save her daughter (Madge Evans) from mistakenly marrying her half-brother (Rex O'Malley). Coward's fans supported this fluff for eighty-two performances.

There were a number of flops in 1928, including another play, *Tin Pan Alley*, with Claudette Colbert and Norman Foster. There was also a cause célèbre at this theatre on October 1, 1928, when the incomparable Mae West opened her new play *The Pleasure Man*. This

BILTMORE THEATRE
47th STREET, WEST OF BROADWAY

Program cover for *Tin Pan Alley*, a 1928 play with Claudette Colbert and Norman Foster.

time, Mae did not appear in her show, but her plot was sufficiently lurid to shock the populace, and the police closed the play after its second performance. *The Pleasure Man* was about an actor who has impregnated so many women that the brother of one of them decides to perform a brutal operation on him that will curtail his love life. The operation is performed at a party largely attended by transvestites and the lover dies under the knife.

Wall Street laid an egg in 1929 and so did the Biltmore Theatre. It housed seven flops, including *Man's Estate*, a Theatre Guild production with Dudley Digges, Elizabeth Patterson, Earle Larimore, Armina Marshall, and Margalo Gillmore.

The 1930s began with an interesting but depressing play by Edwin Justus Mayer called *Children of Darkness*. Set in the notorious debtors' prison of Newgate in London, the drama dealt with the last days of the infamous criminal Jonathan Wild. The seamy play starred Basil Sydney, Mary Ellis, and Eugene Powers and lasted ten weeks.

George Kelly's play *Philip Goes Forth* was a near-hit in 1931, playing for ninety-eight performances. Madge Evans, Thurston Hall, Dorothy Stickney, Cora Witherspoon, and Harry Ellerbe were in the comedy about a young man who fails as a playwright and ends up in his father's business. From May 1931 until January 1934, the Biltmore housed a number of mediocre plays, such as *Her Supporting Cast, Zombie, Border-land,* and *The Scorpion*. One drama, a biographical study called *Carry Nation*, was unsuccessful, but featured this interesting cast: James Stewart, Joshua Logan, Mildred Natwick, Esther Dale, and Katherine Emery.

New Year's Day, 1934, brought a comedy hit at last to the Biltmore. It was called *Big Hearted Herbert* and starred J.C. Nugent as a mean miser who upsets all his family's plans

Claudette Colbert's gams were one of the highlights of the 1927 hit *The Barker*.

until they turn the tables on him. It amused theatregoers for 154 performances. Emmet Lavery's religious play *The First Legion*, with Bert Lytell, John Litel, Charles Coburn, and Frankie Thomas, moved in from the 46th Street Theatre in October and stayed through December.

The Chanin Brothers, who built this theatre, plus five others, lost all six during the depres-

LEFT: George Abbott's hilarious production of *Brother Rat* with Richard Clark, Mary Mason, and Eddie Albert (1936). BELOW LEFT: Ezra Stone, Vaughan Glaser, James Corner in another George Abbott winner *What A Life* (1937). BELOW: Shirley Booth and Jo Ann Sayers in the rollicking hit *My Sister Eileen* (1940).

sion. In 1936 the Federal Theatre Project took over the theatre and presented some of its "Living Newspaper" productions. These consisted of a series of news sketches written by a staff of seventy reporters and writers and about sixteen dramatists. A cast of a hundred actors appeared in such striking productions as *Triple-A Plowed Under* and *1935*. In June 1936 the Federal Theatre presented *Stars on Strings*, a marionette show, at this theatre.

The Biltmore was next taken over by Warner Brothers, the film studio, to serve as a showcase for the productions of the famed producer/playwright/director George Abbott. PLAYBILL magazines for the Biltmore, beginning in 1937 and continuing into the 1940s, stated that the theatre was managed by Bernard Klawans.

George Abbott's production of *Brother Rat*, a comedy about life at the Virginia Military Institute by John Monks, Jr., and Fred F. Finklehoffe, was a huge hit in 1936. The sprightly cast included Eddie Albert, José Ferrer, Frank Albertson, and Ezra Stone and it turned out to be the Biltmore's longest-running show thus far, registering 575 performances. Abbott's next two shows, *Brown Sugar* and *All That Glitters*, were not successful, but his production of Clifford Goldsmith's *What a Life*, a hilarious comedy about a squeaky-voiced high-schooler who is always in trouble (perfectly played by Ezra Stone), turned into a gold mine. Henry Aldrich became such a popular character that he ended up on a successful radio series and, years later, on TV. Eddie Bracken, Betty Field, Joyce Arling, Edith Van Cleve, and Butterfly McQueen were also in the cast of the play, which ran for 538 performances.

George Abbott's 1939 show was a shocker and quite unlike the type of farce comedy in which he excelled. It was called *The Primrose Path* and it was based on Victoria Lincoln's sultry novel *February Hill*. The language was salty and the morals very loose in this saga of a slat-tern and her family. Helen Westley, Betty Field, Betty Garde, and Russell Hardie were in the cast of this moderate success.

In 1940, Warner Brothers and Bernard Klawans produced a play called *Jupiter Laughs*, by A.J. Cronin, starring Jessica Tandy, Alexander Knox, Mary Orr, Edith Meiser, and Philip Tonge. This drama about doctors only ran for 24 performances. But on December 26, 1940, a comedy opened that brought distinction to the Biltmore. It was the fabulous *My Sister Eileen*, by Joseph A. Fields and Jerome Chodorov, based on *The New Yorker* stories of Ruth McKenney. Ms. McKenney had written charming vignettes about her adventures with her wacky blonde sister Eileen when they moved from Ohio to Manhattan. This uproarious comedy, skillfully staged by George S. Kaufman, played for 866 performances. The cast included Shirley Booth as Ruth, Jo Ann Sayers as Eileen, and Morris Carnovsky as their Greek landlord in Greenwich Village. Only one tragic note marred this joyous production. The real Eileen was driving from Ohio to attend the opening night of her sister's play when she was killed in an auto accident.

Another enormously successful comedy, *Janie*, moved here from another theatre for two months in 1942. On March 17, 1943, a play called *Kiss and Tell*, by F. Hugh Herbert, opened and broke all records at this theatre. It ran for 962 performances. The comedy about teenage pregnancy had in its cast Richard Widmark, Jessie Royce Landis, Joan Caulfield, and Robert Keith. It was produced and directed by the incredible George Abbott and was made into a hit movie and a successful radio series.

Bernard Klawans, who continued as manager of the Biltmore, presented (with Victor Payne-Jennings) an adaptation of Emile Zola's *Thérèse Raquin* by Thomas Job called simply *Thérèse* in 1945. Starring Dame May Whitty, Eva Le Gallienne, and Victor Jory, it played for

🎭 Richard Widmark and Joan Caulfield in the wartime comedy hit *Kiss and Tell* (1943).

96 performances. In February 1946 Walter Huston returned once again to this theatre in *Apple of His Eye*, written by Charles Robinson and Kenyon Nicholson (who wrote Huston's big hit *The Barker*, at this theatre in 1927). Jed Harris directed the comedy, which played for 118 performances, and coproduced it with Mr. Huston.

Jed Harris produced another comedy here called *Loco*, with Jean Parker, Elaine Stritch, and Jay Fassett in 1946, but it ran for a brief thirty-seven performances. Paul Bowles's adaptation of Sartre's play about three characters trapped in a room in hell, *No Exit*, only played for a month, but it was memorable for performances given by Claude Dauphin, Annabella, and Ruth Ford. One of the drama critics complained that movie star Annabella's per-

formance gave him a stomachache and she promptly sent him a laxative.

In March 1947 Russian playwright Konstantine Simonov's comedy *The Whole World Over*, with Uta Hagen, Sanford Meisner, and Jo Van Fleet, opened and managed to stay for 100 performances. It was directed by Harold Clurman. On September 29, 1947, Jed Harris returned to this theatre with a fine play—Ruth and Augustus Goetz's excellent adaptation of Henry James's novel *Washington Square*. The play, called *The Heiress*, starred Basil Rathbone, Wendy Hiller, Patricia Collinge, and Peter Cookson and ran for 410 performances. It was directed by Jed Harris and produced by Fred F. Finklehoffe. Mr. Rathbone won a Tony Award for his chilling performance as Ms. Hiller's father.

More hits arrived at the Biltmore: José Ferrer, George Matthews, and Doro Merande in *The Silver Whistle* (1948), a comedy set in an old people's home that ran for 219 performances; *Clutterbuck* (1949), a British comedy by Benn W. Levy about a Don Juan named "Clutterbuck," which was David Merrick's first Broadway production (in association with Irving L. Jacobs).

The 1950s brought a dramatic adaptation of Herman Melville's novel *Billy Budd*. This excellent play, with Charles Nolte in the title role and Dennis King, James Daly, and Lee Marvin in the cast, had an unfortunate opening-night incident. A critic for a major newspaper arrived at the theatre intoxicated. The management called the newspaper and the editor quickly sent another staff critic, without telling the inebriated reviewer. Both critics wrote their reviews; the drunk raved, the sober critic panned it. Unfortunately, the pan appeared in the paper, which helped to shorten the run to 105 performances for this superb drama.

From 1952 to 1961, the Biltmore ceased its legitimate theatre policy. It was leased to the Columbia Broadcasting System. On December 21, 1961, it reverted to being a legitimate house with Harold Prince's production of the hit comedy *Take Her, She's Mine*, directed by the old Biltmore genius George Abbott. Art Carney, Phyllis Thaxter, and Elizabeth Ashley starred in this play about a father's concern when his daughter is ready to go to college. It ran for 404 performances. Ms. Ashley won a Tony for her performance. The actress returned to this theatre in October 1963 in an even bigger hit comedy, *Barefoot in the Park*. Neil Simon's play about the problems of newlyweds (attractively portrayed by Ms. Ashley and Robert Redford, with brilliant support by Mildred Natwick and Kurt Kasznar, directed by Mike Nichols) became the longest-running play at the Biltmore up to this time. It played there from October 1963 to mid-June of 1967. Mike Nichols won a Tony Award for his direction.

Several short-lived plays followed—Dyan Cannon and Martin Milner in *The Ninety-Day Mistress* (1967); Milo O'Shea and Eli Wallach as homosexuals in the British play *Staircase* (1968); and Joe Orton's black comedy *Loot* (1968). Then came one of the high points of the Biltmore's history when the rock musical *Hair* opened there on April 29, 1968. This freewheeling look at the Flower Generation had been an Off-Broadway hit at the downtown New York Shakespeare Festival production by Joseph Papp. It then moved to an uptown disco called Cheetah, but it failed, until a producer named Michael Butler took it over and hired

LEFT: Basil Rathbone and Wendy Hiller in the Jed Harris production of *The Heiress* (1947). RIGHT: Elizabeth Ashley and Robert Redford in Neil Simon's giant hit *Barefoot in the Park* (1963).

director Tom O'Horgan. A very salable commodity was added to this show—total nudity, something that had not been seen on Broadway since some of the 1920s revues—and the show became the biggest hit in town, running a record four years and two months at the Biltmore. With book and lyrics by Gerome Ragni and James Rado and music by Galt MacDermot, *Hair* became a symbol of the 1960s. Among the many performers that the musical introduced were Melba Moore and Diane Keaton.

Some highlights of the 1970s at this theatre included Michael Moriarty in his Tony Award winning performance as a homosexual in *Find Your Way Home* (1974); Jules Feiffer's farce *Knock, Knock* (1976), with Lynn Redgrave and Leonard Frey; Barry Bostwick winning a Tony Award in the musical *The Robber Bridegroom* (1976); Lily Tomlin in her dazzling one-woman show *Appearing Nitely*; an unsuccessful return engagement of *Hair* (1977); a revival of *The Effect of Gamma Rays on Man-in-the-Moon Marigolds* (1978), starring Shelley Winters; Clau-

dette Colbert in her third appearance at this theatre, in *The Kingfisher* (1978), with Rex Harrison and George Rose; Peter Allen in a spectacular personal appearance called *Up in One*.

The 1980s brought such divergent fare as an exciting courtroom drama, *Nuts* (1980), with Anne Twomey; Arthur Miller's play *The American Clock* (1980), which failed; Eva Le Gallienne and Shepperd Strudwick in *To Grandmother's House We Go* (1981); Claudette Colbert again in *A Talent for Murder* (1981), with Jean Pierre Aumont; the longest-running thriller in the American theatre, *Deathtrap* (1982), from the Music Box; and Anthony Shaffer's spoof of mystery plays, *Whodunnit* (1983).

Today, the Biltmore Theatre is owned by the Biltmore Theatre Corp.-Sharcar, Inc., with David J. Cogan, president. It is operated under the direction of the Messrs. Nederlander and has been kept in fine condition. There are few legitimate theatres that have housed as many shows as the Biltmore that were produced and directed by one person—George Abbott.

⚜ BROOKS ATKINSON THEATRE ⚜

The Brooks Atkinson Theatre at 256 West Forty-seventh Street opened in 1926 as the Mansfield Theatre, named in honor of the great classical American actor Richard Mansfield, who died in 1907. The theatre was another house built by the Chanin Brothers, con-struction tycoons, and it was designed by architect Herbert J. Krapp, who seemed to turn out a thea-tre a week in the Roaring Twenties. It followed the lat-est trends—only one bal-cony and an auditorium that was wide rather than deep. According to the New York *Times*, the attractive color scheme was old rose, gold, and light tan.

The opening bill at the Mansfield on the night of February 15, 1926, was a melodrama called *The Night Duel*, by Daniel Rubin and Edgar MacGregor, starring Marjorie Rambeau and Felix Krembs. The *Times* reported that there was an embarrassing bedroom scene in the second act and that it seemed to please the audience. The play only lasted seventeen performances. It was followed by three more failures: *The Masque of Venice*, with Arnold Daly, Osgood Perkins, Selena Royle, and Antoinette Perry; *Schweiger*, with Ann Harding as a wife who discovers that her husband (played by Jacob Ben-Ami) was a child murderer; and

Beau-Strings, with Estelle Winwood as a flirt and Clarence Derwent as one of her interests.

The first moderate hit at the Mansfield opened on September 2, 1926. It was a play by William Anthony McGuire called *If I Was Rich* and it starred vaudeville/ musical comedy favorite Joe Laurie, Jr. It ran for ninety-two performances.

Antoinette Perry (the Tony Awards were named in her honor) again appeared at this theatre in a long-running play with a curious history. *The Ladder*, a show about reincarnation, was disliked by the critics, but it was backed by a millionaire, Edgar B. Davis, who wanted the world to listen to the drama's message, so he kept the play running for 794 performances (often allowing people in free) and lost half a million dollars on it.

The Actors' Theatre revived Eugene O'Neill's Pulitzer Prize play *Beyond the Horizon* (1926) and it ran for seventy-nine performances. This production starred Robert Keith, Thomas Chalmers, and Aline MacMahon. The year ended with a revival of *The Dybbuk*.

Mrs. Fiske revived Ibsen's *Ghosts* for twenty-four performances in January 1927, and the rest of the year brought undistinguished productions.

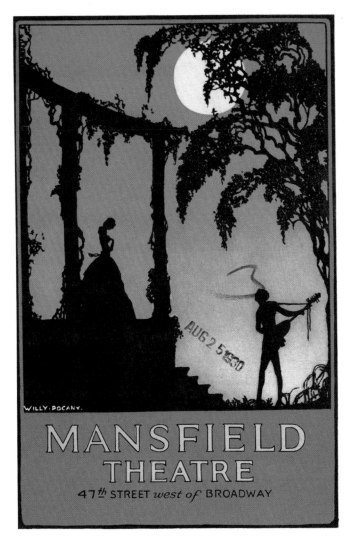

Program cover for the immortal Pulitzer Prize play *The Green Pastures* (1930).

The year 1928 began with something called *Mongolia*, which transferred here from the Greenwich Village Theatre, but only played for three weeks. This was followed by *Atlas and Eva*, a comedy about a family called the Nebblepredders, which expired after 24 labored performances. Finally, on April 26, 1928, Rodgers and Hart came to the rescue with a sprightly musical about U.S. Marines stationed at Pearl Harbor. Called *Present Arms*, it produced one

Rodgers and Hart classic: "You Took Advantage of Me." This song was sung in the show by none other than Busby Berkeley (who also did the dances for the musical), and on the opening night, he forgot the lyrics and made up some of the most foolish words ever sung on the American stage. Lew Fields, who produced this musical, was the father of Herbert Fields, who wrote the show's book. For the next year or so, this theatre was known as Lew Fields' Mansfield Theatre. *Present Arms* ran for 147 performances.

The next Rodgers/Hart/Fields musical at this theatre was a disaster. Called *Chee-Chee*, it was inspired by a novel called *The Son of the Grand Eunuch*, but critics did not find this musical comedy about castration amusing. St. John Ervine, critic for the New York *World*, snapped: "Nasty! Nasty! I did not believe that any act could possibly be duller than the first—until I saw the second."

Herbert and Dorothy Fields next provided a musical called *Hello, Daddy*, which was appropriate since their father, Lew Fields, produced it at his theatre and starred in it. It turned out to be the Mansfield's biggest hit so far, running for 198 performances. The catchy music was the work of Jimmy McHugh.

On February 26, 1930, a classic of the American theatre opened at the Mansfield and won the Pulitzer Prize for the season. It was Marc Connelly's magnificent adaptation of Roark Bradford's stories from the Old Testament, *Ol' Man Adam an' His Chillun*. Connelly's adaptation was called *The Green Pastures* and it had an enormous black cast. Many Broadway producers turned the script down, saying that a play about Old Testament incidents as viewed by southern blacks would never make it on Broadway. They were wrong. Richard B. Harrison, a sixty-six-year-old black, who had never acted before, gave an enthralling performance as de Lawd God Jehovah. *The Green*

🏹 LEFT: Antoinette Perry in the flop play *The Ladder*, which ran for 794 performances. ABOVE: Richard B. Harrison as "De Lawd" and Edna M. Harris as a "sinner" in the classic Marc Connelly play *The Green Pastures* (1930).

Pastures played for 640 performances and was also successful down South and wherever it was staged throughout the world.

During the Great Depression, the Chanin Brothers lost all six of the theatres they had built, including the Mansfield. From early March of 1932 until December of that year, the house was dark. Then, on December 26, it reopened with *Shuffle Along of 1933*, a successor to two former black musicals with similar titles. Once again the show was the work of Eubie Blake, Noble Sissle, and Flournoy Miller, who also appeared in the entertainment. Unfortunately, this edition only ran for seventeen performances.

The Mansfield's bookings in 1933–34 were sparse and undistinguished. A comedy called *Page Miss Glory*, directed by Goerge Abbott, was a moderate hit in November 1934. The cast included James Stewart, Charles D. Brown, Jane Seymour, Royal Beal, and Dorothy Hall. Another moderate hit, *Moon Over Mulberry Street*, moved in from the Lyceum in 1935, and this was followed by Osgood Perkins giving an excellent performance as a playwright who dreams that he is a character in his latest drama. The play was called *On Stage*, but it did not stay there for very long. It had a short run of forty-seven performances.

In January 1937, a lurid exposé of a Manhattan prostitution ring on Park Avenue called *Behind Red Lights* opened and stayed for 176 performances.

In 1940 Barry Fitzgerald, Sara Allgood, and Effie Shannon appeared in a successful revival of O'Casey's *Juno and the Paycock*. This was followed by *Separate Rooms*, a popular comedy that moved here from Maxine Elliott's Theatre. A West Coast revue, *Meet the People*, was a welcome Christmas present in 1940 and stayed for 160 performances. The cast included such bright talents as Jack Gilford, Nanette Farbares (later, Fabray), Jack Williams, Jack Albertson, Peggy Ryan, and many others.

The years 1942 and 1943 brought mostly failures to this theatre. A popular wartime comedy, *Janie*, which had already played at three other theatres, moved in for a few months in 1943–44. Then, on August 30, 1944, a bonanza arrived. *Anna Lucasta*, a play by Philip Yordan, was first done by the American Negro Theatre in Harlem (although the playwright wrote it for white actors). It was so successful that producer John Wildberg transferred it to the Mansfield Theatre with a few changes in the script. Directed by Harry Wagstaff Gribble and

superbly acted by Hilda Simms as the prostitute Anna, Canada Lee, Earle Hyman, and Frederick O'Neal, the drama ran for 957 performances.

Another hit arrived at this theatre on December 3, 1946. Actress Ruth Gordon switched to playwriting, and her autobiographical play, *Years Ago*, was warmly received. It starred Fredric March as her father, Florence Eldridge as her mother, and Bethel Leslie as Ruth Gordon Jones. The play recaptured Ms. Gordon's high school days in Massachusetts when she startled her parents and friends by announcing that she was going to New York to be an actress. The nostalgic hit played for 206 performances.

A lively revival of Marc Blitzstein's proletarian musical *The Cradle Will Rock* opened during the famed blizzard on December 26, 1947. The cast included such luminaries as Alfred Drake, Will Geer, Vivian Vance, Dennis King, Jr., Estelle Loring, Jack Albertson, and Leonard Bernstein, but it only lasted for two weeks at this theatre before it moved to another house. Charles Boyer gave a powerful performance in *Red Gloves* in December 1948, but the Jean-Paul Sartre play was too talky and full of messages for the public. The brilliant revue *Lend an Ear* moved in from another theatre in 1949 and played for three months. A mediocre play, *All You Need Is One Good Break*, was the last legitimate show to play the Mansfield. For the next decade, it functioned as a television playhouse.

When this theatre returned to legitimacy in 1960, producer Michael Myerberg was its owner/manager. The house was renovated and renamed the Brooks Atkinson Theatre in honor of the drama critic of the New York *Times*, who had retired from reviewing the previous spring. According to the PLAYBILL for that occasion, Mr. Atkinson was the first theatre critic in recorded theatrical history to have a theatre named for him.

TOP LEFT: Fredric March, Florence Eldridge in Ruth Gordon's auto-biographical play *Years Ago* (1946). ABOVE: Hilda Simms (standing), Early Hyman, Georgia Burke in *Anna Lucasta* (1944). LEFT: Barry Fitzgerald and Sara Allgood in a revival of *Juno and the Paycock* (1940).

The Brooks Atkinson opened on September 12, 1960, with a revue called *Vintage '60*. Although it was produced by David Merrick, with Zev Bufman, George Skaff, and Max Perkins, it lasted only eight performances. The next tenant, a comedy called *Send Me No Flowers*, with David Wayne and Nancy Olson, wilted after forty performances.

On February 22, 1961, Neil Simon's first play, *Come Blow Your Horn*, opened and it flourished for 677 performances. The cast featured Hal March, Sarah Marshall, Warren Berlinger, Lou Jacobi, and Pert Kelton. In late 1962, Sidney Kingsley's play *Night Life*, with Neville Brand, Walter Abel, Carmen Matthews, Carol Lawrence, Salome Jens, and Bobby Short, presented a realistic nightclub onstage, but the drama only lasted 63 performances. Peter Ustinov's comedy *Photo Finish* offered Ustinov as a writer with alter egos played by Dennis King, Donald Davis, and John Horton. Eileen Herlie, Jessica Walters, and Paul Rogers were also in the cast of this charade that ran for 160 performances in 1963.

The year 1964 started out disastrously at the Brooks Atkinson. Tennessee Williams decided to rewrite his unsuccessful play *The Milk Train Doesn't Stop Here Anymore*, and this time he turned it into, of all things, a Kabuki-style drama. The great Tallulah Bankhead made her last Broadway appearance in this error, and Tab Hunter, Ruth Ford, and Marian Seldes all went down the drain with her. It only played five times.

Josephine Baker made a dazzling personal appearance here in 1964, followed by the very controversial play, Rolf Hochhuth's *The Deputy*, which accused Pope Pius XII of having failed to denounce the Nazi extermination of the Jews. Emlyn Williams played the pope. The drama was picketed by Catholic organizations, but it managed to run for 318 performances. Julie Harris, Estelle Parsons, and Lou Antonio were next in a comedy called *Ready When You Are, C.B.!* Ms. Harris was praised for her acting, but the show closed after 80 performances. A revival of *The Glass Menagerie*, with Maureen Stapleton, George Grizzard, Pat Hingle, and Piper Laurie, was well received and lasted 176 performances in 1965.

From November 1965 until November 1967 the Brooks Atkinson housed a series of undistinguished plays. Peter Ustinov's *Halfway Up the Tree*, a generation gap comedy—with the younger generation winning out—was a moderately amusing play, with Eileen Herlie, Anthony Quayle, Sam Waterston, and Graham Jarvis; and Peter Nichols's macabre comedy *A Day in the Death of Joe Egg* had memorable performances by Albert Finney, Zena Walker, and Elizabeth Hubbard. Ms. Walker won a Tony Award as best featured actress in a drama.

Lovers and Other Strangers, a quartet of revue-style playlets by Renee Taylor and Joseph Bologna, in which they appeared, was amusing in 1968, as was *Jimmy Shine*, a Murray Schisgal comedy starring Dustin Hoffman that ran for 153 performances in 1968–69.

After a series of mishaps, the Brooks Atkinson booked *Lenny*, a play about the late Lenny Bruce. Written by Julian Barry, the stinging biographical study gave Cliff Gorman a part that won him a Tony Award for his tour de force performance. Brilliantly directed by Tom O'Horgan, who also wrote the play's music, *Lenny* presented a corrosive portrait of the drug-riddled, foul-mouthed comic, whose fame increased after he died. This "dynamite shtick of theatre," as critic Clive Barnes labeled it, played for 453 explosive performances.

In 1973 the Negro Ensemble Company transferred its successful play *The River Niger* from Off-Broadway to the Brooks Atkinson, where it remained for 280 performances. Written by Joseph A. Walker and directed by Douglas Turner Ward, who also appeared in the play,

it won a Tony Award as the best drama of the season. In January 1974 Michael Moriarty gave a stunning performance as a homosexual hustler in *Find Your Way Home*, by John Hopkins, and was rewarded with a Tony. Jane Alexander costarred with him. The British comedy *My Fat Friend*, with Lynn Redgrave and George Rose, brought laughter to this theatre in 1974, and was followed by a revival of John Steinbeck's powerful play *Of Mice and Men*, with James Earl Jones as Lenny and Kevin Conway as George.

On March 13, 1975, a comedy with only two performers—Ellen Burstyn and Charles Grodin—opened at the Brooks Atkinson and it stayed for 1,453 performances, making it this theatre's record holder. It was Bernard Slade's *Same Time, Next Year*—a merry romp about a couple who meet every year in a motel for a sexual tryst, unknown to their respective spouses. Ms. Burstyn won a Tony Award for her beguiling performance.

Jack Lemmon returned to Broadway in another play by Bernard Slade—*Tribute*—in 1978, and his performance was rated better than the play. The British comedy *Bedroom Farce* had some hilarious moments and won Tony Awards for Michael Gough and Joan Hickson as best featured actors in a play.

Teibele and Her Demon, a play by Isaac Bashevis Singer and Eve Friedman, did not succeed in 1979, but *Talley's Folly*, one of Lanford Wilson's cycle plays about the Talley family, moved here from Off-Broadway's Circle Rep with its original cast—Judd Hirsch and Trish Hawkins—and scored a triumph. Directed by Marshall W. Mason, the play won the Pulitzer Prize and the Drama Critics Circle Award for best play.

Four unsuccessful plays followed: *Tricks of the Trade* (1980), with George C. Scott and his wife, Trish Van Devere; *Mixed Couples* (1980), with Julie Harris, Geraldine Page, and Rip Torn;

 Ellen Burstyn and Charles Grodin in the smash comedy about infidelity *Same Time, Next Year* (1975).

Edward Albee's adaptation of *Lolita* (1981), with Blanche Baker as the nymphet and Donald Sutherland as Humbert Humbert; and *Wally's Café* (1981), with Rita Moreno, James Coco, and Sally Struthers.

The British play *The Dresser* (1981), by Ronald Harwood, starred Tom Courtenay as a dresser to an aging drunk actor, played by Paul Rogers, and the fascinating drama played for 200 performances. Christopher Durang's Off-Broadway hit *Beyond Therapy* did not repeat its success on Broadway in 1982. Liv Ullmann and John Neville appeared in a revival of Ibsen's *Ghosts* for a few weeks, and the British comedy *Steaming* won a Tony Award for Judith Ivey as best supporting actress in a play. Patrick Meyers's thrilling play *K2* was about two mountain climbers—Jeffrey DeMunn and Jay Patterson—trapped on a small ledge on the second-

highest mountain in the world. The incredible set for this drama won a Tony Award for its designer, Ming Cho Lee.

The next show at this theatre was the British hit comedy *Noises Off*, starring Dorothy Loudon, Brian Murray, Paxton Whitehead, Victor Garber, and Linda Thorson.

The Brooks Atkinson is owned and operated by the Messrs. Nederlander, with Arthur Rubin as general manager. It has been refurbished in recent years and its capacity of 999 seats makes it ideally suited for the staging of dramas and comedies.

 Paul Rogers (seated) and Tom Courtenay in the British play *The Dresser* (1981).

⚜ ROYALE THEATRE ⚜

The Royal Theatre at 242 West Forty-fifth Street was one of the six legitimate theatres built by the Chanin Brothers in the 1920s. In describing the new house, the New York *Times* reported that it was "comfortable, with plenty of leg room around the seats." The theatre was done in modern Spanish style, had two murals, "Lovers of Spain" by Willy Pogany, on the walls, and the general color scheme was cardinal red, orange, and gold. Not surprisingly, once again the architect was the busy Herbert J. Krapp.

With a seating capacity of a little over 1,000, the Royale opened on January 11, 1927, with a musical comedy called *Piggy*. The popular comic Sam Bernard played a monocled Englishman whose son (Paul Frawley) falls in love with an American girl. Brooks Atkinson in the *Times* called it an "average musical comedy" and highly praised the dancing of Goodee Montgomery, whom he identified as the daughter of the late and still lamented Dave Montgomery of the famed Montgomery and Stone team. The following day, the *Times* carried a correction. Miss Goodee was Montgomery's niece. Shortly after this show opened, the producer changed its name to *I Told You So* (a very rare

practice in the theatre) and it ran for seventy-nine performances.

The Royale's next musical, *Judy*, starred the bubbly Queenie Smith and romantic Charles Purcell. One of the songs was titled "When Gentlemen Grew Whiskers and Ladies Grew Old." *Judy* pleased the nostalgia crowd for 104 performances.

A musical version of Oscar Wilde's *The Importance of Being Ernest*, retitled *Oh, Ernest!*, did not last long, but a black revue called *Rang Tang* fared better in 1927, running for 119 performances. The dancing in this show was highly praised by the critics. The *Times* referred to the revue as "a blackamoor folderol."

The Winthrop Ames's Gilbert and Sullivan Opera Company moved into the Royale in September 1927 and performed *The Mikado*, *Iolanthe*, and *The Pirates of Penzance* for a very successful three months. A popular, but aging entertainer named Mitzi next appeared in *The Madcap*, a very silly musical about an older woman (Mitzi) who pretends to be much younger in order to win Lord Clarence Steeple (Sydney Greenstreet). Arthur Treacher was also in this nonsense, which ran for 103 performances.

After its diet of musicals only, the Royale

ABOVE: John Halliday and Jane Cowl in S.N. Behrman's thoughtful comedy, *Rain From Heaven* (1935). TOP RIGHT (from left): Frieda Inescort and Selena Royle in Rachel Crothers's comedy *When Ladies Meet* (1932). RIGHT: Standard program cover for the Royale in the 1920s and early 1930.

played its first straight show in 1928. It was *Sh! The Octopus*, described by an overzealous press agent as a "sneaky, snaky, slimy mystery." The murderous doings took place in a lighthouse, and since there is little prospect that this show will be revived, it can be revealed that the plot turned out to be nothing but a dream.

The Royale had its first bona fide hit on April 9, 1928, when Mae West starred in her own play, *Diamond Lil*, a melodrama of the 1890s in the Bowery. This devil's brew bubbled for 323 performances. The year 1929 ended at the Royale with an item called *Woof, Woof*, a musical that featured not one, but two live whippet races onstage. They only ran 46 times.

The Second Little Show, a revue successor to the highly successful *The Little Show*, opened at the Royale on September 2, 1930, but did not measure up to the first edition. Although the score was by the illustrious Howard Dietz and Arthur Schwartz, it was a song by Herman Hupfeld that swept the nation —"Sing Something Simple." It managed only sixty-three performances. A popular farce called *Stepping Sisters* played two engagements at this theatre in 1930–31. Mae West returned to the Royale in 1931 with her latest play, *The Constant Sinner*, but it wasn't sinful enough and ran for only sixty-four performances. Mae announced that she might do some matinees of *Macbeth* and play Lady Macbeth herself, but the project, unfortunately, never got off the ground. Instead, Fritz Leiber and his Chicago Civic Shakespeare Society arrived in *The Merchant of Venice* (1931). His company included Helen Menken, Tyrone Power (Sr.), William Faversham, Pedro De Cordoba, Viola Roache, and Whitford Kane.

Rachel Crothers had another hit play, *When Ladies Meet*, which opened at the Royale on October 6, 1932, starring Frieda Inescort, Walter Abel, Spring Byington, and Selena Royle.

The Theatre Guild production of Maxwell Anderson's exposé of corruption in the nation's capital, *Both Your Houses*, was brilliantly acted by Shepperd Strudwick, Morris Carnovsky, Walter C. Kelly, Mary Philips, J. Edward Bromberg, and others, but it only managed to play for seventy-two performances. A comedy called *Every Thursday*, starring Queenie Smith, opened in May of 1934, and it was the last play at the Royale before the theatre changed its name.

John Golden, the famous theatrical producer, owned the John Golden Theatre on West Fifty-Eighth Street between Broadway and Seventh Avenue, but he lost it in 1933. In 1934 he leased the Royale and renamed it the Golden Theatre. The first production under the new management was Norman Krasna's comedy *Small Miracle*, which opened on September 26, 1934. Directed by George Abbott, this unusual play took place in a theatre lobby and chronicled the lives of the theatre's patrons who congregated there. The large cast included Ilka Chase, Joseph Spurin-Calleia, Myron McCormick, Elsbeth Eric, and many others. It prospered for 118 performances.

In November 1934 the Abbey Theatre Players from Dublin opened at the Golden in a repertoire of plays that were changed weekly. Headed by Barry Fitzgerald, the company presented such Irish classics as *The Plough and the Stars*, *The Far-off Hills*, *The Shadow of the Glen*, *The Playboy of the Western World*, and *Drama at Inish*. On Christmas Eve, the Theatre Guild presented one of S.N. Behrman's most thoughtful drawing room comedies, *Rain from Heaven*, with Jane Cowl, John Halliday, Lily Cahill, Ben Smith, and Thurston Hall. Contemporary problems—fascism, Nazism, communism, Lindberg hero worship—were brilliantly discussed by intellectuals of opposing viewpoints during a country weekend in England.

The remainder of 1935 was devoted to a comedy, *The Bishop Misbehaves*, starring Walter Connolly, which moved here from the Cort Theatre, and an acerbic play, *A Touch of Brimstone*, with Roland Young as a very nasty theatrical producer who took perverse delight in mistreating people. (Shades of Jed Harris?)

During 1936 the Golden Theatre had a series of short-run shows. Some of the more interesting ones were the return of eighty-year-old actor William Gillette, after four years of retirement, in a revival of *Three Wise Fools*, with Charles Coburn; Nazimova in *Ghosts*, which returned after a tour and played for a month at a $1.65 top; and *Double Dummy*, a "farce-satire" about contract bridge, with Martha Sleeper, Dudley Clements, and John McGovern.

From 1937 until 1940 the Golden Theatre ceased functioning as a legitimate theatre. It became the CBS Radio Theatre. When this occurred, producer John Golden leased the Masque Theatre next door and turned it into the John Golden Theatre and it has remained so ever since.

In October 1940 the former Golden Theatre was taken over by the Magoro Operating Corporation, which restored this theatre's original name: the Royale. It has kept that name ever since. To clarify matters: first, this theatre was the Royale, then it became the Golden, then the CBS Radio Theatre, and, finally, the Royale again.

The hit Cole Porter musical *DuBarry Was a Lady* moved from the 46th Street Theatre to the Royale on October 21, 1940, minus one of its stars—Ethel Merman—who was succeeded by Gypsy Rose Lee. Bert Lahr was still the star of the show. It stayed for two months. This was followed by Elmer Rice's *Flight to the West* (1940), from the Guild Theatre, and Ethel Barrymore in her hit *The Corn Is Green* (1940), which transferred from the National Theatre. Paul Muni returned in a revival of Elmer Rice's *Counsellor-at-Law* (1942), one of his earlier hits. It ran for 258 performances. The daffy ZaSu Pitts arrived in a melodramatic farce, *Ramshackle*

Inn (1944), and her Hollywood fans supported this ramshackle play for 216 performances.

The critics scorned *School for Brides*, a Chicago hit that came East with Roscoe Karns and a bevy of beauties in the summer of 1944, but the public bought it for 375 performances. Michael Todd's spectacular production of *Catherine Was Great*, with the mistress of triple entendre, Mae West, moved here from the Shubert and pulverized the local yokels for three more months. Another sex comedy that was a smash in Chicago—*Good Night, Ladies* (1945)—came East and was assassinated by the New York Drama Critics Circle. The public listened to their betters this time and the farce left after 78 performances. A stage adaptation of Lillian Smith's best-seller *Strange Fruit* expired after 60 performances in 1945.

The distinguished veteran producer Arthur Hopkins presented Louis Calhern as Justice Holmes and Dorothy Gish as his loving wife in Emmet Lavery's *The Magnificent Yankee* in January 1946 and it ran a respectable 160 performances. Tennessee Williams's first Broadway play, *The Glass Menagerie*, with triumphant performances by the great Laurette Taylor, Eddie Dowling, Julie Haydon, and Anthony Ross, moved here from the Playhouse in 1946. This was followed by a moderately successful revival of *The Front Page*, with Lew Parker and Arnold Moss. The radiant Ina Claire returned to the stage in George Kelly's amusing comedy *The Fatal Weakness*, about a romantic woman (Ms. Claire) who loves to attend weddings, even if the groom happens to be a former husband of hers.

A stylish revival of Wilde's *The Importance of Being Earnest* starred John Gielgud (who also staged it), Margaret Rutherford, and Robert Flemyng in 1947 and achieved a run of 81 performances. Gielgud and Flemyng returned to the Royale in May in a revival of William Congreve's artificial bore *Love for Love*, which

the Belasco in 1949 and stayed for four months. *Dance Me a Song*, an intimate revue, was not a hit, but it served to introduce the delightful comic Wally Cox, who wrote his own very funny monologues. This was followed by a revival of Shaw's *The Devil's Disciple*, with Maurice Evans, Dennis King, Victor Jory, and Marsha Hunt, staged by Margaret Webster for 111 performances. Next came a London hit, Christopher Fry's verse play *The Lady's Not for Burning*, starring John Gielgud (who also directed it), Richard Burton, and Pamela Brown, which made pleasant rhymes for 151 performances. Sidney Kingsley's powerful dramatization of Arthur Koestler's novel *Darkness at Noon* moved

ABOVE: Herald for Ina Claire in George Kelly's romantic comedy *The Fatal Weakness* (1946). RIGHT: Audrey Christie and Sam Levene in Moss Hart's theatre comedy *Light Up The Sky* (1948).

left town after 48 showings. In December 1947 Judith Anderson returned from a triumphant tour in *Medea* and continued to kill her helpless babes for five more months. Moss Hart's acidulous comedy about theatre folks trying out a show in Boston, *Light Up the Sky*, arrived in November 1948 and provoked hysteria for 214 performances. Sam Levene played a vulgar producer, Audrey Christie acted his loudmouth wife, and Broadway insisted that the characters were modeled after Billy Rose and his then wife, Olympic swimmer Eleanor Holm.

Alfred de Liagre's memorable production of *The Madwoman of Chaillot* moved here from

🦋 Back cover of souvenir program for *New Faces* of 1952.

here from the Alvin and played for three more months in 1951.

Borscht Capades, described as an "English-Yiddish revue," pleased the critics and ran for ninety performances. Another revue—Leonard Sillman's *New Faces of 1952*, which opened here on May 16, 1952—turned out to be the best show of this series and one of the finest revues in Broadway history. Staged by the great revue director John Murray Anderson, the cast included such bright talents as Paul Lynde, Ronny Graham, June Carroll, Eartha Kitt, Robert Clary, Alice Ghostley, Carol Lawrence, and many others. The smash ran for 365 performances and was one of the few Broadway revues that was filmed by Hollywood.

Billy Rose presented a stage adaptation of André Gide's novel *The Immoralist*, with Geraldine Page as a wife who has married a homosexual, played by Louis Jordan. In the cast was the young James Dean as a North African homosexual who attempts to lure the husband to the local date grove. The daring play ran for 104 performances in 1954.

A British musical, *The Boy Friend*, by Sandy Wilson, opened at the Royale on September 30, 1954, and captivated Manhattan. This diverting parody of 1920s musicals introduced Julie Andrews to Broadway and she was a delight. The spoof ran for 485 performances. This theatre had another smash hit in Thornton Wilder's *The Matchmaker*, which opened on December 5, 1955. The play had a very curious history. Wilder first wrote it as *The Merchant of Yonkers*, but it flopped on Broadway in 1938, despite direction by the famed Max Reinhardt, and Jane Cowl and Percy Waram in the leading roles. But this raucous version—staged by Tyrone Guthrie and vividly performed by Ruth Gordon, Loring Smith, Robert Morse, Eileen Herlie, and Arthur Hill—rang the bell for 486 performances. Mr. Guthrie won a Tony Award for his galvanic staging of this comedy, which was later converted to the celebrated musical *Hello, Dolly!*

The Tunnel of Love, a minor comedy by Joseph Fields and Peter DeVries, managed to run for 417 performances in 1957, probably because of the popularity of its leading man, Tom Ewell. Nancy Olson, Darren McGavin, and Elizabeth Wilson were also in this comedy about a childless suburban couple who wish to adopt a baby.

Laurence Olivier gave a memorable performance as a seedy vaudeville actor in John Osborne's rather boring play *The Entertainer* (1958). The cast included Olivier's wife, Joan Plowright, Brenda de Banzie, Peter Donat, and Jeri Archer, who played Britannia as a topless statue who did not move. David Merrick, the producer of this British play, did not allow Ms. Archer to take a curtain call, stating that she would be too distracting to the audience.

ABOVE: Sir Laurence Olivier in John Osborne's *The Entertainer* (1958). TOP RIGHT: Julie Andrews (center) and flappers in Sandy Wilson's spoof of 1920s musicals, *The Boy Friend* (1954). RIGHT: Bette Davis in Tennessee Williams's *The Night of the Iguana* (1961).

🎭 Lauren Bacall in the long-running comedy *Cactus Flower* (1965).

The 1950s came to a dazzling close at this theatre with the lunatic French revue *La Plume de Ma Tante*, which opened on November 11, 1958, and stayed for 835 performances. Robert Dhery conceived, wrote, and starred in this uproarious vaudeville explosion, and the entire cast won Tony Awards as the best featured performers in a musical.

Highlights of the 1960s at this theatre included Laurence Olivier and Anthony Quinn in Jean Anouilh's *Becket* (1960), which moved here from the St. James; *From the Second City* (1961), a hit Chicago revue with Alan Arkin, Barbara Harris, Paul Sand, and others; Tennessee Williams's *The Night of the Iguana* (1961), starring Bette Davis, Patrick O'Neal, Alan Webb, and Margaret Leighton, who won a Tony Award for her luminous performance; Charles Boyer in S.N. Behrman's high comedy about an art

dealer, *Lord Pengo* (1962), with Agnes Moorehead, Brian Bedford, and Henry Daniell; Coral Browne and Keith Michell in Anouilh's *The Rehearsal* (1963); Margaret Leighton, John Williams, Alan Webb, Peter Donat, and Douglas Watson in Enid Bagnold's *The Chinese Prime Minister* (1964); Frank D. Gilroy's *The Subject Was Roses* (1964), the Pulitzer Prize play with Jack Albertson (who won a Tony Award for his performance), Irene Dailey, and Martin Sheen; Jason Robards in Eugene O'Neill's *Hughie* (1964); Lauren Bacall, Barry Nelson, Robert Moore, and Brenda Vaccaro in *Cactus Flower* (1965), adapted from a French comedy by Abe Burrows, which ran for 1,234 performances; Donald Pleasence in Robert Shaw's play *The Man in the Glass Booth* (1968), directed by Harold Pinter.

The 1970s brought Robert Marasco's chilling

🎭 Martin Sheen (seated), Irene Dailey and Jack Albertson in *The Subject Was Roses* (1964).

Child's Play (1970), with Ken Howard, Pat Hingle, Fritz Weaver, and David Rounds; Michael Weller's fascinating play *Moonchildren* (1972); and the record-breaking musical *Grease*, which moved to the Royale from the Broadhurst in 1972 and stayed until April 13, 1980. It became the longest-running musical in Broadway history with 3,388 performances. (In September 1983, it was surpassed by *A Chorus Line*, which now holds first position.)

An unusual event occurred at this theatre in February 1980. The British play *Whose Life Is It Anyway?*, in which Tom Conti won a Tony Award for his performance as a man who is paralyzed from the neck down, was revised to make the hero a heroine. Mary Tyler Moore played the part in the revised version, which ran at the Royale for ninety-six performances. The experiment was considered a success.

Next came a screwball musical, *A Day in Hollywood, A Night in the Ukraine*, which moved here from the John Golden Theatre and won a Tony Award for Priscilla Lopez as best featured actress in a musical and another for cochoreographers Tommy Tune and Thommie Walsh.

The Royale's most recent tenants have been *Duet for One*, a short-lived play starring Anne Bancroft and Max von Sydow, and the long-running *Joseph and the Amazing Technicolor Dream Coat*, which moved here from the Entermedia Theatre on January 27, 1982. The Andrew Lloyd Webber/Tim Rice musical had a number of actors in the leading role of Joseph, including Bill Hutton, Richard Hilton, Doug Voet, Allen Fawcett, Andy Gibb, and David Cassidy.

The Royale is a Shubert Organization theatre and is perfect for the staging of dramas, comedies, and intimate musicals. It is ideally located on West Forty-fifth Street, traditionally known as "the street of hits."

⚜ JOHN GOLDEN THEATRE ⚜

The John Golden Theatre at 252 West Forty-fifth Street was originally named the Theatre Masque. It was the fifth theatre built by the Chanin Brothers, and once again they chose Herbert J. Krapp as their architect. This house was their smallest, with 800 seats, and the Chanins announced that it aimed to be "the home of fine plays of the 'artistic' or 'intimate' type." They also reiterated their philosophy that their theatres were built to afford ease and comfort to actors as well as playgoers.

The New York *Times* reviewed the first production at the Theatre Masque, an Italian play called *Puppets of Passion,* which opened on February 24, 1927, and the paper liked the new playhouse more than the new play. "Like all the Chanin houses," wrote critic Brooks Atkinson, "the Theatre Masque is pleasing and comfortable. The architecture is modern Spanish in character, and the interior of the house is decorated in pastel shades, trimmed in grayish blues and reds." Of the play, which had Frank Morgan in the cast, Atkinson wrote that it moved along at a funereal pace. It expired after twelve performances.

The theatre's next attraction fared better. It ran for fifteen performances. This was a play called *The Comic,* with J.C. Nugent, Patricia Collinge, and Rex O'Malley, and the program stated that it was written by one Lajos Luria, a pseudonym for a famous serious European dramatist who wouldn't use his real name on a comedy.

During the remainder of 1927 this theatre housed a revival of the Gilbert and Sullivan operetta *Patience*; a play about the corruption of the Harding administration in Washington, *Revelry*; Lionel Atwill in a sorry swashbuckler, *The King Can Do No Wrong*; and finally, a misguided comedy called *Venus,* by the usually skillful Rachel Crothers, who, this time out, wrote a futuristic play about man's first flight to the planet Venus. Her play was visible for only eight performances.

Things did not improve much in 1928. There were eight productions produced here and only one ran more than a hundred performances. This was an ethnic comedy called *Relations,* written by and starring Edward Clark. *The Scarlet Fox,* written by and starring Willard Mack, ran for seventy-nine performances; and *Young Love,* by Samson Raphaelson, starring Dorothy Gish and James Rennie, lasted for eighty-seven performances.

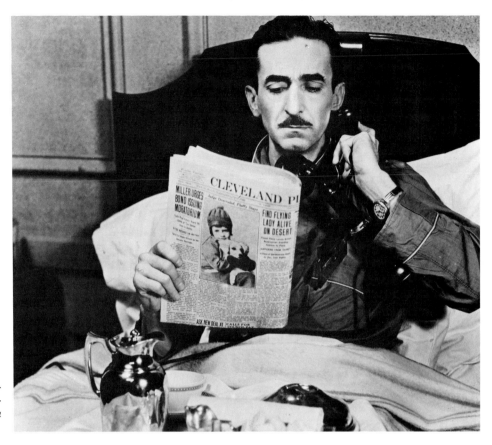

Osgood Perkins as a best-selling novelist besieged by female fans in *Goodbye Again* (1932).

Theatre Masque's biggest hit in 1929 was a macabre drama called *Rope's End*, by British playwright Patrick Hamilton. The play detailed the grisly murder of an Oxford undergraduate by two upperclassmen, just for kicks. Although the playwright denied it, he was obviously influenced by the similar murder of a young boy in Chicago by Leopold and Loeb, two intellectuals who also committed a thrill kill. In *Rope's End*, the murderers put their victim's body in a chest, then invite his father and aunt to dinner. The meal is served on the chest. Alfred Hitchcock made a rarely shown film of this play and called it *Rope*.

In early 1930 the hit play *Broken Dishes*, with Bette Davis and Donald Meek, moved here from the Ritz and played for three months. A comedy about life in Greenwich Village, *Up Pops*

the Devil, with Roger Pryor, Sally Bates, Brian Donlevy, and Albert Hackett (who coauthored the play with Frances Goodrich) ran for 146 performances that year. An interesting but unsuccessful drama, *Brass Ankle*, by DuBose Heyward (who later wrote *Porgy and Bess* with the Gershwins) starred Alice Brady in 1931.

A Norman Krasna farce about Hollywood, *Louder, Please!*, was a moderate success in 1931. It starred Lee Tracy as a loudmouth publicity man and it was directed at top speed by George Abbott. A much bigger hit was *Goodbye Again*, a comedy in which Osgood Perkins felicitously played a novelist who tries to renew an old affair while on a publicity tour for his latest book. This romantic trifle kept the Theatre Masque full for 212 performances in 1932–33.

The 1934 hit was a play about kidnapping

🎭 Sir Cedric Hardwicke and Julie Haydon in Paul Vincent Carroll's spiritual play *Shadow and Substance* (1938).

derful mimic Cecilia Loftus was Mrs. Watson.

On February 2, 1937, the Masque became the John Golden Theatre, making it the third house named after the illustrious theatrical producer. Its first play was *And Now Good-bye*, a drama based on a James Hilton novel, starring Philip Merivale as a reverend who falls in love with a parishioner. It was not successful.

A radiant play, *Shadow and Substance*, by Paul Vincent Carroll arrived in January 1938 and was acclaimed by the drama critics. It had shining performances by the ethereal Julie Haydon as the servant to an intellectual snob and by Sir Cedric Hardwicke, who played her employer. The spiritual play found favor and stayed for 206 performances. The following year, another memorable play by Paul Vincent Carroll, *The White Steed*, moved here from the Cort. It starred Jessica Tandy and Barry Fitzgerald.

On December 5, 1941, a Victorian thriller called *Angel Street* opened here, with Judith Evelyn, Vincent Price, and Leo G. Carroll. Produced by Shepard Traube, in association with Alexander H. Cohen, it was not expected to succeed, and consequently, only a three-day supply of PLAYBILL magazines was ordered. The producers underestimated their show. It played for 1,293 times, making it the longest-running play in this theatre's history up to that time.

Rose Franken's comedy *Soldier's Wife* found an audience in 1944 and ran for 255 performances. The play, which had a star-studded cast —Martha Scott, Frieda Inescort, Lili Darvas, Glenn Anders, and Myron McCormick—was not a war play. It was about a woman who wrote a best-seller and the problems it incurred on her family.

The remainder of the 1940s brought a number of shows to this theatre, but none was outstanding. Among them were: *The Rich Full Life* (1945), with Judith Evelyn and Virginia Weidler; S.N. Behrman's *Dunnigan's Daughter*

called *Post Road*, with delirious performances by Lucile Watson and Percy Kilbride. The following year brought J.B. Priestley's *Laburnum Grove*, starring Edmund Gwenn, Elizabeth Risdon, and Melville Cooper, which moved here from the Booth. In 1936 *Russet Mantle*, a pleasant play about Santa Fe characters by Lynn Riggs, moved in and stayed for 116 performances. There was much praise for the actors —Evelyn Varden, John Beal, Martha Sleeper, Margaret Douglass, Jay Fassett, and others.

The last show to play the Masque before it changed its name was *The Holmses of Baker Street*, in which Sherlock's daughter (Helen Chandler) proved that she was as good a sleuth as her old man. Cyril Scott played Sherlock, Conway Wingfield was Dr. Watson, and the won-

Charles Dickens (1952); Cornelia Otis Skinner in *Paris '90* (1952), a monodrama that moved here from the Booth; the long-running comedy *The Fourposter* (1952–53), which moved here from the Ethel Barrymore.

On October 2, 1953, the witty Victor Borge opened at this theatre in a one-man show called *Comedy in Music*. Mr. Borge played the piano and indulged in dead-pan patter and lampoons that kept audiences in stitches for 849 performances.

In 1956, comic Bert Lahr gave one of his most unforgettable performances as Gogo in Samuel Beckett's *Waiting for Godot*. It was a radical departure for this famed revue and musical comedy star and the critics hailed

ABOVE: Sketch of Victor Borge in *Comedy in Music* on souvenir program (1953). RIGHT: Vincent Price and Judith Evelyn in the celebrated thriller *Angel Street* (1941).

(1945), with June Havoc, Dennis King, Richard Widmark, Jan Sterling, and Luther Adler; *January Thaw* (1946), with Robert Keith and Lulu Mae Hubbard; and *I Like It Here* (1946), with Oscar Karlweis and Bert Lytel.

From mid-1946 until February 1948 the John Golden was leased as a motion picture theatre. It returned to legitimacy on February 29, 1948, with Maurice Chevalier in a one-man show of songs and impressions.

Highlights of the 1950s at the John Golden included Grace George and Walter Hampden in *The Velvet Glove* (1950), which moved here from the Booth; Emlyn Williams in a solo performance of six scenes from the works of

🦋 Bert Lahr as "Gogo" in Samuel Beckett's surrealistic *Waiting for Godot* (1956).

him. Also in the cast were E.G. Marshall, Kurt Kasznar, and Alvin Epstein.

Menasha Skulnik appeared in a comedy, *Uncle Willie*, in late 1956 and stayed for 141 performances. The play was a variant of *Abie's Irish Rose*, focusing on an Irish and a Jewish family who are neighbors.

John Osborn's vitriolic hit *Look Back in Anger* moved here from the Lyceum in 1958 and stayed for six months. *A Party with Betty Comden and Adolph Green*, with the popular duo singing their witty lyrics from Broadway musicals and Hollywood films, was welcomed in 1958–59, as was the *Billy Barnes Revue* from the West Coast. The British duo of Michael Flanders and Donald Swann scored a hit in their two-man revue *At the Drop of a Hat* (1959–60).

One of the John Golden's most cherished entertainments was the brilliant Alexander H. Cohen production of *An Evening with Mike Nichols and Elaine May*. Even their biographies in PLAYBILL, which they wrote themselves, were hilarious. The duo presented some of their classic comedy sketches that satirized everyday foibles and they kept the John Golden Theatre quaking with laughter for 306 performances in 1960–61.

An Evening with Yves Montand (1961) also proved a hit, with the French actor/singer charming audiences in a one-man show. Robert Redford appeared here in *Sunday in New York*, a fair comedy by Norman Krasna that moved to the Golden from the Cort Theatre in 1962. On October 27, 1962, a tornado of mirth called *Beyond the Fringe* arrived from England and fractured audiences for 673 performances. This Alexander H. Cohen import was a delirious revue written and performed by Alan Bennett, Peter Cook, Jonathan Miller, and Dudley Moore; Mr. Cohen staged the uproar.

In 1964 Victor Borge returned to the Golden with another edition of his *Comedy in Music, Opus 2*, which was good enough for 192 performances. Another hit revue, *Wait a Minim*, opened here in 1966, bringing eight extremely personable and talented performers from South Africa. Their zany entertainment delighted theatregoers for 457 performances. The remainder of the 1960s brought seven shows, but only two of them were of much interest: John Bowen's British play *After the Rain* (1967) with Alec McCowen, and the British actor Roy Dotrice in his one-man show, *Brief Lives*, about an English antiquarian named John Aubrey.

Highlights of the 1970s included *Bob and Ray—The Two and Only* (1970), a two-

ABOVE: PLAYBILL covers for *An Evening with Mike Nichols and Elaine May* (1960) and David Rabe's *Sticks and Bones* (1972). RIGHT: Dudley Moore (at piano), Alan Bennett and Jonathan Miller (standing on piano) and Peter Cook in the witty British revue *Beyond the Fringe* (1962).

ABOVE: Jessica Tandy and Hume Cronyn in the Pulitzer Prize play *The Gin Game* (1977). RIGHT (from left): Kathy Bates and Anne Pitoniak in the Pulitzer Prize play, *'night, Mother* (1983).

man show featuring the popular radio comics Bob Elliott and Ray Goulding; David Rabe's *Sticks and Bones* (1972), which won a Tony Award for best play of the season; *Words and Music* (1974), a revue featuring the songs of Sammy Cahn, who appeared in the show with Kelly Garrett, Jon Peck, and Shirley Lemmon; Robert Patrick's *Kennedy's Children* (1975), with Shirley Knight, who won a Tony Award as best supporting actress of the season; Tom Stoppard's *Dirty Linen* and *New-Found-Land* (1977), two plays in one, performed without intermission; D.L. Coburn's *The Gin Game* (1977), a Pulitzer Prize play that starred Hume Cronyn and Jessica Tandy, who won a Tony Award for her performance; a revival of Lillian Hellman's *Watch on the Rhine* (1980); *A Day in Hollywood, A Night in the Ukraine* (1980), a double bill combining a revue about Hollywood

musicals of the 1930s with a parody of a Marx Brothers movie, with Priscilla Lopez winning a Tony Award for her performance and Tommy Tune and Thommie Walsh also winning a Tony for their choreography; *Tintypes* (1980), a diverting revue of turn-of-the-century songs, which moved to the John Golden from the Off-Broadway Theatre of St. Peter's Church; Beth Henley's Pulitzer Prize play *Crimes of the Heart* (1981), which transferred here from the Off-Broadway Manhattan Theatre Club; and the current tenant, Marsha Norman's Pulitzer Prize play *'night, Mother*, with Kathy Bates as a daughter who announces to her mother (Anne Pitoniak) that she intends to commit suicide.

The John Golden is currently a Shubert Organization Theatre. It has been very successful as a house for intimate revues, one- and two-man shows, and dramatic plays with small casts. In the past six years, it has presented three Pulitzer Prize plays, an enviable record for any theatre.

⚜ MAJESTIC THEATRE ⚜

The Majestic Theatre at 245 West Forty-forth Street, right off the corner of Eighth Avenue, was the sixth and last of the houses built by the Chanin Brothers. With a seating capacity of 1,800 seats, it was the largest legitimate theatre in the Times Square district and was primarily suited for the staging of lavish musical comedies and revues.

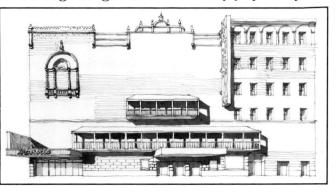

Architect Herbert J. Krapp used the same stadium-style design for this house as he had for the Chanins' first theatre, the 46th Street. The orchestra was built on a steep slope, and patrons had to climb stairs to reach the rear section of the orchestra. There was only one balcony. The New York *Times* described the architecture and decoration of the interior as being in the Louis XV style with a color scheme of gold and ivory. "The house curtain, the valence, the box drapes and panels on the side walls are of gold and rose silk damask," the paper reported. "As in other Chanin houses, the seats are said to be three inches wider than the ordinary theatre chair."

The Majestic Theatre opened on March 28, 1927, with a revue curiously called *Rufus LeMaire's Affairs*, probably because the show's producer was named Rufus LeMaire. Despite such talents as Ted Lewis, Charlotte Greenwood, and Peggy Fears, the show was a dud and only played fifty-six times. This was succeeded by a black revue, *Rang Tang*, that moved here from the Royale Theatre and stayed for two months. A Sigmund Romberg musical play called *The Love Call* was next, but this, too, didn't tarry more than eighty-one performances. An extremely elaborate Gilbert Miller production, *The Patriot*, had John Gielgud in the cast and, considering the reviews, should have run longer than twelve performances in 1928. George Kelly's play *Behold the Bridegroom*, which critic Burns Mantle named one of the year's ten best plays, moved to the Majestic from the Cort Theatre in February 1928. It starred Judith Anderson, Jean Dixon, Mary Servoss, Thurston Hall, and Lester Vail, but it ran only eighty-eight performances.

Ziegfeld's enormous hit *Rio Rita* (1928) moved to the Majestic after playing some months at the splendid new Ziegfeld Theatre. An unusual event occurred on September 18,

1928. Champion boxer Jack Dempsey made his Broadway debut at the Majestic in a drama called, aptly, *The Big Fight*, in which he had to knock out another boxer to win the hand of a manicurist named Shirley. The critics rated his boxing better than his acting and the novelty wore off after thirty-one rounds.

The Majestic's biggest hit thus far was a revue called *Pleasure Bound*, with Phil Baker, Jack Pearl, Grace Brinkley, and others. The dances were by the young Busby Berkeley and the show made it to 136 performances. The Shuberts produced a new version of *Die Fledermaus* called *A Wonderful Night*, and the star was a young stilt walker from England called Archie Leach, who became better known in Hollywood as Cary Grant. This Johann Strauss bauble played for 125 performances.

In February 1930 *The International Revue* opened here and it should have been a triumph. It cost $200,000 to mount (an exorbitant amount for that depression era) and it had such luminaries in the cast as Gertrude Lawrence, Harry Richman, Jack Pearl, ballet star Anton Dolin, the great Spanish dancer Argentinita, Moss and Fontana, and the Chester Hale Girls. It also had two song hits by Dorothy Fields and Jimmy McHugh that have become standards: "On the Sunny Side of the Street" and "Exactly Like You." But the revue was earthbound. On the opening night, it was so long that the second act did not begin until 11:00 P.M., and the highly touted Argentinita laid an egg.

The Shuberts' next venture, an operetta called *Nina Rosa*, by Sigmund Romberg, Otto Harbach, and Irving Caesar, ran 129 times. It starred Ethelind Terry (the famed star of *Rio Rita*) and Guy Robertson and it had a novel setting—the Peruvian Andes. A revival of Romberg's *The Student Prince* in 1931 fared less well, running for 45 performances. The depression was felt by this theatre in 1932, when it was dark for many months.

In January 1933 much was expected of *Pardon My English*, a musical by George and Ira Gershwin and Herbert Fields. The producers were Alex Aarons and Vinton Freedley, who had produced a series of highly successful Gershwin shows, and the stars were Jack Pearl, Lyda Roberti ("the Polish bombshell"), Josephine Huston, and the dance team of Carl Randall and Barbara Newberry. The net result was probably the Gershwins' biggest flop. It ran for only forty-three performances. According to Gerald Bordman in his book *American Musical Theatre*, the fact that this musical was set in Germany disturbed many theatregoers, since Hitler had recently assumed power.

The successful team of Ray Henderson and Lew Brown decided to give the depression a kick in the slats by writing and producing an opulent revue, *Strike Me Pink*, at the Majestic in March 1933. The show, backed by gangster Waxey Gordon, smacked of the Roaring Twenties. Opening-night top was $25.00 (outrageous for those dark days), and the tickets were printed on gold stock. The stars included the ebullient Jimmy Durante, the hot tamale Lupe Velez (then married to Tarzan, Johnny Weissmuller), and that cool socialite Hope Williams. The result was neither a flop nor a smash, but a pleasant run of 122 performances.

An ingenious musical, *Murder at the Vanities*, moved to the Majestic from the New Amsterdam in November 1933 and stayed for four months. It focused on some backstage murders during a performance of Earl Carroll's *Vanities* and thus combined thrills with lush scenes from a typical Carroll revue. Bela Lugosi was in the cast, but he didn't do it. Since producers are constantly threatening to revive this novelty, we shall not divulge the murderer's (or murderess's) identity.

An impresario named S.M. Chartock took over the Majestic in the spring of 1934 and staged a Gilbert and Sullivan festival of five

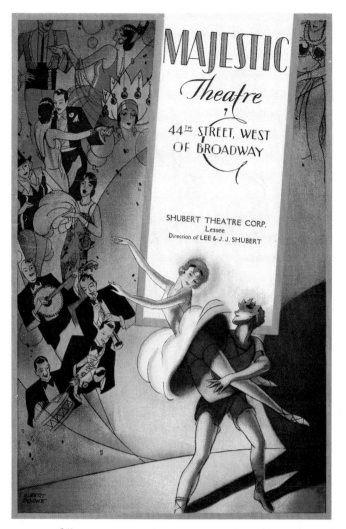

Program cover for *A Wonderful Night* with Archie Leach (Cary Grant) in the cast (1930).

and more successful musicals that had opened in other theatres and would end their Broadway runs here, usually at reduced prices. In 1937 there was an unsuccessful attempt to revive two old thrillers, *The Bat* and *The Cat and the Canary*. A new operetta, *Three Waltzes*, employing the music of Johann Strauss, Sr., and Jr., was a moderate success that year. It starred Kitty Carlisle, Glenn Anders, and Michael Bartlett and ran for 122 performances.

At the end of 1938 Gertrude Lawrence moved into this theatre from the Plymouth with her huge hit *Susan and God*, and this was followed in February 1939 with the lively musical *Stars in Your Eyes*, with such personalities as Ethel Merman, Jimmy Durante, Richard Carlson, Mildred Natwick, and the Russiana ballerina Tamara Toumanova. The show, with a bright score by Arthur Schwartz and Dorothy Fields, a witty book about a lusty Hollywood star (Merman) trying to seduce her innocent leading man (Carlson), and direction by Joshua Logan, had a glittering opening night, which *Life* magazine photographed. But despite a rave review in the New York *Times*, it only ran for 127 performances, and producer Dwight Deere Wiman blamed the short run on the fact that the highly publicized World's Fair opened in Flushing Meadows that spring. Perhaps the most remarkable aspect of *Stars in Your Eyes* was its chorus line, which numbered such future ballet luminaries as Alicia Alonso, Jerome Robbins, Nora Kaye, and Maria Karnilova.

The next musical at the Majestic, *Yokel Boy*, was not as good as *Stars in Your Eyes*, but ran longer. It also dealt with Hollywood studios—and not very kindly. Buddy Ebsen, Judy Canova, Lois January, and Phil Silvers led the cast and one hit tune emerged: "Comes Love."

Clare Boothe's hit anti-Nazi play *Margin for Error* moved here from the Plymouth in 1940; and Olsen and Johnson's *Hellzapoppin* transferred from the Winter Garden in 1941. In Jan-

operettas. During 1935 a series of quick failures played at this theatre. The only show to stay longer than a few weeks was the *Earl Carroll Sketch Book*, described as a "Hysterical Historical Revue," or American history as seen through the eyes of a chorus girl. This amusing show, starring Ken Murray and the usual near-nude Carroll girls, moved here from the Winter Garden and stayed for almost three months.

Beginning in 1936 the Majestic booked more

🖼 The successful 1942 revival of George Gershwin's opera, *Porgy and Bess*, with J. Rosamond Johnson, Todd Duncan, and Anne Brown.

uary 1942 producer Cheryl Crawford presented the first Broadway revival of Gershwin's opera, *Porgy and Bess*, and this production proved to be an artistic and a commercial success. Crawford removed the operatic recitatives and made the work more of a Broadway musical than an opera, and the public flocked to it for thirty-five weeks. Many members of the original cast (Todd Duncan, Anne Brown, Warren Coleman, Ruby Elzy, and J. Rosamond Johnson) were in this revival, and they brought luster to a work that had failed in its premiere engagement in 1935.

Paul Green and Richard Wright's powerful play *Native Son*, directed by Orson Welles, played a return engagement at the Majestic in 1942, followed by the frothy hit comedy *Junior Miss*, which moved here from the Lyceum Theatre in 1943. One of this theatre's biggest hits to this time opened on August 4, 1943. It was the new musical version of that favorite Franz Lehár/Victor Leon/Leo Stein operetta *The Merry Widow*, and the cast included Marta Eggerth and her husband, Jan Kiepura, David Wayne, Gene Barry, Melville Cooper, and Ruth Matteson. It waltzed for 321 performances.

Cole Porter's *Mexican Hayride*, with Bobby Clark and June Havoc, moved here from the

Winter Garden in 1945, and this was followed by one of the treasures of the American Musical Theatre: Rodgers and Hammerstein's lilting *Carousel*. A musical adaptation of Molnár's play *Liliom*, the work opened to rapturous reviews in April 1945. Critic John Chapman in the New York *Daily News* stated that it was one of the finest musical plays he had ever seen, and Richard Rodgers later confessed that of all the musicals he had written, this was his favorite. John Raitt was memorable singing his "Soliloquy," and he and Jan Clayton shared the lovely ballad "If I Loved You." The musical ran 890 performances.

The hit soldier revue *Call Me Mister* moved to this theatre in 1947 from the National, and this was followed by another Rodgers and Hammerstein musical, *Allegro*, a rather pretentious chronicle about a man named Joseph

BELOW: Jan Clayton and John Raitt in Rodgers and Hammerstein's memorable *Carousel* (1945). RIGHT: Mary Martin clowns in the Pulitzer Prize musical *South Pacific* (1949).

Taylor, Jr., which critic Woollcott Gibbs described in *The New Yorker* as "a shocking disappointment." It ran for 315 performances.

On April 7, 1949, Rodgers and Hammerstein's *South Pacific* opened here, starring Mary Martin and Ezio Pinza, and immediately became the hottest ticket in town. Based on James A. Michener's Pulitzer Prize book *Tales of the South Pacific*, it won a Pulitzer Prize for drama in 1950, the Tony Award, the New York Drama Critics Circle Award, and the Donaldson Award for best musical of the season. With direction by Joshua Logan (who also coauthored

supporting players (Barbara Cook, David Burns), best authors (Meredith Willson and Franklin Lacey), best composer and lyricist (Willson), best musical director (Herbert Greene), and best producers (Kermit Bloomgarden, Herbert Greene, Frank Productions). This bonanza about a con man who sells musical instruments to schools, then skips town before delivering them, ran for 1,375 performances.

Much was expected of *Camelot*, the Majestic's next musical, in late 1960. Written by Alan Jay Lerner and Frederick Loewe, directed by

◢ LEFT: Program cover sketch for the musical *Fanny* (1954). BELOW: Julie Andrews charms Richard Burton in the Lerner/Loewe musical *Camelot* (1960).

the book with Oscar Hammerstein II) and with some of Richard Rodgers's most inspired melodies, the musical ran for 1,925 performances and won Tony Awards for Ms. Martin, Mr. Pinza, supporting performers Juanita Hall and Myron McCormick, director Joshua Logan, and Rodgers, Hammerstein, and Logan for their book, lyrics, and music.

The remainder of the 1950s at this theatre saw the production of some musicals of varying merit that enjoyed respectable runs. Rodgers and Hammerstein's *Me and Juliet*, a musical about the theatre, was second rate R&H, but ran for 358 performances in 1953–54; *By the Beautiful Sea*, a musical by Arthur Schwartz and Herbert and Dorothy Fields, starring Shirley Booth, ran a moderate 268 performances in 1954; *Fanny* (1954–56), a musical adaptation of Marcel Pagnol's trilogy (*Marius, César,* and *Fanny*), by S.N. Behrman, Joshua Logan, and Harold Rome, starring Walter Slezak (who won a Tony Award for his performance) and Ezio Pinza, ran for 888 performances; and the phenomenal Meredith Willson musical *The Music Man* (1957–60) won Tony Awards for best musical, best actor (Robert Preston), best

Moss Hart, whose previous show had been the sensational *My Fair Lady*, it costarred Julie Andrews of that show and movie star Richard Burton. The critics gave it very mixed reviews, and after a few weeks it appeared that the expensive musical was not long for Broadway. Then, a miracle happened. Ed Sullivan presented four musical numbers from the show on his popular TV show, *Toast of the Town*, and the following morning, there was a long line of ticket buyers at the Majestic Theatre. Richard Burton won a Tony Award for his performance as King Richard and the musical played for 873 performances.

The remainder of the 1960s was devoted to a revival of *The School for Scandal* (1963), starring Ralph Richardson and John Gielgud (who also directed it); Judy Holliday in her last Broadway show, the lamentable musical *Hot Spot* (1963); *Tovarich* (1963), the musical version of the play of the same name, which moved here from the Broadway Theatre with Tony Award winner Vivien Leigh and Jean Pierre Aumont; Mary Martin in the flop musical *Jennie* (1963), supposedly based on the early career of actress Laurette Taylor; a misguided musical, *Anyone Can Whistle* (1964), with a beguiling score by Stephen Sondheim, a murky book by Arthur Laurents, and good performances by Angela Lansbury, Lee Remick, and Harry Guardino, which only lasted nine performances; an unsuccessful musical version of Clifford Odets's *Golden Boy* (1964–65), with Sammy Davis, Jr.; *Funny Girl* (1966), from the Winter Garden; the long-running classic *Fiddler on the Roof*, which moved here from the Imperial in 1967 and stayed until December 1970.

The 1970s saw a flop musical version of *The Teahouse of the August Moon* called *Lovely Ladies, Kind Gentlemen* (1970); the Tony Award winning musical *1776* (1971), here from the St. James Theatre; a fairly successful musical version of the popular movie *Some Like It Hot*,

From bottom: Hinton Battle, Stephanie Mills, James Wigfall, and Tiger Haynes in the long-running hit *The Wiz* (1975).

PLAYBILL
MAJESTIC THEATRE

ABOVE: PLAYBILL cover for David Merrick's *42nd Street*. BELOW: Liza Minnelli gives a Tony Award-winning performance in *The Act* (1977).

retitled *Sugar* (1972), with Robert Morse and Tony Roberts as the musicians who must masquerade as women to hide from gangsters and Cyril Ritchard as the old man who falls for one

of them; *A Little Night Music* (1973–74), the Tony Award winning musical from the Shubert Theatre; the unsuccessful Jerry Herman/Michael Stewart musical *Mack and Mabel* (1974), about Mack Sennett and Mabel Normand; the delightful black musical *The Wiz*, based on *The Wizard of Oz*, which won Tony Awards for best musical, best score (Charlie Smalls), best director (Geoffrey Holder), best supporting performers (Ted Ross, Dee Dee Bridgewater), best costume designer (Geoffrey Holder), and best choreographer (George Faison) and ran for 1,661 performances; Liza Minnelli and Barry Nelson in a pallid musical, *The Act* (1977), for which Ms. Minnelli won a Tony Award; Henry Fonda and Jane Alexander in *The First Monday in October* (1978); two unsuccessful musicals, *Ballroom* (1978) and Richard Rodgers's last show, *I Remember Mama*, a 1979 musical version of the John Van Druten play, which Rodgers and Hammerstein had produced in 1944; a revival of *The Most Happy Fella* (1979); a personal appearance by Bette Midler (1979–80); the final performances of *Grease* (1980), from the Royale Theatre; *Blackstone!* (1980), a magic show; and a revival of the 1947 musical *Brigadoon* with Agnes de Mille recreating her dances that won a Tony Award in 1947.

The Majestic's current long-running tenant is David Merrick's spectacular musical *42nd Street*, which moved here in 1981 from the Winter Garden and has been selling out ever since. At this writing, Jerry Orbach and Lee Roy Reams of the original cast are still in the Tony Award winning musical, which also won a Tony for its choreographer, Gower Champion, who died on the afternoon of the show's opening.

The Majestic Theatre is owned by the Shubert Organization and is one of the world's finest musical comedy houses. It has been renovated in recent years and its sloped orchestra section still offers better viewing than is available at most other theatres.

ST. JAMES THEATRE

The St. James Theatre at 246 West Forty-fourth Street was built by Broadway booking agent Abraham Erlanger and opened as Erlanger's Theatre in the fall of 1927. The theatre was designed by the architectural firm of Warren and Wetmore, with interiors by John Singraldi.

With an ample capacity of 1,600 seats, Erlanger's Theatre was aimed primarily for the production of musicals. According to the New York *Times*, it cost $1,500,000 to build and was the least ornate of all the theatres constructed in the Times Square district at the time. "In the auditorium," reported the paper, "there has been a studied attempt to create an intimate rather than a theatrical atmosphere. The interior design is Georgian, the color scheme coral and antique gold. Murals decorate the side walls and the proscenium arch. Two large boxes on either side of the proscenium are known as the President's and the Governor's boxes. The main entrance is through wide doors to a spacious marble lobby extending all the way across the

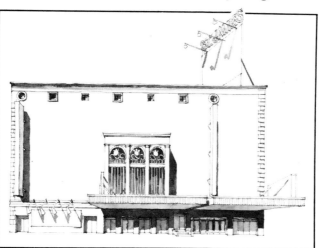

building. The façade, stretching along West 44th Street, is of marble, stone and stucco on a granite base and is also said to be representative of Georgian architecture."

The opening attraction at Erlanger's on the night of September 26, 1927, was George M. Cohan's musical *Merry Malones*, which, with typical Cohan modesty, he wrote, produced, and starred in. It was a hit and got the new theatre off to a good start. It played for 192 performances, was strangely interrupted by a short engagement of a flop play called *The Behavior of Mrs. Crane*, then returned for 16 additional performances.

Erlanger's was the scene of the last musical George M. Cohan wrote. It was called *Billie* and was based on Cohan's 1912 play *Broadway Jones*. He did not appear in it, but it managed to run for 112 performances in 1928–29. This was followed by the popular musical *Hello, Daddy!*, which moved here from the Mansfield Theatre. It was the show that Herbert and Dor-

the infectious musical *Fine and Dandy*, with a funny book by Donald Ogden Stewart and a score by Kay Swift and Paul James that included two standards: "Can This Be Love?" and the rousing title tune. Joe Cook was the comic and he fractured theatregoers with his acrobatics, juggling, daffy gadgets, and inane patter. The hit thrived for 246 performances.

From May 1931 until March 1932 this theatre was taken over by the Civic Light Opera Company, which presented a successful repertory of Gilbert and Sullivan operettas and other musical entertainments. Then a dark period followed, during which it was decided to rename the theatre the St. James. On December 7, 1932, the theatre reopened with this new name (inspired by the St. James Theatre in London), and the star, appropriately, was London's favorite revue comedienne, Beatrice Lillie, in a new revue called *Walk a Little Faster*. Her costars were the famed comedy team of Bobby Clark and Paul McCullough, and the score was by Vernon Duke and E.Y. Harburg. The show was

LEFT: Standard program cover in the early years, when the St. James was known as Erlanger's Theatre. BELOW: Ina Haywood and Robinson Newbold in this theatre's first production, *The Merry Malones* (1927).

othy Fields wrote for their father, Lew Fields, who starred in it. The remaining shows of 1929 were an unsuccessful revue, *Murray Anderson's Almanac*, with Jimmie Savo and Trixie Friganza, and Noel Coward as one of the contributors, and a moderately successful comedy, *Ladies of the Jury*, with Mrs. Fiske as an opinionated juror who sways the other jurors to her way of thinking.

Mrs. Fiske appeared again at Erlanger's in 1930 in a brief revival of Sheridan's comedy *The Rivals*, in which she played Mrs. Malaprop. Next came this theatre's biggest hit thus far,

Beatrice Lillie, Bobby Clark and Paul McCullough cavort in the sleek revue *Walk A Little Faster* (1932).

staged by Monty Woolley and Albertina Rasch, the production was designed and conceived by Boris Aronson, and the orchestrations were by the fabulous Russell Bennett and Conrad Salinger. So what went wrong? Who knows, but the revue was only a moderate success, running for 121 performances. One gem has survived from this show: the beautiful Duke/Harburg song "April in Paris," which the notoriously tone-deaf drama critics didn't even mention.

After this sophisticated revue, the St. James reverted to Gilbert and Sullivan for several months. An event more balletic than theatrical occurred at this theatre in January 1934. Concert impresario Sol Hurok brought over the Monte Carlo Ballet Russe and the famed company presented its repertory of ballets from January through April. The lead dancers included Leonide Massine, Irina Baronova, David Lichine, André Eglevesky, Tamara Toumanova, and Sono Osato. It was the beginning of America's intense ballet craze.

Bobby Clark and Paul McCullough returned to the St. James in another gilded revue, *Thumbs Up*, produced by Eddie Dowling, who also starred in the show with his comical wife, Ray Dooley. Two great dancers—Hal Le Roy and Jack Cole—were also in the show, as well as the popular Pickens sisters. It ran for 156 performances and introduced two song hits: James Hanley's "Zing Went the Strings of My Heart" and Vernon Duke's haunting "Autumn in New York."

On December 5, 1935, *May Wine*, a Sigmund Romberg, Oscar Hammerstein II, and Frank Mandel operetta that disguised itself as "a musical play," waltzed into the St. James for 212 performances. Among the large cast were Walter Slezak, Walter Woolf King, Leo G. Carroll, and Jack Cole.

John Gielgud moved his highly successful *Hamlet* from the Empire Theatre to the St. James in January 1937, and Maurice Evans followed him in the title role of the highly praised revival of Shakespeare's *Richard II*, staged by Margaret Webster. This was the first revival of this tragedy in America since Edwin Booth played it in 1878 and it was a triumph. It ran for 132 performances.

A truly delightful fantasy called *Father Malachy's Miracle* opened here on November 17, 1937. The beloved comic Al Shean (of Gallagher and Shean fame) played Father Malachy, a kindly priest who tired of a noisy dance hall across the way from his church and prayed that it would be transported to an island. It happened and he got into a lot of trouble because he had not consulted the church hierarchy before working a miracle. Mr. Shean was hailed for his acting and the fantasy ran for 125 performances.

On October 12, 1938, another dramatic milestone occurred at this theatre. The first full-length production of *Hamlet* in America was presented by Maurice Evans, Joseph Verner

ABOVE: Lillian Gish and John Gielgud in *Hamlet* which moved to the St. James in 1937. BELOW: Maurice Evans and Henry Edwards in the uncut revival of *Hamlet* (1938).

Reed, and Boris Said. Staged by the Shakespearean expert Margaret Webster, it ran from 6:45 P.M. until 8:15, with a dinner intermission, then resumed from 8:45 until 11:15. Later, the dinner intermission was extended from a half-hour to an hour, bringing the final curtain down at 11:45. The production was a success, running for ninety-six performances. Ophelia was played by Katherine Locke, Gertrude by Mady Christians, and Rosencrantz by Alexander Scourby. Mr. Evans, of course, played Hamlet. In January 1939 Evans switched to playing the rotund Sir John Falstaff in a revival of Shakespeare's *Henry IV* (Part 1) with Edmond O'Brien as Henry, Prince of Wales. It was another success, running for seventy-four performances.

Shakespeare was interrupted for a brief moment by the arrival from the West Coast of the last Earl Carroll *Vanities*, a sorry revue with Jerry Lester and, worst of all, microphones onstage! According to Gerald Bordman in *American Musical Theatre*, this was really the beginning of that monster of our present-day musical theatre: amplification.

Shakespeare returned to the St. James with a splendid production of *Twelfth Night*, co-presented by the Theatre Guild and Gilbert Miller. The cast included Helen Hayes (Viola), Maurice Evans (Malvolio), June Walker (Maria), Wesley Addy (Orsino), and Sophie Stewart (Olivia) in this delightful revival staged by Margaret Webster in the fall of 1940. In March 1941, a dramatic thunderbolt hit this theatre. It was *Native Son*, the dramatization of Richard Wright's novel of the same name by Mr. Wright and Paul Green. Produced by John Houseman and Orson Welles and directed by Welles, this powerful drama stunned theatregoers with its story of a black man who accidentally kills a white woman. It ran for 114 performances and was chosen one of the season's ten best plays by critic Burns Mantle.

The Boston Comic Opera Company and the

Jooss Ballet Dance Theatre presented an exciting season of their works (including Kurt Jooss's brilliant dance drama *The Green Table*) at the St. James from January to March 1942. This event was followed by the hit play *Claudia*, transferred from the Booth, which stayed at this theatre until November. The Theatre Guild then moved in with Philip Barry's comedy *Without Love*, starring Katharine Hepburn, Elliott Nugent, and Audrey Christie. It was definitely not another winner like *The Philadelphia Story*, being a flimsy notion about a platonic marriage, and after 110 performances, it departed. The best thing about the show was the stunning wardrobe designed for Ms. Hepburn by that supreme couturier Valentina.

On March 31, 1943, a musical play opened at the St. James that was rumored to be hopeless. In fact, the opening night was not sold out, and that was astounding, considering that it was a Theatre Guild production and that it was the work of Richard Rodgers and Oscar Hammerstein II, with choreography by Agnes de Mille and staging by Rouben Mamoulian. The show was *Oklahoma!*, and after the opening night, you needed powerful friends or ticket brokers to get you into the St. James. It became the hottest ticket since *Show Boat* in 1927. At the first matinee the following day, the St. James lobby was jammed with blue-haired ladies and rabid musical comedy lovers all trying to get seats for the show that revolutionized the American musical theatre. Enough has been written about the significance of this musical—integrated book and musical numbers, ballets woven into the plot, and the dispension of the usual chorus line—not to warrant repetition. Notably, it launched the great team of Rodgers and Hammerstein, saved the Theatre Guild from unavoidable bankruptcy,

Joan Roberts, Joseph Buloff, Betty Garde and Celeste Holm in the Rodgers and Hammerstein blockbuster *Oklahoma!*

in the leads, the romantic musical based on the popular novel *Anna and the King of Siam* proved an immediate hit and played for 1,246 performances. It also proved to be Gertrude Lawrence's last Broadway show. She passed away while it was still running and was succeeded by Constance Carpenter. In tribute to the great British star, all theatre marquee lights were dimmed for one minute on the night after her death.

Two more successful musicals followed *The King and I* at this theatre. *The Pajama Game* opened in May 1954 and stayed for 1,061 performances; *Li'l Abner* opened in November 1956 and ran for 693 performances.

In 1957 the Shuberts, who owned the St. James at this point, sold the theatre to Scar-

LEFT: Jane Lawrence and Ray Bolger in Frank Loesser's delightful musical *Where's Charley?*. BELOW: Jean Arthur enchants in the 1950 revival of *Peter Pan* which moved here from the Imperial.

(once again), and directed the course of musicals for decades to come. It ran for 2,248 performances.

Although the musical that followed *Oklahoma!* into this theatre—Frank Loesser's *Where's Charley?*—did not match the artistry of its predecessor, it featured a winning performance by Ray Bolger, who stopped the show at every performance with his engaging number "Once in Love with Amy." George Abbott wrote the libretto and directed the show, which ran for 792 performances. The choreography was by George Balanchine.

The successful revival of *Peter Pan*, starring Jean Arthur and Boris Karloff, with some songs by Leonard Bernstein, moved here from the Imperial Theatre in October 1950 and stayed until mid-January 1951. On March 29, 1951, Rodgers and Hammerstein presented their latest creation, *The King and I*, directed by playwright John Van Druten and choreographed by Jerome Robbins. With Gertrude Lawrence and a practically unknown actor, Yul Brynner,

borough House Inc., which leased it to Jujamcyn Amusement Corporation. When *Li'l Abner* closed in 1958, the theatre was dark for almost six months and stripped to its skeleton. The noted stage and interior designer Frederick Fox was engaged to rebuild the house and redecorate it from its original shell. He designed a new marquee and houseboards, new box office and lobby, new foyer walls and floors, a brand-new smoking loggia, a new lighting system and chandelier, sculpture, murals, specially woven fabrics for seats, walls, and carpeting, new house and asbestos curtains, new stairs, and an improved stage and dressing rooms. The latest equipment was installed, including a closed-circuit TV system so that technicians backstage could follow the action onstage. The new St. James was hailed as one of the most beautiful theatres in America.

The first production in the renovated theatre was Rodgers and Hammerstein's *Flower Drum Song*, one of their lesser efforts, which managed to run from December 1, 1958, until May 7, 1960. It was succeeded by *Once Upon a Mattress*, the popular Off-Broadway musical starring Carol Burnett, which started at the downtown Phoenix Theatre and moved to Broadway when it turned into a hit. The score was by Richard Rodgers's daughter, Mary, and Marshall Barer, and Ms. Burnett was praised for her zany performance.

Highlights of the 1960s at this theatre included Laurence Olivier and Anthony Quinn in Anouilh's *Becket* (1960); the Comden/Green, Jules Styne, Garson Kanin musical *Do Re Mi* (1960), starring Nancy Walker and Phil Silvers; *Subways Are for Sleeping*, another Comden/Green/Styne collaboration, with Sydney Chaplin, Carol Lawrence, Orson Bean, and Phyllis Newman (who won a Tony for her performance) in 1961; an uninspired Irving Berlin musical, *Mr. President* (1962), also his last Broadway show, starring Robert Ryan and Nanette Fabray; the

Yul Brynner dances with Gertrude Lawrence in *The King and I*, her last show.

exciting John Osborn play *Luther* (1963), starring Albert Finney, which won the Tony Award for best play of the season.

On January 16, 1964, *Hello, Dolly!* exploded at this theatre and by the time it closed on December 27, 1970, it had chalked up 2,844 performances, making it the longest-running Broadway musical up to that time. The David Merrick production, with a score by Jerry Herman, book by Michael Stewart (based on Thornton Wilder's *The Matchmaker*), direction and choreography by Gower Champion, won ten Tony Awards. During its run at the St. James, Carol Channing was succeeded by the following stars: Ginger Rogers, Martha Raye, Betty Grable, Bibi Osterwald, Pearl Bailey, Thelma Carpenter, Phyllis Diller, and Ethel Merman.

In 1971 Joseph Papp then brought his musical success *Two Gentlemen of Verona* from Central Park to this theatre and it stayed for 613 performances, winning a Tony Award for best musical. The cast included Raul Julia, Clifton Davis, and Jonelle Allen, and all three received Tony nominations.

A revival of *A Streetcar Named Desire* in 1973, with Lois Nettleton, Alan Feinstein, Barbara Eda-Young, and Biff McGuire, was well received, but lasted only 53 performances; a revival of the 1920s musical *Good News* (1974), with Alice Faye and John Payne (who was replaced by Gene Nelson during previews), fared even worse, with only 16 repetitions. A revival of Molière's *The Misanthrope*, starring Alec McCowen, Diana Rigg, and others, played 94

LEFT: Carol Channing sings the title song of *Hello, Dolly!* and wins a Tony Award for her performance (1964). BELOW: The PLAYBILL cover for the Tony Award-winning musical *Two Gentlemen of Verona* (1971).

LEFT: Souvenir program cover for *Barnum* (Australian production). RIGHT: Twiggy in the "new" Gershwin musical *My One and Only* (1983).

performances in 1975, and *A Musical Jubilee*, a revue of popular American songs, ran for 92 performances. A revival of *My Fair Lady* opened in March 1976, with Christine Andreas, Ian Richardson, Brenda Forbes, and George Rose, who won a Tony for his performance, and it had a run of 384 performances.

In February 1978 Comden/Green and Cy Coleman brought in their musical version of the play *Twentieth Century* and called it *On the Twentieth Century*. John Cullum and Kevin Kline won Tony Awards for their performances, and the musical played 460 times.

From the spring of 1979 to the following spring, this theatre booked four unsuccessful productions. They were the Alan Jay Lerner/ Burton Lane musical *Carmelina*; *Broadway Opry '79*; *The 1940's Radio Hour*; and the British import *Filumena*, directed by Laurence Olivier and starring his wife, Joan Plowright, and Frank Finlay.

On April 30, 1980, the hit musical *Barnum* arrived and won a Tony Award for its star, Jim

Dale, as well as for its sets (David Mitchell) and costumes (Theoni V. Aldredge). The fanciful musical about the mighty Barnum ran for 854 performances.

The last two tenants at this theatre have been the unsuccessful musical *Rock and Roll: The 1st 5,000 Years* (1982) and the hit *My One and Only*, a new version of the old Gershwin musical *Funny Face*. After many troubles on the road, this musical opened on Broadway on May 1, 1983, to some very enthusiastic notices, especially for its two stars, Twiggy and Tommy Tune, and for tap dancer Charles ("Honi") Coles. Mr. Tune won a Tony for his performance and another for his choreography with Thommie Walsh, and Mr. Coles also won a Tony for his performance. It is still running at this time.

The St. James was the first theatre to be acquired by the firm of Jujamcyn Theatres in the 1950s and is still owned by this organization. It has been kept in top condition and has been extremely successful as both a musical comedy and a dramatic house.

⚜ NEIL SIMON THEATRE ⚜

The Neil Simon Theatre was, until recently, one of Manhattan's most illustrious musical comedy houses, the Alvin. The theatre was named after the men who built it and produced shows there—Alex Aarons and Vinton Freedley. Having made considerable money producing musicals, Aarons and Freedley built their own playhouse. This building opened at 250 West Forty-second Street, facing the stately Guild Theatre (now the Virginia Theatre).

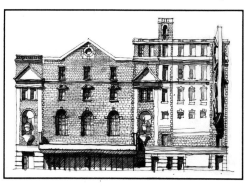

Critic Brooks Atkinson of the New York *Times* wrote about their theatre: "The new Alvin Theatre, set defiantly across the street from the scholarly Theatre Guild, seems to have all the best features of the modern playhouse—even an old English lounge where refreshments may be had. The auditorium is decorated with pastel shades of blue and gray, with ivory and gold decorations. The Alvin can serve 1,400 drama gluttons at one sitting."

Designed by the ubiquitous Herbert J. Krapp, the new house had three floors of offices above it where Aarons and Freedley had their headquarters. The theatre contained a spacious lobby in black marble and an inner lobby of simple design. There was only one balcony. The ample orchestra pit could accommodate forty-eight musicians, and the stage was spacious enough to allow for the production and staging of the most elaborate musicals.

The Alvin opened auspiciously on November 22, 1927, with the Aarons/Freedley production of *Funny Face*, a hit musical by George and Ira Gershwin, Paul Gerard Smith, and Fred Thompson. The cast included Fred and Adele Astaire, Victor Moore, Allen Kearns, Betty Compton, William Kent, and the duo pianists Phil Ohman and Victor Arden. The memorable score featured such gems as "He Loves and She Loves," "'S Wonderful, "My One and Only," "The Babbitt and the Bromide," and the title song. The Astaires captivated theatregoers for 250 performances.

The following November, Aarons and Freedley tried again with another Gershwin musical, *Treasure Girl*, but this time they failed. The star was Gertrude Lawrence, and her supporting cast included Paul Frawley, Walter Catlett, Clifton Webb, Mary Hay, and Ohman and Arden at the ivories, but the show's book was uninspired and the critics complained that Ms. Lawrence had to play a disagreeable liar. Clifton Webb's

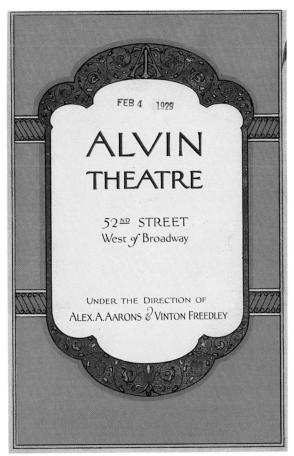

ABOVE: Standard program cover for the Alvin Theatre in the 1920s. RIGHT: Helen Hayes loses her head in Maxwell Anderson's *Mary of Scotland* (1933).

"With a Song in My Heart" and "Yours Sincerely." In the cast were Inez Courtney, Glenn Hunter, Charles Ruggles, and Joyce Barbour. *Spring Is Here* lasted 104 performances. *Heads Up!*, the next Rodgers and Hart musical, had a book by John McGowan and Paul Gerard Smith and contained a lovely song that is sometimes heard in supper clubs —"A Ship Without a Sail." The cast included Ray Bolger, Victor Moore, Betty Starbuck, Jack Whiting, Barbara Newberry, and Lewis Parker (later, Lew). Victor Moore won

and Mary Hay's dancing was applauded, and the Gershwin tunes included "I Don't Think I'll Fall in Love Today," "Feeling I'm Falling," and "I've Got a Crush on You." The musical expired after sixty-nine performances.

In 1929 the Theatre Guild production of *Wings Over Europe,* a startling drama about the destructive power of atomic energy, moved here from the Martin Beck Theatre. This was followed by two Rodgers and Hart musicals in succession. The first was *Spring Is Here,* with a book by Owen Davis from his play *Shotgun Wedding.* It was not one of Rodgers and Hart's triumphs, but a pleasant show with two songs that lasted:

raves for his comedy routines. The musical ran for 144 performances.

In 1930 the Theatre Guild's production of Shaw's *The Apple Cart*, with Claude Rains and Violet Kemble Cooper, moved here from the Martin Beck. Then, on October 14, 1930, one of this theatre's historic musicals opened. It was the Aarons/Freedley production of George and Ira Gershwin's *Girl Crazy*, with a book by Guy Bolton and John McGowan. The cast included Ginger Rogers, Willie Howard, Allen Kearns, William Kent, and the Foursome. But it was Ethel Merman, making her Broadway debut, who shook the Alvin with her electrifying rendition of the classic "I Got Rhythm." The musical ran for 272 performances.

Eugene O'Neill's great trilogy, *Mourning Becomes Electra*, moved here from the Guild Theatre across the street in 1932.

Jerome Kern's *Music in the Air* was an enormous hit in 1932 at this theatre. It did not have another theatrical booking until May 29, 1933, when The Players chose it as the house for their twelfth annual revival of a classic play. They revived *Uncle Tom's Cabin* for a week, but it was so popular that it played for three. The distinguished cast included Otis Skinner as Uncle Tom, Fay Bainter as Topsy, Thomas Chalmers as Simon Legree, Elizabeth Risdon as Eliza, Minnie Dupree as Aunt Ophelia, Cecilia Loftus as Aunt Chloe, and Gene Lockhart as Gumption Cute.

The Alvin housed a distinguished play in the fall of 1933. It was the Theatre Guild production of Maxwell Anderson's verse play *Mary of Scotland*, starring Helen Hayes in the title role, Helen Menken as Queen Elizabeth, and Philip Merivale as the Earl of Bothwell.

On the night of November 21, 1934, one of the depression's most glittering first-night audiences gathered at the Alvin to roar its approval of Cole Porter's felicitous musical *Anything Goes*. This show had a very shaky history. The original libretto by Guy Bolton and P.G. Wodehouse involved a group of zany characters on a luxury liner that is shipwrecked. Just as the musical was about to go into rehearsal, the luxury liner *Morro Castle* burned off the coast of Asbury Park and the musical's plot seemed very unfunny. In desperation, the producers hired two New Yorkers—Howard Lindsay and Russel Crouse—to quickly write a new libretto and the show went into rehearsal with only a portion of the first act on paper. They kept the action on a luxury liner, but forgot about the shipwreck notion. The result was a triumph of mirth and melody, with Ethel Merman as Reno Sweeney (a parody of Aimee Semple MacPherson) traveling with her band of singers, called "Angels." Victor Moore was Public Enemy No. 13, disguised as Reverend Dr. Moon (with a machine gun in his violin case), and William Gaxton was a playboy in pursuit of Hope Harcourt (Bettina Hall). Porter wrote his greatest score thus far—"I Get a Kick Out Of You," "You're the Top," "All Through the Night," "Blow, Gabriel, Blow," and the infectious title song. The musical became the most representative show of the 1930s— glamorous, screwball, slightly risqué, very topical, and very sophisticated. It ran for 420 performances.

In October 1935 the Gershwins and DuBose Heyward brought their magnificent opera *Porgy and Bess* to the Alvin. The reception was mixed and it played only 124 times. In October of 1936 Vinton Freedley hoped to strike gold again with another Ethel Merman/ Cole Porter show. This one was called *Red, Hot and Blue!* and there was trouble from the very start. Both Ethel and her costar, Jimmy Durante, wanted top billing. After much haggling, Mrs. Porter came up with a solution: a criss cross arrangement of the two names so that each could be construed as having top billing. The other star, Bob Hope, took to lying down and mugging during one of Ethel's song numbers and she threatened "to

Ethel Merman and chorus belt out Cole Porter's rousing "Blow, Gabriel, Blow" in *Anything Goes* (1934).

sit on the son of a bitch" if he didn't stop. He stopped. The show was not another *Anything Goes*. The plot, by Howard Lindsay and Russel Crouse, was about a national lottery. The winner was the person who could find one "Peaches Le Fleur," who had a birthmark on her behind because she once sat on a hot waffle iron. The Supreme Court got into the lottery and began examining show girls in cellophane skirts to see if they had the winning mark. The dippy show ran for 181 performances and the most memorable moments were provided by Durante

as a polo-playing convict and three great Porter songs: "It's De-Lovely," "Ridin' High," and "Down in the Depths (On the Ninetieth Floor)."

On November 2, 1937, George M. Cohan returned to this theatre as President Roosevelt in the satirical musical *I'd Rather Be Right*, and the occasion turned into one of Broadway's most flamboyant opening nights. The fact that no living U.S. president had ever been portrayed onstage (and in a satire, no less) and the added lure that the show was the creation of Rodgers and Hart, George S. Kaufman, and Moss Hart made this a must-see event. Reported Lucius Beebe in *Stage* magazine: "Probably no theatrical event has occasioned such civic tumult since the Astor Place Riots. All New York wanted in, as the phrase has it. New York seemed completely overwhelmed by the return of Mr. Cohan, and popular rejoicing and Morris dancing in Longacre Square complemented the most insufferable crush, confusion, and amiable uproar Fifty-second Street has ever known."

Although *I'd Rather Be Right* was not as biting as *Of Thee I Sing*, Cohan's affectionate portrayal of FDR and his delightful tap dancing made the show one of the season's sold-out delights. Only one Rodgers and Hart song was played outside of the show: "Have You Met Miss

BELOW: Polo-playing convict Jimmy Durante taps Ethel Merman's wire in *Red, Hot and Blue!* (1936). RIGHT: George M. Cohan as F.D.R. gives a fireside chat in *I'd Rather Be Right* (1937).

Jones?" The musical ran for 289 performances.

In November 1938 Rodgers and Hart and George Abbott brought to the Alvin their memorable musical *The Boys from Syracuse*, based on Shakespeare's *The Comedy of Errors*, with Eddie Albert and Ronald Graham as one set of twins, Jimmy Savo and Teddy Hart as the other set, and Muriel Angelus, Marcy Wescott, Wynn Murray, Betty Bruce, and Burl Ives. With choreography by George Balanchine and such lilting songs as "This Can't Be Love," "Falling in Love With Love," and "Sing For Your Supper," the exuberant musical ran for 235 performances.

In February 1940, to aid the Finnish Relief Fund, the Lunts brought back their 1935 revival of *The Taming of the Shrew*. It was a short engagement but a notable one for a worthy war cause. In April of that year, they returned to this theatre in Robert E. Sherwood's *There Shall Be No Night*, which was awarded the Pulitzer Prize. It was a powerful denunciation of war and, in particular, Russia's invasion of Finland. The play showed the devastating effects of this

Lynn Fontanne, Montgomery Clift and Alfred Lunt in the Pulitzer Prize play *There Shall Be No Night* (1940).

attack on a Finnish family. The supporting cast included Montgomery Clift, Richard Whorf, Sydney Greenstreet, Elizabeth Fraser, and Phyllis Thaxter. It ran for 115 performances, took a vacation, then resumed for 66 additional performances.

On January 23, 1941, the Alvin housed one of the American Musical Theatre's finest works: *Lady in the Dark*, by Moss Hart, Kurt Weill, and Ira Gershwin. Gertrude Lawrence scored one of her greatest triumphs in it, bumping and grinding to one of the musical's greatest tunes, "The Saga of Jenny." Danny Kaye also stopped the show with his tongue-twister "Tschaikowsky." The supporting cast included Bert Lytell, Macdonald Carey, Victor Mature, and Margaret Dale, and its opulent sets and costumes and choreography by Albertina Rasch made it one of the most memorable musicals ever seen on Broadway. Brooks Atkinson in the New York *Times* called it "a work of theatre art." It ran for 467 performances.

On January 7, 1943, there was a unique opening night at the Alvin for the latest Cole Porter/Ethel Merman musical, *Something for the Boys*. This was the date that a new government ruling went into effect because of the war.

No private automobiles could be driven to places of entertainment, therefore Fifty-second Street was jammed up with taxi cabs, all honking to get through the crush. The musical, with Paula Laurence, Allen Jenkins, Betty Garrett, Bill Johnson, Jed Prouty, Betty Bruce, and—in the chorus—Dody Goodman, was a smash hit. Its plot, by Herbert and Dorothy Fields, was even more foolish than that of *Red, Hot and Blue!* Ms. Merman played a defense worker who got carborundum in her teeth fillings, which turned her into a radio receiving set. At the show's climax, she saves an army plane from crashing by receiving landing instructions via her teeth. Wartime audiences ate this up for 422 performances.

A series of failures played this theatre during 1944 and 1945. They were a musical called *Jackpot*, with Nanette Fabray, Benny Baker, Allan Jones, Wendell Corey, and Betty Garrett; *Helen Goes to Troy*, a new musical version of Offenbach's operetta *La Belle Hélène*, with Ernest Truex and Jarmila Novotna; *The Firebrand of Florence*, a musical version of the play *The Firebrand*, by Kurt Weill, Ira Gershwin, and Edwin Justus Mayer, with Lotte Lenya; and *Hollywood Pinafore*, George S. Kaufman's modern interpretation of Gilbert and Sullivan's *Pinafore*, with Victor Moore, William Gaxton, and Shirley Booth. More successful was a revival of *The Tempest*, as interpreted by Margaret Webster and Eva Le Gallienne and starring Vera Zorina, Arnold Moss, Canada Lee, and Frances Heflin.

Betty Comden, Adolph Green, and Morton Gould combined talents on *Billion Dollar Baby*, an interesting musical about the Roaring Twenties. Mitzi Green, Joan McCracken, Helen Gallagher, Danny Daniels, William Tabbert, and David Burns gave vivid performances, and the show amused postwar audiences for 220 performances.

Ingrid Bergman scored a triumph in Maxwell Anderson's *Joan of Lorraine* (1946), with Sam Wanamaker and Romney Brent also giving memorable performances in this unconventional interpretation of the story of Joan of Arc.

In 1947 *Life with Father* moved to the Alvin from the Bijou Theatre and ended its record run here of 3,224 performances, making it the longest-running straight play in the history of the American theatre—a record that it still holds.

On October 8, 1947, Maurice Evans opened his highly successful revival of Shaw's *Man and Superman* and starred in it for 294 performances. This was followed by one of the Alvin's fondest bookings: *Mister Roberts*, the navy comedy that opened on February 18, 1948, and stayed in port at the Alvin until January 6, 1951, after 1,157 performances. The Thomas Heggen/Joshua Logan play starred Henry Fonda, who won a Tony Award for his performance in the title role. Other Tony Awards went to the play, to its producer, and to its authors.

Highlights of the 1950s at this theatre included Sidney Kingsley's adaptation of Arthur Koestler's novel *Darkness at Noon* (1951), which won a Tony Award for its star, Claude Rains; the musical version of Betty Smith's novel *A Tree Grows in Brooklyn* (1951), by Ms. Smith,

Ingrid Bergman plays Saint Joan in Maxwell Anderson's play-within-a-play *Joan of Lorraine* (1946).

🎭 From left: David Wayne, Henry Fonda and Robert Keith sample some homemade Scotch in the memorable *Mister Roberts* (1948).

George Abbott, Arthur Schwartz, and Dorothy Fields, starring Shirley Booth, Johnny Johnston, Marcia Van Dyke, and Nathaniel Frey; Henry Fonda again in *Point of No Return* (1951), Paul Osborn's dramatization of John P. Marquand's novel of the same name, with Leora Dana, Frank Conroy, and John Cromwell.

In 1952 Bette Davis rashly starred in a revue called *Two's Company* and the decision was ill-advised. It closed after 91 performances. Mary Martin and Charles Boyer starred in a humdrum comedy, *Kind Sir*, by Norman Krasna in 1953. The spring of 1954 brought the successful Phoenix Theatre production of *The Golden Apple*, which won the New York Drama Critics Circle Award for best musical of the season; and this was followed in December 1954 by *House of Flowers*, a musical by Truman Capote and Harold Arlen, directed by Peter Brook and starring Pearl Bailey, Diahann Carroll, Ray Walston, Juanita Hall, and dancers Alvin Ailey, Geoffrey Holder, and Carmen de Lavallade. Although the score, sets, costumes, and cast were praised, the musical had a weak book and it did not recoup its large investment.

On October 20, 1955, *No Time for Sergeants* opened and convulsed theatregoers for 796 performances. Ira Levin's comedy, based on Mac Hyman's novel, starred Andy Griffith as an amiable southerner who throws the army into an uproar by his friendly simplicity; Roddy McDowall was his army buddy.

The late 1950s at this theatre brought some musicals that were only moderately successful: *Oh, Captain* (1958), with Tony Randall, Abbe Lane, Susan Johnson, and Alexandra Danilova, and *First Impressions*, a musical version of *Pride and Prejudice* (1959), starring Hermione Gingold, Farley Granger, Polly Bergen, Phyllis Newman, and Ellen Hanley. During these years, there were also engagements of Jerome Robins' *Ballets: U.S.A.* and *Bells Are Ringing,* the musical that moved here from the Shubert.

The 1960s brought Frank Loesser's unsuccessful musical *Greenwillow* (1960), starring Anthony Perkins, Ellen McCown, Pert Kelton, and

🎭 LEFT: Zero Mostel chastises Raymond Walburn in the antic musical *A Funny Thing Happened on the Way to the Forum* (1963). BELOW: Medium Beatrice Lillie in her last show, *High Spirits*, with ghostly Tammy Grimes (1964).

Maurice Chevalier at 77, a personal appearance by the French singer, occurred in 1965, as did the Broadway debut of Liza Minnelli in an unsuccessful musical, *Flora, The Red Menace*. Other unsuccessful shows followed: a musical version of the best-selling book *The Yearling* (1965); a musical adaptation of the Superman comic strip called *It's a Bird...It's a Plane...It's Superman* (1966); an all-star revival of *Dinner at Eight* (1966); a musical version of *The Man Who Came To Dinner*, called *Sherry!* (1967). Finally, a palpable hit arrived in October 1967, when Tom Stoppard's coruscating play *Rosencrantz and Guildenstern Are Dead* opened. The dazzling work, which offered *Hamlet* as seen through the eyes of two of its minor characters, won a Tony Award as the best drama of the season. It was brilliantly acted by John Wood, Paul Hecht, and Brian Murray. It played for 421 performances.

Another powerful drama, *The Great White Hope*, by Howard Sackler, opened here in 1968 and won the Pulitzer Prize, New York Drama Crit-

Cecil Kellaway; the Ballets Africains and *West Side Story*, from the Winter Garden (1960); Lucille Ball in a moderately entertaining musical, *Wildcat* (1961); *Irma La Douce* (1961), the hit musical from the Plymouth Theatre; an unsuccessful revue, *New Faces of 1962*; and a huge hit, *A Funny Thing Happened on the Way to the Forum*, the Stephen Sondheim/Burt Shevelove/Larry Gelbart musical based on several plays of Plautus, directed by George Abbott and starring Zero Mostel, David Burns, Jack Gilford, John Carradine, and Raymond Walburn. This antic production tickled theatregoers for 966 performances.

Beatrice Lillie made her last Broadway appearance at the Alvin in 1964 in *High Spirits*, an uproarious musical version of Noel Coward's comedy *Blithe Spirit*, by Hugh Martin and Timothy Gray, staged by Coward. Miss Lillie was brilliant as the medium, Madam Arcati, and she was splendidly assisted by Tammy Grimes, Edward Woodward, and Louise Troy. The musical ran for 376 performances.

ics Circle Award, and Tony Award for best play. James Earl Jones and Jane Alexander won Tony Awards for their memorable performances as the first black heavyweight champion of the world and his tragic girlfriend. The play ran for 557 performances.

In the spring of 1970 Harold Prince arrived with an exciting, off-beat musical, *Company*, by Stephen Sondheim and George Furth, and the series of sketches about a popular bachelor (played by Dean Jones briefly, then succeeded by Larry Kert) and his demanding friends won seven Tony Awards, including best musical, best book, best music, best lyrics, and best direction. Boris Aronson's magnificent set—a skeletal apartment house with running elevators—also won a Tony.

Shenandoah, a musical that arrived from the Goodspeed Opera House in Connecticut in 1975, starred John Cullum, who won a Tony Award for his performance in this Civil War musical. Next came a veritable gold mine for this theatre, another winner from the Goodspeed Opera House, called *Annie*. This musical adaptation of the popular comic strip by Martin Charnin, Thomas Meehan, and Charles Strouse played at the Alvin for almost five years before moving to another theatre. It received Tony Awards for best musical, best book, best score, best sets, best costumes, best choreography, and best actress (Dorothy Loudon). Andrea McArdle was highly praised for her acting of Annie and the beguiling orphans also received raves. It was a great family show and ran for 2,377 performances.

After *Annie* left the Alvin, the theatre had five musical failures in succession: *Merrily We Roll Along; The Little Prince and the Aviator* (which closed during previews); *Little Johnny Jones; Do Black Patent Leather Shoes Really Reflect Up?*, and *Seven Brides for Seven Brothers*. Next came a revival of *Your Arms Too Short to Box with God*, starring Al Green and

Andrea McArdle as Little Orphan Annie is menaced by Dorothy Loudon as Janine Ruane and Robyn Finn look on in *Annie* (1977).

Patti LaBelle, for several months, followed by the theatre's current attraction, Neil Simon's play *Brighton Beach Memoirs*, which won the New York Drama Critics Circle Award as the season's best play. It stars Matthew Broderick, who won a Tony Award for his performance, Zeljko Ivanek, Elizabeth Franz, Peter Michael Goetz, Joyce Van Patten, and Mandy Ingber.

This theatre is currently owned by the Messrs. Nederlander. On Wednesday, June 29, 1983, the Alvin was officially renamed the Neil Simon Theatre in honor of America's most prolific playwright, whose current hit is flourishing here. Through its long and distinguished career, this house has successfully staged both brilliant dramas and outstanding musicals. It is one of Broadway's most prized legitimate theatres.

ETHEL BARRYMORE THEATRE

In 1927, when Ethel Barrymore was appearing at Maxine Elliott's Theatre in Somerset Maugham's hit play *The Constant Wife*, playwright Zoe Atkins told her that the Shuberts wanted her to star in a new play for them and were willing to build a theatre in her name if she consented. Miss Barrymore read the play, a religious drama called *The Kingdom of God*, liked it, and thereupon agreed to switch to Shubert management.

The Ethel Barrymore Theatre, designed by Herbert J. Krapp, opened on the night of December 20, 1928, with Ethel Barrymore in *The Kingdom of God* by Spanish playwright G. Martinez Sierra. The star played Sister Gracia, a character who aged from nineteen to seventy. Wrote Brooks Atkinson in the New York *Times*: "As the curtain raiser for a splendid new theatre that fittingly bears her own name, Ethel Barrymore has chosen a quiet and elusive piece by that dexterous Spaniard, G. Martinez Sierra. For Miss Barrymore, it serves as a vehicle." Critic Heywood Broun was more enthusiastic. He wrote: "Miss Barrymore's performance is the most moving piece of acting I have ever seen in the theatre."

The new Barrymore Theatre, with over 1,000 seats, was ideal for dramas, comedies, and intimate musicals. Ms. Barrymore chose for her next appearance at her theatre one of those Hungarian romances in which the lovers are named He and She. *The Love Duel*, as it was called, starred Barrymore as She and Louis Calhern as He and it was directed (as *The Kindgom of God* had been) by E.M. Blythe (who happened to be Ethel Barrymore). This Hungarian trifle ran for eighty-eight performances.

In 1929 John Drinkwater's hit comedy *Bird in Hand* moved to the Barrymore from the Morosco for three months. This was followed by a fascinating drama called *Death Takes a Holiday*, in which Philip Merivale played death on vacation, masquerading as Prince Sirki. Unfortunately, Death falls in love with Grazia (Rose Hobart) and takes her with him (willingly) as he returns to "the other side." This fanciful play engrossed theatregoers for 181 performances.

The popular comedy *Topaze* moved here from the Music Box in 1930, with Frank Morgan, Catherine Willard, and Clarence Derwent. Miriam Hopkins appeared very fleetingly in another of those Hungarian romances, *His Majesty's Car*. Ethel Barrymore returned in blackface to do a

LEFT: Ethel Barrymore as Sister Gracia in *The Kingdom of God*, the play that opened the theatre built for her by the Shuberts (1928). RIGHT: Philip Merivale as the Grim Reaper prepares to take Rose Hobart with him to the "other side" in *Death Takes a Holiday* (1929).

play about blacks called *Scarlet Sister Mary*. The critics felt that whites should not attempt to portray blacks when blacks did it so much better and this curious drama ran for only twenty-three performances. It did, however, serve to introduce Miss Barrymore's daughter, Ethel Barrymore Colt, in her Broadway debut.

The beautiful Billie Burke returned to the stage in 1930 in Ivor Novello's play *The Truth Game*, in which he also appeared. The *Times* labeled the work "a perfect matinee comedy" and the ladies flocked to it for 105 perform-

ances. The following year brought Edna Best, Basil Rathbone, and Earl Larimore in a French triangle situation, *Melo*, but it was only moderately successful. Later in the year, Ethel Barrymore returned in Lee Shubert's revival of *The School for Scandal*, and this time the actress introduced her son, John Drew Colt, to Broadway.

Socialite/actress Hope Williams starred in something called *The Passing Present* in 1931, with Maria Ouspenskaya, but this made way after 16 performances for a more deserving

From left: Alfred Lunt, Lynn Fontanne and Noel Coward in Coward's *menage-a-trois* comedy *Design for Living* (1933).

production called *Whistling in the Dark*. Starring the amusing Ernest Truex as a detective-story writer who is forced by a gang of gunmen to concoct a perfect crime, the comedy delighted Barrymore patrons for 144 performances.

Here Today, a "comedy of bad manners," by George Oppenheimer, directed by George S. Kaufman, amused first-nighters in September 1932 mainly because the acid-mouth character played by Ruth Gordon was supposed to be no less than acid-mouth Dorothy Parker. But the general public did not take to this evening of bitchiness and the play folded after thirty-nine performances. John Van Druten's more civilized comedy hit *There's Always Juliet* moved here next from Henry Miller's Theatre.

On November 29, 1932, the Barrymore Theatre housed its first musical, Cole Porter's *Gay Divorce*, and it was a hit. Fred Astaire, without his sister Adele for the first time, danced with the blonde Claire Luce, who once rode a live ostrich in the *Ziegfeld Follies*. Astaire and Luce singing and dancing Porter's haunting "Night and Day" helped to turn this into a hit. The scintillating cast included the venomous Luella Gear and the wry Eric Blore and Erik Rhodes, who would repeat their roles when Astaire appeared in the movie version. *Gay Divorce* had to move to the Shubert to make way for another event at this theatre. The musical played for 248 performances.

On January 24, 1933, Alfred Lunt, Lynn Fontanne, and Noel Coward dazzled first-nighters in *Design for Living*, a comedy Coward had promised to write for them and himself as a starring vehicle. Master Coward, who did not relish long runs, limited this engagement to 135 performances, but it could have run all season. It presented what one critic described as the most amoral situation ever viewed on the Broadway stage: two men in love with the same woman, but when she was not available, in love with themselves. It proved an acting triumph for this gilded trio.

A mystery play, *Ten-Minute Alibi*, with Bramwell Fletcher, John Williams, and Joseph Spurin-Calleia, was a moderate success in the fall of 1933. This was succeeded by *Jezebel*, a southern drama by Owen Davis, originally written for Tallulah Bankhead. When she became ill, Miriam Hopkins stepped in, but the play was not a success. It later made an excellent film for Bette Davis.

The year 1934 was not a bountiful one for this theatre. No fewer than seven failures paraded across its stage. Theatregoers looked forward to Noel Coward's play *Point Valaine*, starring the Lunts, Osgood Perkins, Louis Hayward, and Broderick Crawford, in January 1935, but the play was sordid and overly melodramatic, with Lunt spitting in Fontanne's face in one scene. This turgid tale of tropical lust expired none too soon after fifty-six performances.

The hit play *The Distaff Side* moved here from the Longacre Theatre in March 1935. Later in the year, Philip Merivale and his wife, Gladys Cooper, brought their revivals of *Othello* and *Macbeth*, but they were not successful. A historical play, *Parnell*, with George Curzon as the Irish hero, fared better, playing for ninety-eight performances. Irwin Shaw provided excitement in 1936 with his one-act war play *Bury the Dead*, paired with another short work, *Prelude*, by J. Edward Shugrue and John O'Shaughnessy, which moved theatregoers for ninety-seven performances. In the fall of 1936, the British playwright/actor Emlyn Williams starred in his terrifying play *Night Must Fall*, based on an actual case in the British courts. He played a charming psychopath who carries one of his victims' head around in a hat box. May Whitty (later Dame May Whitty) was his next victim.

On December 26, 1936, Clare Boothe's play *The Women* opened at this theatre with about forty women in the cast and not one male. Critic Brooks Atkinson called it "a kettle of venom" in the New York *Times* and said he disliked it. It promptly became the Barrymore's longest-running play to date, spewing its venom for 657 performances with such brittle actresses as Ilka Chase, Margalo Gillmore, Betty Lawford, Arlene Francis, Audrey Christie, and Marjorie Main.

In October 1938 the Playwrights' Company presented the Maxwell Anderson/Kurt Weill mu-

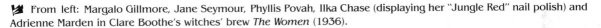 From left: Margalo Gillmore, Jane Seymour, Phyllis Povah, Ilka Chase (displaying her "Jungle Red" nail polish) and Adrienne Marden in Clare Boothe's witches' brew *The Women* (1936).

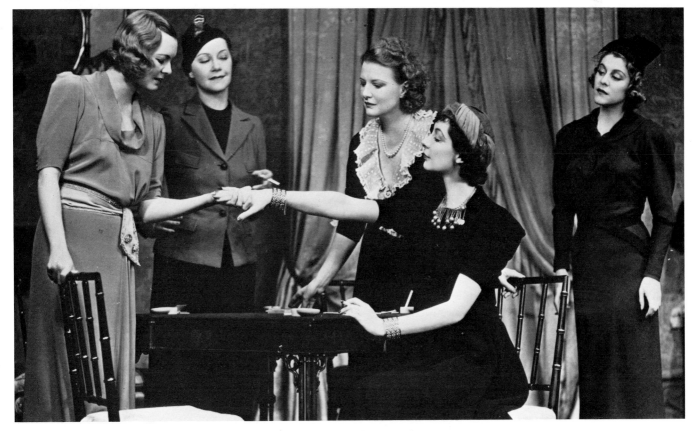

Ferrer, and Carl (later Karl) Malden. It ran for 105 performances.

Highlights of the 1940s at the Barrymore included Ethel Barrymore's last appearance at her theatre, in a weak play by Vincent Sheean called *An International Incident*. On Christmas night, 1940, Rodgers/Hart and John O'Hara brought a landmark musical here which shocked some of the critics. It was *Pal Joey*, the tough chronicle of a Chicago heel (Gene Kelly) who is kept by a rich adulteress (Vivienne Segal). The memorable score contained "Bewitched, Bothered and Bewildered," "I Could Write a Book," and some great musical comedy numbers that stopped the show. The cast also included June Havoc, Van Johnson, Leila Ernst, and Jack Durant. It ran for 270 performances. When it was revived in the 1950s, it shocked no one and it had a triumphant run of 540 performances. George Abbott, who produced and

ABOVE: Vivienne Segal and Gene Kelly in the amoral *Pal Joey* (1940). RIGHT: Gertrude Musgrove, Judith Anderson, Katharine Cornell in *The Three Sisters* (1942).

sical *Knickerbocker Holiday*, starring Walter Huston as Peter Stuyvesant. It is chiefly remembered today for Huston's magnificent rendition of the classic "September Song."

The spring of 1939 brought Katharine Cornell in a rarity—a modern comedy by S.N. Behrman called *No Time for Comedy*. Her costar was Laurence Olivier, who played her playwright husband, who is swayed from writing hit comedies to attempting a stuffy drama by his mistress (Margalo Gillmore). The public took to Cornell in high-fashion gowns by Valentina, and the comedy ran for 185 performances, with Olivier turning into a matinee idol.

The last show to play this theatre in the 1930s was Maxwell Anderson's *Key Largo*, a moderate hit with Paul Muni, Uta Hagen, José

staged *Pal Joey*, brought another musical hit here on October 1, 1941. It was the prep-school show *Best Foot Forward*, detailing what happens when a movie queen visits a campus as a publicity stunt. The star was Rosemary Lane, but the show was stolen by Nancy Walker, June Allyson, and Maureen Cannon as students. It ran for 326 performances.

This was followed by a musical failure, *Count Me In*, written by Walter Kerr (before he was a critic) and Leo Brady, with such talents as Charles Butterworth, Luella Gear, Hal LeRoy, Mary Healy, and Gower and Jeanne (Champion).

The rest of the 1940s are remembered for Katharine Cornell's production of Chekhov's *The Three Sisters* (1942), in which she starred with Ruth Gordon and Judith Anderson. The distinguished cast also included Dennis King, Edmund Gwenn, Alexander Knox, McKay Morris, Kirk Douglas, Tom Powers, and Marie Paxton. This splendid production was directed by Ms. Cornell's husband, Guthrie McClintic, and played for 123 performances. Ralph Bellamy and Shirley Booth appeared in an enormous success, *Tomorrow the World*, by James Gow and Arnaud d'Usseau in 1943, which showed what happened to an American family who sheltered a twelve-year-old boy (Skippy Homeier) who was brought up in Germany as a Nazi.

A series of revivals played this theatre in the mid-1940s: Katharine Cornell and Brian Aherne in *The Barretts of Wimpole Street* (1945); Gertrude Lawrence, Raymond Massey, and Melville Cooper in *Pygmalion* (1945); Elisabeth Bergner, John Carradine, and Canada Lee in *The Duchess of Malfi* (1946); and José Ferrer in his acclaimed revival of *Cyrano de Bergerac*, which moved here from the Alvin Theatre (1946).

Gian-Carlo Menotti's twin opera bill, *The Telephone* and *The Medium* (1947), received high praise, especially for Maria Powers's electrifying performance in the latter.

Gertrude Lawrence makes a fair lady in Shaw's *Pygmalion* (1945 revival).

On December 3, 1947, the Barrymore Theatre presented its most distinguished offering, Tennessee Williams's *A Streetcar Named Desire*. Jessica Tandy won a Tony Award for her unforgettable performance as Blanche du Bois, and the inspired acting of Marlon Brando, Kim Hunter, and Karl Malden made this a historic night in the American theatre. The haunting play won the Pulitzer Prize and the New York Drama Critics Circle Award for best play of the season and ran for 855 performances. During the run, Anthony Quinn and Uta Hagen succeeded Brando and Tandy.

Gian-Carlo Menotti returned with another superb opera, *The Consul*, in 1950, a harrowing work about postwar Europe, with magnificent performances by Patricia Neway and Marie Powers. Irene Mayer Selznick, who produced *A Streetcar Named Desire*, piloted another hit at this theatre in 1950 when she presented Rex

Harrison and his then wife, Lili Palmer, in John Van Druten's beguiling comedy about witchcraft, *Bell, Book and Candle*. The silken duo enchanted audiences for 233 performances. Another huge hit opened on October 24, 1951, when Jessica Tandy and her husband, Hume Cronyn, starred in Jan de Hartog's two-character comedy *The Fourposter*, which won a Tony Award for the season's best play and another Tony for its director, José Ferrer. The play, about events in the thirty-five-year married life of a couple simply named Agnes and Michael, ran for 632 performances.

A spirited revival of Shaw's *Misalliance*, with William Redfield, Roddy McDowall, Richard Kiley, Tamara Geva, and Jerome Kilty, moved here from the New York City Center in 1953. Later that year, Robert Anderson's first Broadway play, *Tea and Sympathy*, with Deborah Kerr, John Kerr, and Leif Erickson, presented a poignant study of a young prep-school student who is suspected of being gay. The drama ran for 712 performances. John Kerr won a Tony Award for his performance.

In February 1955 Paul Newman returned to the stage in a thriller by Joseph Hayes called *The Desperate Hours*. It was one of those plays in which three criminals hide out in a pleasant family's house and terrorize them. The excellent cast also included Karl Malden, Nancy Coleman, Patricia Peardon, George Grizzard, James Gregory, and Mary Orr. *The Desperate Hours* won a Tony Award as best play and production and also one for Robert Montgomery's direction.

Marcel Marceau played an engagement here in 1955, followed by another Irene Mayer Selznick production, the exquisite Enid Bagnold play *The Chalk Garden*, with sparkling performances by Gladys Cooper, Fritz Weaver, Siobhan McKenna, Betsy von Furstenberg, Percy Waram, and Marian Seldes. The unusual drama played for 182 performances.

The British actress Maggie Smith made her Broadway debut at the Barrymore in June 1956 as one of Leonard Sillman's *New Faces of 1956*. But it was female impersonator T. C. Jones who drew raves, for his impersonations of Tallulah Bankhead, Bette Davis, and other stars, and who kept the revue running for 220 performances.

The Barrymore's next hit was a dramatization of Thomas Wolfe's *Look Homeward Angel*, by Ketti Frings in 1957, which was awarded the Pulitzer Prize and the New York Drama Critics Circle Award for best play. It starred Anthony Perkins, Jo Van Fleet, Arthur Hill, Hugh Griffith, Rosemary Murphy, and many others and ran for 564 performances. Another fine drama, *A Raisin in the Sun*, by Lorraine Hansberry, opened here in March 1959, starring Sidney Poitier, Claudia McNeil, Diana Sands, Ruby Dee, and Louis Gossett. It won the New York Drama Critics Circle Award for best play and had a lengthy run of 530 performances.

The smash hit comedy *A Majority of One*, starring Gertrude Berg and Cedric Hardwicke, moved here in 1959 from the Shubert Theatre and stayed for eight months. Some highlights of the 1960s included Henry Fonda and Mildred Natwick in Ira Levin's comedy *Critic's Choice* (1960); Michael Redgrave, Sandy Dennis, and Googie Withers in Graham Green's comedy *The Complaisant Lover* (1961); Henry Fonda and Olivia de Havilland in Garson Kanin's play *A Gift of Time* (1962); James Baldwin's play *The Amen Corner* (1965); Lee Remick and Robert Duvall in Frederick Knott's thriller *Wait Until Dark* (1966); an engagement of Les Ballets Africains (1966); Peter Shaffer's off-beat twin bill—*Black Comedy* and *White Lies* (1967)—with Geraldine Page, Lynn Redgrave, Donald Madden, Michael Crawford, Peter Bull, and Camila Ashland; *Noel Coward's Sweet Potato* (1968), a revue of Coward's songs with Dorothy Loudon, George Grizzard, Carole Shelley, and Arthur Mitchell; a revival of *The Front Page* with

🐾 ABOVE: Marlon Brando rapes Jessica Tandy in *A Streetcar Named Desire* (1947). TOP RIGHT: Rex Harrison seduces Lili Palmer in *Bell, Book and Candle* (1950). BOTTOM RIGHT: Hume Cronyn marries Jessica Tandy in the long-running comedy *The Fourposter* (1951).

best play; the inventive musical *I Love My Wife* (1977), by Michael Stewart and Cy Coleman; Anthony Perkins and Mia Farrow in Bernard Slade's *Romantic Comedy* (1979); Jean Kerr's *Lunch Hour* (1980), with Sam Waterston and Gilda Radner; Katharine Hepburn and Dorothy Loudon in Ernest Thompson's *The West Side Waltz* (1981); and Jessica Tandy, Hume Cronyn, and Keith Carradine in *Foxfire*, by Mr. Cronyn and Susan Cooper. Ms. Tandy won a Tony Award for her performance in this play with music. The theatre's most recent tenant was the musical *Baby*.

The Ethel Barrymore Theatre has always been owned by the Shubert Organization, which has kept this prized house in excellent order. It has housed some of the theatre's most honored plays and is also perfect for revues, musicals, and personal appearances.

ABOVE: Deborah Kerr is kind to John Kerr in *Tea and Sympathy* (1953). RIGHT: Katharine Hepburn at the ivories and Dorothy Loudon on the fiddle in *West Side Waltz* (1981).

Robert Ryan, Bert Convy, Doro Merande, Peggy Cass, and Julia Meade (Helen Hayes later joined the cast) in 1969.

The 1970s brought to this theatre *Conduct Unbecoming* (1970), the British thriller with Jeremy Clyde and Michael Barrington; Alec McCowen in *The Philanthropist* (1971); Melvin Van Peebles's unusual vignettes of black life entitled *Ain't Supposed to Die a Natural Death* (1971); Pirandello's *Emperor Henry IV* (1973), with Rex Harrison; the New Phoenix Repertory Company with revivals of *The Visit*, *Chemin de Fer*, and *Holiday* (1973); Jessica Tandy, Hume Cronyn, and Anne Baxter in two plays by Noel Coward, *Noel Coward in Two Keys* (1974); John Wood in his Tony Award performance in Tom Stoppard's *Travesties* (1975), which also won a Tony Award for best play; Robert Duvall in David Mamet's *American Buffalo* (1977), winner of New York Drama Critics Circle Award for

♜ MARK HELLINGER THEATRE ♜

This theatre was one of the last movie palaces built in Manhattan. It opened on April 22, 1930, as the Hollywood Theatre, one of Warner Brothers' flagship houses. The architect was Thomas W. Lamb, the distinguished designer of some

Niessen, Patricia Bowman, Mitzi Mayfair, Ella Logan, and Judy, Pete, Zeke, and Anne Canova, but the show only registered thirty-five performances. The experiment was not successful, and in 1935 the Hollywood returned to showing

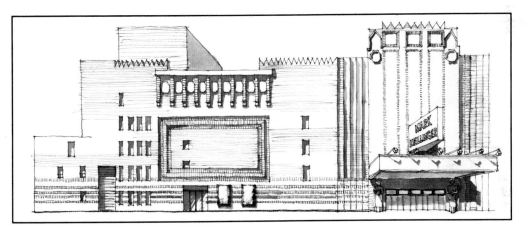

of America's most opulent movie houses. The Hollywood was typical of his ornate splendor, with columns, grand staircases, and baroque curlicues. The entrance to this theatre was originally on Broadway, but later it was switched to Fifty-first Street.

During the depression, Warner Brothers converted their huge movie house to a policy of live entertainment and, with Lew Brown, presented a variety show named *Calling All Stars* on December 13, 1934. The cast was composed of such headliners as Lou Holtz, Phil Baker, Jack Whiting, Martha Ray (later, Raye), Gertrude

films, including a reserved-seat, two-a-day engagement of the Warner Brothers/Max Reinhardt movie *A Midsummer Night's Dream*.

In October 1936 the Hollywood Theatre became the 51st Street Theatre when it presented George Abbott's version of *Uncle Tom's Cabin*, called *Sweet River*. The play was spectacular, with a very large cast and choir and mammoth sets by Donald Oenslager, but the critics were not impressed and the epic only achieved five performances.

The 51st Street Theatre went back to being the Hollywood Theatre to show major Warner

Brothers releases until November 1939, when *George White's Scandals* moved here from the Alvin Theatre. The 1939 edition of this popular revue was the last of the series and it featured the Broadway debut of Hollywood's tap dancing star Ann Miller, who garnered raves. Other headliners in the show included Ella Logan, Willie and Eugene Howard, Ben Blue, Collette Lyons, and Victor Arden and his Orchestra. The show ran for 120 performances.

In the spring of 1940 this theatre once again switched its name to the 51st Street Theatre when Laurence Olivier and Vivien Leigh opened there in *Romeo and Juliet*. Olivier designed and directed the production and played Romeo, Ms. Leigh was Juliet, Dame May Whitty was the Nurse, Cornel Wilde was Tybalt (he also directed the dueling scenes), Edmond O'Brien was Mercutio, Wesley Addy was Benvolio, and Halliwell Hobbes was Capulet. Motley designed the sets and costumes, Robert Edmond Jones created the lighting, and the play should have been a triumph, but it was a disaster. The leading stars, who had invested their own money in the revival, lost all of it. Major blame was placed upon Olivier's direction and the production managed only thirty-six performances.

The theatre went back to being the Hollywood and showing films until Christmas night, 1941, when Eddie Cantor returned to Broadway after a thirteen-year absence in Hollywood and starred in a hit musical called *Banjo Eyes*, based on the popular comedy *Three Men on a Horse*. The impressive cast also featured Jacqueline Susann (yes, the future novelist), Virginia Mayo, Bill Johnson, Audrey Christie, June Clyde, Lionel Stander, and the dancing De Marcos. The score was by Vernon Duke and lyrics by John La Touche and Harold Adamson. The musical could have run longer than 126 performances but it closed due to Cantor's illness.

During the war years, the Hollywood Theatre reverted to showing films and in 1947 it

OPPOSITE: Laurence Olivier and Vivienne Leigh in their star-crossed production of *Romeo and Juliet* (1940). RIGHT: Bert Lahr as Queen Victoria and the leader of a space brigade in the 1951 revue *Two on the Aisle* (1951).

renamed itself the Warner Brothers Theatre during the showing of the film version of *Life with Father*.

In 1949 tycoon Anthony B. Farrell bought the theatre and rechristened it the Mark Hellinger in honor of the esteemed Broadway columnist. The name has remained ever since. Mr. Farrell, a manufacturer from Albany who got bitten by the show biz bug, bought the theatre for a million and a half dollars and spent another fortune producing a revue called *All for Love* that opened at the Mark Hellinger on January 22, 1949. The theatre, beautifully refurbished by Mr. Farrell, looked great, but the show did not. It managed to run for 121 performances but not at a profit. Farrell took a $12,000 weekly loss, and when the revue closed in May *Variety* estimated that its producer had lost a half million dollars on it. The talented cast included Paul and Grace Hartman and Bert Wheeler.

S.M. Chartock presented a three-week season of Gilbert and Sullivan in the fall of 1949. Anthony B. Farrell fared better with his next musical in his theatre. Even though the critics were not wild about *Texas, Li'l Darlin'*, with Kenny Delmar, theatregoers disagreed with them and supported this show for 293 performances.

The Hartmans returned to Mr. Farrell's theatre in their hit revue *Tickets, Please!*, which moved here from the Coronet Theatre in 1950. A very lavish revue, *Bless You All*, was produced at the Hellinger in December 1950 by Herman Levin and Oliver Smith. It starred Pearl Bailey, Jules Munshin, Mary McCarty, Donald Saddler, Valerie Bettis, and Gene Barry, but it was not a success. The score was by Harold Rome and the sketches by Arnold Auerbach.

A far more successful revue was *Two on the Aisle*, starring Bert Lahr and Dolores Gray, by Betty Comden, Adolph Green, Julie Styne, Nat Hiken, and William Friedberg, which opened on July 19, 1951, and ran for 279 performances. Lahr's great clowning and Gray's belting were a dynamic combination. The following year brought another musical, *Three Wishes for Jamie*, with Bert Wheeler, John Raitt, Charlotte Rae, Anne Jeffreys, and Ralph Morgan, with a score by Ralph Blane, and this fairy tale set to music ran for 91 performances.

Gilbert and Sullivan returned to the Mark Hellinger in the fall of 1952, followed by the National Theatre of Greece in their repertory of classical plays presented by Guthrie McClintic.

In February 1953 *Hazel Flagg* opened at this theatre. It was a musical version of the satiric film *Nothing Sacred*, by Hecht and MacArthur, and Hecht wrote the show's libretto to a score by Jule Styne and Bob Hilliard. Helen Gallagher played the title role and she was ably assisted by Jack Whiting, Benay Venuta, Thomas Mitchell, and Sheree North. One hit tune emerged from the show: "How Do You Speak to an Angel?", which became popular before the show opened. This was followed in March 1954 by *The Girl in Pink Tights*, starring dancer Zizi Jeanmaire. It was Sigmund Romberg's last Broadway show and, unfortunately, it was not a success. It ran for 115 performances. The Ballets Espagnols: Teresa and Luisillo played a profitable engagement here later that year.

The charming musical about the Amish —*Plain and Fancy*—opened here on January 27, 1955, and proved an immediate hit. It starred Shirl Conway, Richard Derr, Gloria Marlowe, Barbara Cook, Nancy Andrews, Daniel Nagrin, Stefan Schnabel, and many others. The hit song was "Young and Foolish" and the musical ran for 461 performances.

On the evening of March 15, 1956, the Mark Hellinger presented its most distinguished production. It was Herman Levin's presentation of the Alan Jay Lerner and Frederick Loewe masterpiece *My Fair Lady*, adapted from Shaw's *Pygmalion*. Brilliantly directed by Moss Hart, with choreography by Hanya Holm, sets by Oliver Smith, and costumes by Cecil Beaton, the musical was one of Broadway's finest moments. It starred Rex Harrison and Julie Andrews and they made theatrical history. It won the Tony Award and New York Drama Critics Circle Award for best musical and countless other awards. It ran for 2,717 performances and is constantly revived. It is one of the landmarks of American musical theatre and is the most honored show ever to play the Mark Hellinger.

In 1962, when *My Fair Lady* left this theatre, *The Sound of Music* moved in from the Lunt Fontanne and stayed for seven months. This was succeeded by an Italian import, *Rugantino* (1964), probably the only show ever presented on Broadway with running subtitles, since it was acted and sung in Italian. Despite the translation, which was flashed across the top of the proscenium, the musical was a flop. Another musical that did not pay off was the Comden/Green/Jule Styne show *Fade Out—Fade In*, starring the popular TV star Carol Burnett and Jack Cassidy. George Abbott directed the show about a movie usher who becomes a movie star, but there were book problems, and Ms. Burnett became ill, which eventually closed the musical.

On a Clear Day You Can See Forever (1965) had a stunning score by Burton Lane and Alan Jay Lerner and brilliant performances by Barbara Harris and John Cullum, but this unusual musical about ESP had script troubles. Nevertheless, it ran for eight months.

During the latter 1960s, the Mark Hellinger housed a number of shows with illustrious stars and creators, but none was a commercial hit. This included a musical called *A Joyful Noise* (1966), choreographed by Michael Bennett.

✄ LEFT: Souvenir program for *My Fair Lady*. BELOW: Julie Andrews and Rex Harrison in Lerner and Loewe's classic *My Fair Lady* (1956).

Illya, Darling (1967) starred Melina Mercouri in the same role she played in the hit movie *Never on Sunday*. It ran for 319 performances, but did not recoup its investment. *I'm Solomon*, a Biblical disaster starring Dick Shawn, came and went in 1968. Marlene Dietrich made one of her public appearances here in 1968, as did Les Ballets Africains.

Jerry Herman, who had two solid hits in his career—*Hello, Dolly!* and *Mame*—came up with a clinker named *Dear World* (1969), based on the sparkling play *The Madwoman of Chaillot*. Angela Lansbury won a Tony Award for her performance and that was the only redeeming feature of this pretentious musical. In 1969 Katharine Hepburn made her musical comedy debut in *Coco* at this theatre. Her acting was far better than her guttural singing, and the Alan Jay Lerner/André Previn show ran for 332 performances because of her star power. A horror named *Ari* opened here in 1971, followed by *Man of La Mancha* from another theatre. Then came a musical that brought out New York's worst-dressed people for the opening. The show was *Jesus Christ Superstar* and every creep in Manhattan showed up for the opening. It was a grisly sight: a Biblical spectacle onstage and the dregs of society in the audience. The musical by Andrew Lloyd Webber and Tim Rice, staged by Tom O'Horgan, ran for 720 performances on Broadway and had considerably more dignity than its audiences.

Katharine Hepburn as Coco Chanel in the spectacular musical *Coco* (1959).

🎭 Ann Miller and Mickey Rooney do some patriotic clowning in *Sugar Babies* (1979).

The remainder of the 1970s at this theatre was a mixed bag. Martha Graham brought her Dance Company for an engagement, which was always welcome. Then there was an all-male *As You Like It* from Britain that did not fare well in 1974. A revival of *The Skin of Our Teeth* folded its tents quickly in the same year, as did the horrendous musical *1600 Pennsylvania Avenue*, by no less than Alan Jay Lerner and Leonard Bernstein. *Timbuktu!*, a musical with Eartha Kitt, was not much better in 1978, nor was *Platinum*, a musical of the rock world starring Alexis Smith in that same year.

Sarava, a musical about South America, was another clinker in 1979. This was succeeded by an engagement of Nureyev with the Joffrey Ballet and another forgettable musical, *The Utter Glory of Morrisey Hall*, with Celeste Holm in 1979. Finally, the Mark Hellinger housed a show worthy of its dimensions. The burlesque revue *Sugar Babies*, starring Mickey Rooney

(making his Broadway debut at the same theatre where he once played "Puck" on the screen in *A Midsummer Night's Dream*) and Ann Miller, who had appeared here in the 1939 *George White's Scandals*, turned into this theatre's biggest hit since *My Fair Lady*. Its combination of old-time burlesque sketches with musical favorites of yesteryear made it a winning combination. It ran for 1,208 performances.

The Mark Hellinger's most recent tenant was the magical musical *Merlin*, starring the great magician Doug Henning and Chita Rivera. The show had the most spectacular effects ever seen on Broadway, but the book and the score were mediocre. It managed to run for 199 performances.

The Mark Hellinger is a Nederlander Theatre and has been kept in splendid condition. Its gigantic capacity of over 1,600 seats qualifies it for musical spectacles of the most elaborate caliber.

⚜ CIRCLE IN THE SQUARE THEATRE ⚜

The new Circle in the Square Theatre opened on November 15, 1972, with Theodore Mann as artistic director and Paul Libin as managing director. The nonprofit organization is the uptown successor to Circle in the Square in Greenwich Village. The handsome new theatre was designed by architect Allen Sayles and has lighting by Jules Fisher.

The theatre, located in the Uris Building at Fiftieth Street, west of Broadway, is situated below the former Uris Theatre, now renamed the Gershwin Theatre. It has 650 seats, more than double the number of its Off-Broadway parent. At the time of the new theatre's opening, Theodore Mann told PLAYBILL: "Every seat here has a perfect view. Essentially, the design is based on the old theatre—with almost exactly the same stage space. But we have the latest technical facilities—we can trap the stage, have enough height to fly the scenery—from an artistic and scenic point of view. And look at the ceiling in the auditorium. I don't know of any other theatre like this that has a visible grid above the audience where electricians and stage hands can walk about. All our lighting will come from there. This is a whole new innovation in the Broadway area—the arrival of institutional theatres."

The new theatre is much more cheerful than its predecessor on Bleecker Street, with bright red seats and red-and-gray checked carpet bearing the Circle in the Square cube symbol, which is repeated in the solid cube lights in the handsome lobby.

"We owe a lot to Brooks Atkinson for the design of this theatre," Mr. Mann stated. "When we were building the first one, I asked Mr. Atkinson what the essential ingredient should be. He replied, 'When you walk in the door, you should see the stage—that should predominate—not the audience.' So, when you walk into our theatre, the first thing you see is the stage—and it works."

The new Circle in the Square opened auspiciously with a revival of an edited version of Eugene O'Neill's *Mourning Becomes Electra*, with Colleen Dewhurst. Critics praised the production and the new theatre, expressing satisfaction that although the house was larger and more modern, it preserved the intimacy and ambiance of its downtown predecessor.

In 1973 the theatre presented Irene Papas

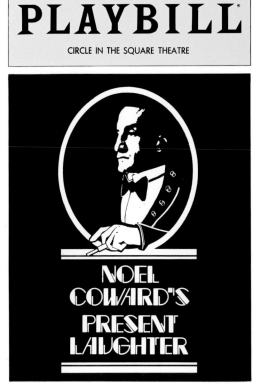

NOEL COWARD'S PRESENT LAUGHTER

✍ LEFT: Ellis Rabb (in wheelchair) berates Patricia O'Connell and Richard Woods in the 1980 revival of *The Man Who Came to Dinner*. ABOVE: PLAYBILL cover sketch of George C. Scott in the scintillating 1982 revival of Noel Coward's *Present Laughter*.

in *Medea*; Siobhan McKenna in *Here Are Ladies*; Lillian Gish, George C. Scott, Nicol Williamson, Barnard Hughes, and Julie Christie in *Uncle Vanya*; Anne Jackson and Eli Wallach in *The Waltz of the Toreadors*; and James Earl Jones in *The Iceman Cometh*.

The year 1974 offered a new play, *An American Millionaire* by Murray Schisgal; Jim Dale in *Scapino*; Rita Moreno in *The National Health*; and Raul Julia in the musical *Where's Charley?*

In 1975 Circle in the Square staged Eugene O'Neill's *All God's Chillun Got Wings*, directed by George C. Scott; Arthur Miller's *Death of a Salesman*, starring Mr. Scott; *Ah, Wilderness!*, with Geraldine Fitzgerald; and Tennessee Williams's *The Glass Menagerie*, with Maureen Stapleton and Rip Torn.

The 1976 season highlighted Vanessa Redgrave in Ibsen's *The Lady from the Sea*; Rodgers and Hart's *Pal Joey*, with Christopher Chadman and Joan Copeland; Mildred Dunnock in *Days in the Trees*, by Marguerite Duras; and Tennessee Williams's *The Night of the Iguana*, starring Richard Chamberlain and Dorothy McGuire.

Four revivals were presented in 1977: Paul

Rudd and Pamela Payton-Wright in *Romeo and Juliet*; Wilde's *The Importance of Being Earnest*; John Wood, Mildred Dunnock, and Tammy Grimes in Molière's *Tartuffe*; and Lynn Redgrave in Shaw's *Saint Joan*.

In 1978 Circle in the Square staged Feydeau's *13 Rue De L'Amour*, with Louis Jourdan and Patricia Elliott; Kaufman and Hart's *Once in a Lifetime*, with John Lithgow, Treat Williams, Max Wright, and Jayne Meadows Allen; Gogol's

▼ From left: William Atherton, Michael Moriarty and John Rubinstein hold court in the 1983 revival of Herman Wouk's *The Caine Mutiny Court-Martial.*

The Inspector General, with Theodore Bikel; and Shaw's *Man and Superman*, with George Grizzard, Philip Bosco, and Laurie Kennedy.

The 1979 season included two new plays: *Spokesong*, by Stewart Parker, with John Lithgow, Virginia Vestoff, Joseph Maher, and Maria Tucci, and *Loose Ends*, by Michael Weller, with Kevin Kline and Roxanne Hart.

The 1980 productions included *Major Barbara*, with Philip Bosco and Laurie Kennedy; *Past Tense*, by Jack Zeman, with Barbara Feldon and Laurence Luckinbill; and Ellis Rabb in *The Man Who Came to Dinner*.

In 1981 Irene Papas returned in *The Bacchae*; E.G. Marshall, Irene Worth, and Rosemary Murphy appeared in *John Gabriel Borkman*; Ralph Waite and Frances Sternhagen headlined *The Father*; and a new American play, *Scenes and Revelations*, by Elan Garonzik, was presented.

The 1982 season opened with Joanne Woodward in *Candida*, followed by *Macbeth*, starring Nicol Williamson. Next came Percy Granger's new play, *Eminent Domain*, with Philip Bosco and Betty Miller. In the summer of 1982, George C. Scott was hailed in a hilarious revival of Noel Coward's light comedy *Present Laughter*.

The year 1983 began with a scintillating revival of Molière's *The Misanthrope*, with Brian Bedford, Carole Shelley, and Mary Beth Hurt. This was followed by an exciting revival of Herman Wouk's *The Caine Mutiny Court-Martial*, with John Rubinstein, Michael Moriarty, and William Atherton. Later, Joe Namath joined the cast, making his Broadway debut. The most recent tenant was a revival of Shaw's *Heartbreak House* starring Rex Harrison and Rosemary Harris.

The Circle in the Square uptown theatre has proven to be ideally designed for the organization's policy of presenting revivals of distinguished plays and premieres of new works.

GEORGE GERSHWIN THEATRE

The George Gershwin Theatre was originally named the Uris. When it opened in 1972 it was the first large Broadway theatre to be built since the Earl Carroll in 1931. Occupying six stories of the new Uris Building on the site of the old Capitol movie palace at Broadway and Fifty-first Street, the huge theatre, with over 1,900 seats, was designed by the late set designer Ralph Alswang. At the time of the theatre's opening, Mr. Alswang told PLAY-BILL: "The Uris represents what I think is

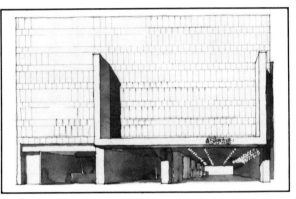

the total philosophy of a modern musical comedy house—seating, sight lines, acoustics—the economy and aesthetics of this kind of theatre. I was given a completely free hand by the Uris people and by the Nederlanders and Gerard Oestreicher, who have a thirty-year lease on the house."

The designer stated that the whole theatre was done in a sensuous Art Nouveau style. The auditorium is on the second floor and is reached by escalators. "The bar, the plaster wall running 200 feet on a reverse curve and the Lalique lighting fixtures are all Art Nouveau shapes," Alswang stated. "Most people want to sit in the orchestra, so we have 1,280 seats downstairs and a very small balcony with 660 seats with projecting side sections to replace box seats. We have dark proscenium panels that serve as light towers and that are removable if the production demands it. The flexible stage floor can be taken apart like a Tinker Toy or be extended as a thrust stage. And for the first time in theatre history, there is a water curtain instead of an asbestos curtain in the event of an on-stage fire."

Another "first" for a legitimate theatre is a revolutionary automatic rigging system called Hydra-Float. Mr. Alswang estimated that the theatre's building cost would amount to about $12.5 million.

A special feature of the theatre is the inclusion of a theatre Hall of Fame with the names of stage greats inscribed in bas-relief on the walls of an impressive rotunda. Another rotunda on the theatre's other side may be used for theatrical exhibitions. The Hall of Fame rotunda was suggested to the Nederlanders by Earl Blackwell.

The Uris opened on November 18, 1972,

PLAYBILL covers for the opening production, *Via Galactica* (1972); the musical *Seesaw* (1973); and the Tony Award-winning revival of *Porgy and Bess* (1976).

with a spectacular rock musical, *Via Galactica*, with Raul Julia and Virginia Vestoff as space beings in the year 2972. Unfortunately, the special effects were more dazzling than the show and it closed after only seven performances.

The theatre's next tenant was much more successful. It was *Seesaw*, a musical version of William Gibson's hit comedy *Two for the Seesaw*. It had a book by Michael Bennett, music by Cy Coleman, lyrics by Dorothy Fields, and starred Ken Howard and Michele Lee. Tommy Tune won a Tony Award as best supporting actor in a musical and Michael Bennett received another for his choreography. On March 23, 1973, Mayor John V. Lindsay replaced Ken Howard in the "My City" number for seven minutes. The musical ran for 296 performances.

In September 1973 the Uris presented a revival of the operetta *The Desert Song*, but it was not for today's audiences. It closed after 15 performances. The next booking was unusual. The brilliant movie musical *Gigi* was converted to a stage musical, which is not the usual order of creativity. Alan Jay Lerner and Frederick Loewe added some songs to the score, which won a Tony Award. The cast included Alfred Drake, Agnes Moorehead (later succeeded by Arlene Francis), Karin Wolfe, Daniel Massey, and Maria Karnilova. It ran for 103 performances.

During 1974, the Uris housed personal appearances by a series of celebrated artists. These included Sammy Davis, Jr.; the rock group Mott the Hoople; Enrico Macias and his La Fete Orientale Co.; Andy Williams and Michel Legrand; Anthony Newley and Henry Mancini; Johnny Mathis; The Fifth Dimension; Raphael in Concert; and Nureyev and Friends.

These concert bookings continued in 1975 with the Dance Theatre of Harlem; Count Basie, Ella Fitzgerald, and Frank Sinatra. The first New York production of Scott Joplin's opera *Treemonisha* opened here in October of that year. The Houston Grand Opera Association production of this work, which had been lost for many years, was conceived and directed by Frank Corsaro and it ran for sixty-four performances. This was followed by the American Ballet Theatre, Margot Fonteyn and Rudolf Nureyev, Paul Anka, Dance Theatre of Harlem, D'Oyly Carte Opera Company, and Al Green.

The Houston Grand Opera and Sherwin M. Goldman presented an acclaimed revival of George Gershwin's opera, *Porgy and Bess*, in 1976, and the production received a Tony Award as the most innovative production of a revival. Clamma Dale was especially praised for her singing and acting of Bess.

ABOVE (from left): Willard White, Carmen Balthrop and Betty Allen in the first New York production of Scott Joplin's opera *Treemonisha* (1975). BELOW: Angela Lansbury and Len Cariou as the cannibalistic twosome in the multi-award-winning *Sweeney Todd* (1979).

Bing Crosby made a rare appearance on Broadway at the Uris in 1976 with his wife, Kathryn, members of his family, and Rosemary Clooney, Joe Bushkin, and others. *Bing Crosby on Broadway* played a limited engagement of twelve performances during the Christmas holiday season. Nureyev appeared next in a dance concert, followed by the Ballet of the Twentieth Century.

A splendid revival of Rodgers and Hammerstein's *The King and I* opened here on May 2, 1977, starring Yul Brynner and Constance Towers. Produced by Lee Guber and Shelly Gross, it was an immediate hit and became the Uris's longest-running show to date: 719 performances.

On March 1, 1979, a ghoulish event occurred at this theatre. It was *Sweeney Todd*, the grisly musical by Stephen Sondheim and Hugh Wheeler, based on a version of *Sweeney Todd* by Christopher Bond. The work received critical acclaim and won Tony Awards for best musical, best score (Sondheim), best book (Wheeler), best musical actress (Angela Lansbury), best musical actor (Len Cariou), best director (Hal Prince), best scenic design (Eugene Lee), and best costume design (Franne Lee). The shocker about a London barber who slits his customers' throats in revenge for an injustice suffered by him was not everyone's cup of blood, but the highly imaginative production ran for 557 performances.

In 1980, the Uris presented Roland Petit's Ballet National de Marseilles, Makarova and Company, and Nureyev and the Boston Ballet. On January 1, 1981, Joseph Papp presented the New York Shakespeare Festival production of *The Pirates of Penzance*, which had been a hit in Central Park the preceding summer. The cast included Kevin Kline, who received a Tony Award for best actor in a musical, Linda Ronstadt, Estelle Parsons, Rex Smith, George Rose, and Tony Anzio. The production received addi-

tional Tony Awards for being the best revival of a show and for best direction (Wilford Leach). It ran for 772 performances.

On August 18, 1981, the Uris presented a revival of Lerner and Loewe's classic *My Fair Lady*, with its original star, Rex Harrison. Nancy Ringham played Eliza Doolittle, Milo O'Shea played her father, and Cathleen Nesbitt, who was in the original cast in 1956, recreated her role of Mrs. Higgins. The revival ran for 124 performances.

The long-running musical *Annie* moved into the Uris from the Eugene O'Neill Theatre in January 1982 and stayed here for a year. It ended its run at the Uris, having chalked up 2,377 performances.

Barry Manilow made a personal appearance here in February 1983, and this was followed by a Houston Grand Opera revival of the Jerome Kern/Oscar Hammerstein II classic *Show Boat*, starring Donald O'Connor.

On the evening of June 5, 1983, during the annual Tony Award telecast, the name of the Uris was officially changed to the Gershwin Theatre, in honor of composer George Gershwin and his lyricist brother, Ira, who contributed many distinguished musicals and the opera *Porgy and Bess* to the Broadway theatre.

The Gershwin Theatre's most recent tenant was the revival of *Mame*, starring the original Mame, Angela Lansbury, the original Miss Gooch, Jane Connell, and these three repeaters: Anne Francine, Willard Waterman, and Sab Shimono.

The Gershwin Theatre is a Nederlander Theatre, under the direction of the Messrs. Nederlander and Gerald Oestreicher. It has the largest seating capacity of any Broadway theatre (excepting the New York State Theatre and the City Center). It was designed for lavish musicals and has also been successful as a showcase house for personal appearances and dance companies.

✍ ABOVE: PLAYBILL cover for the popular revival of *The Pirates of Penzance* (1980). TOP RIGHT: Linda Ronstadt, Tony Azito and policemen in the Gilbert and Sullivan caper. BELOW RIGHT: Angela Lansbury in the 1983 revival of *Mame*.

⚬ MINSKOFF THEATRE ⚬

The Minskoff Theatre, perched on the third floor of One Astor Plaza, the fifty-five-story office tower on the site of Broadway's old Astor Hotel, derives its name from Sam Minskoff and Sons, builders and owners of the high rise. The modern theatre, with a very large seating capacity of 1,621 seats, was designed by the architectural firm of Kahn and Jacobs and offers a spectacular view of the Great White Way from the glass front of the building on all levels of the theatre.

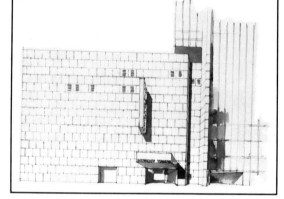

The theatre features an arcade that runs from Forty-fourth to Forty-fifth streets. Inside the spacious lobby, dual escalators take playgoers to the third level of the Grand Foyer of the house. Here there are coat-checking concessions and bars. Additional escalators rise to the fourth, or orchestra, level.

At the time of the theatre's opening in 1973, Robert A. Jacobs, partner-in-charge of Kahn and Jacobs, told PLAYBILL: "A theatre that is thirty-five feet in the air is quite an innovation. According to the old building code in Manhattan, a theatre's orchestra floor had to be within three feet of the sidewalk. We think we've created one of the most exciting, three-dimensional processional routes for the theatregoers —a series of forms, changes in ceiling heights, and spatial explosions. The whole processional, from the moment you enter and rise thirty-five feet to the theatre level, is a theatrical event in itself. Our forms are purely architectural, beautifully proportioned in relation to the processional drama you're going through."

Mr. Jacobs stated that his firm had kept everything simple in the theatre's decor, without hiring what he called "exotic interior desecraters." The decorations consisted of color used in paint, carpeting, and in vinyl on walls. The theatre was done primarily in white and gold, with charcoal-gray seats, which are roomy, comfortable, and offer an excellent view. The orchestra floor rakes steeply toward the stage. Hundreds of small, clear G lamps sparkle in the lobbies, and crystal-basket lights glow in the auditorium. The ceiling is broken into two sections with a narrow grid between them for the stage lights. The proscenium has removable mesh panels on both sides, and the mezzanine, with 590 seats, has

🔖 Debbie Reynolds and ensemble exhume the 1919 hit *Irene*, the Minskoff's opening production (1973).

narrow side projections instead of box seats.

The stage has an innovation: all the flies are on the upstage wall instead of on the side wall. Part of the stage is trapped and can be extended out over the orchestra pit. The dressing rooms are sumptuous and the rest rooms are large, cheerful, and comfortable.

The Minskoff Theatre opened on March 13, 1973, with a lavish revival of the 1919 musical *Irene*. Debbie Reynolds played the title role and sang the show's classic "Alice Blue Gown." The cast also included Patsy Kelly, Monte Markham, Janie Sell, Ruth Warrick, Carmen Alvarez, and George S. Irving, who won a Tony Award for his performance. The musical ran until the fall

of 1974. It was succeeded by two special shows: *Charles Aznavour on Broadway* and *Tony Bennett and Lena Horne Sing*.

The 1975 season at the Minskoff was extremely varied. It began on a sober note with Henry Fonda in his one-man show *Clarence Darrow*. The raucous Bette Midler was next in her salty revue *Clams on the Half Shell*. In the fall of that year, Pearl Bailey and Billy Daniels brought their version of *Hello, Dolly!* to the theatre. The 1976 attractions included a short-lived rock version of *Hamlet* called *Rockabye Hamlet*, with Meat Loaf playing a priest. This was followed by the Dutch National Ballet and the Chinese Acrobats of Taiwan.

The 1977 season brought Merce Cunningham and Dance Company, followed by the long-running musical *Pippin*, which moved here from the Imperial. The year ended with engagements of Cleo Laine and *Star Wars Concert Live*.

Nureyev made a dance appearance at the Minskoff in 1978 with the Murray Lewis Dance Company. Next came a musical version of the play *Look Homeward, Angel*, called simply, *Angel*. Its cast included Fred Gwynne, Frances Sternhagen, Don Scardino, Leslie Ann Ray, Patti Allison, and Joel Higgins, but the Thomas Wolfe

classic did not succeed as a musical and it closed after five performances. Another unsuccessful musical opened in 1978. It was called *King of Hearts* and it was adapted from the film of the same name. The cast included Donald Scardino, Millicent Martin, Pamela Blair, Gary Morgan, Timothy Scott, and Michael McCarty. It expired after forty-eight performances.

In late 1978 an elaborate spectacle, *Ice Dancing*, opened here. It was followed by Bejart —Ballet of the Twentieth Century. A musical called *Got Tu Go Disco* was a quick failure in 1979. Appearances by Shirley Bassey and the Chinese Acrobats and Magicians of Taiwan followed.

A revival of *West Side Story* in 1980 was moderately successful, running for 341 performances. A revival of Cole Porter's *Can-Can*, however, proved a disaster in 1981, despite the dancing of Zizi Jeanmaire and the choreography of Roland Petit. It folded after 5 showings.

In the fall of 1981 the successful revival of *The Pirates of Penzance* moved here from the Uris Theatre and stayed for over a year.

The most recent offering at the Minskoff was the Alan Jay Lerner/Charles Strouse musical *Dance a Little Closer*, an ill-advised musical adaptation of Robert E. Sherwood's Pulitzer Prize play *Idiot's Delight*. It starred Len Cariou, Liz Robertson, and George Rose, but it was clobbered by the critics and closed on its opening night. This production was followed by *Marilyn: An American Fable*, a musical about Marilyn Monroe.

The Minskoff Theatre is owned by the Minskoff Organization and is under the direction of this firm and James M. Nederlander. It is an ideal house for large-scale musicals, dance companies, and personal-appearance shows. As an added attraction, it houses a downtown branch of the Theatre Collection of the Museum of the City of New York, where there are continuous theatrical exhibitions.